Upper Intermediate

English for
BUSINESS LIFE

IAN BADGER PETE MENZIES

Course Book

with Business
Grammar Guide
and detachable
Answer Key

Marshall Cavendish
Education

Acknowledgements

The authors would like to thank the following for their great advice and support in the preparation of *English for Business Life*: Simon Ross, Lucy Brodie, Carol Goodwright, John Russell, Keith Dalton, Jo Barker, Graham Hart, Teresa Miller and Fiona Walker. Special thanks to Valerie Lambert for her work on the Business Grammar Guide.

We would also like to thank our business 'students' from organisations including UPM-Kymmene, Metso Paper, BEMIS, Peterson Packaging, Vattenfall, the International Maritime Organisation, GE Finance, ABN Amro (Investment Bank), Dresdner Kleinwort Wasserstein (UK), Panasonic Europe, Nokia and Marketing Akademie Hamburg for providing the inspiration and feedback that underpins *English for Business Life*.

Finally, the authors would like to thank their families for their support and forbearance during the writing process! – Gerry, Ollie and Elly Badger, Helen Glavin and Miranda Glavin.

Photo acknowledgements

Pg 13 ©British Airways, Pg 14 ©Lloyd Sutton/Masterfile, Pg 17 ©Adverstising Archives, Pg 18 ©Rex Features, Pg 19 ©Rex Features, Pg 21 ©Photolibrary, Pg 22 ©Photolibrary, Pg 25 ©Najiah Feanny/Corbis Saba, Pg 26 ©Bettmann Corbis, Pg 27 ©James Leynse/Corbis, Pg 29 ©Photolibrary, Pg 30© Simon Whitmore/Getty Images, Pg 33 ©Still Pictures, Pg 34 ©Ecoscene/Chris Knapton, Pg 35 ©Scott Barbour/Getty Images, Pg 37 ©Torsten Blackwood/Getty Images, Pg 38 ©Taxi/Getty Images Pg 41 ©Randy Faris/Corbis, Pg 43 ©Photodisc Blue/Getty Images, Pg 45 ©Dennis Galante/Corbis, Pg 46 ©Norbert Schaefer/Corbis, Pg 47 ©Jlp/Zefa/Corbis, Pg 49 ©Rex Features, Pg 50 ©Martin Gray/National Geographic/Getty Images, Pg 53 ©Martin Hayhow/Getty Images, Pg 54 ©Uppa, Pg 57 ©Photolibrary, Pg 58 ©Danny Lehman/Corbis, Pg 59 ©SIME/Giovanni Simeone/4Cornersimages, Pg 61 ©Photonica/Getty Images, Pg 62 ©Helen Ashford/Photos.com, insert ©P. Winbladkh/zefa/Corbis, Pg 63 ©Helen King/Corbis, Pg 65 ©Glen Lear/Getty Images, Pg 66 ©Rex Features, Pg 67 ©Royalty Free/Corbis, Pg 69 ©Helen King/Corbis, Pg 70 ©Photographers Choice/Getty Images, Pg 71 ©Rex Features Pg 73 ©Damir Frkovic/Masterfile, Pg 75 ©Tanaka/Getty Images, Pg 77 ©Richard Drury/The Image Bank/Getty Images, Pg 78 ©Image 100/Alamy, Pg 81© Photolibrary, Pg 82 ©Photolibrary, Pg 85 ©Ross M Horowitz/Iconica/Getty Images, Pg 87©Altrendo images/Getty Images, Pg 89 ©Stephen Chemin/Getty Images, Pg 90 ©Purestock/Alamy, Pg 93 ©Colin Anderson/Brand X Pictures/Alamy, Pg 94 ©Wei Yan/Masterfile, Pg 95 ©Jeff Greenberg/Alamy, Pg 97 ©Masterfile, Pg 98 main ©Zia Soleil/Iconica/Getty Images, a ©Bruce Ayres/Stone/Getty Images, b ©Jeff Morgan/Alamy, c ©SW Productions/Brand X Pictures/Alamy, Pg 99 ©Rex Features, Pg 101 ©Jason Dewey/Stone/Getty Images, Pg 102 ©Masterfile, Pg 105 ©Garry Black/Masterfile, Pg 106 ©R.Ian Lloyd/Masterfile, Pg 107 ©Rex Features, Pg 109 ©Michael Pasdzior/Getty Images, Pg 111 ©Will & Deni McIntyre/Stone/Getty Images, Pg 113 ©Bryan Mullennix/Alamy, Pg 115c ©Rex Features, Pg 115 ©Photonica/Getty Images, Pg 117 ©Sandra Baker/Tips Images, Pg 118 ©Seizo Terasaki/Taxi/Getty Images, Pg 121 ©Stone/Getty Images, Pg 122 t ©Herbert Kehrer/Corbis, bl ©PBNJ Productions/Brand X Pictures/Alamy, br ©Chad Johnston/Masterfile, Pg 123 ©Tips Images, Pg 125 ©Stone/Getty Images, Pg 126 ©Terry Husebye/Stone/Getty Images, Pg 129 ©William Edward King/Iconica/Getty Images, Pg 130 ©AllrightImages/face to face Bildagentur GmbH/Alamy.

Illustrations, layout and editorial arrangement
© Marshall Cavendish Ltd 2007

Text © Ian Badger & Pete Menzies 2007

First published 2007 by Marshall Cavendish Education

Marshall Cavendish Education is a member of the Times Publishing Group

ISBN (13-digit) 978-0-462-00767-0

Marshall Cavendish Education
119 Wardour Street
London W1F 0UW

Designed by Hart McLeod, Cambridge

Printed and bound by Times Offset (M) Sdn Bhd

Contents

Contents chart

UNIT	EXPRESSIONS	LANGUAGE CHECK	PRACTICE
1 Business travel	Why don't you come and see what we are doing? How do I get to the site? We've moved the meeting to the afternoon. The best beaches are only a few kilometres away.	Countability: *some / any / none* *much / many / a lot of* *(a) few / little* *all / whole* Vocabulary: *rural, urban, industrial, temperature (20°C = 68°F), set up, pick up, come up*	Setting up a visit Confirming a visit in writing Listening to travel advice
2 Representing your company	I'd like to welcome you to Van Breda. The organisation consists of three divisions. This is what we are working on at the moment. Mel, this is Donna Ng. She's with the group from Shanghai.	Articles: (*a, the, –*) Present tenses: Simple (*work / works*) and Continuous (*is / are working*) Vocabulary: *slippery, sharp, wet, mission, aim, objective, show round, look round, run through*	Showing someone round A web page presenting the company Writing a letter introducing your company
3 Following up	How are you getting on? How is it going? I managed to get hold of the figures you wanted. Generally, I think it was well worth going. I'm just calling to thank you for organising such an interesting programme.	More on present tenses Simple: *I wonder why …, I gather …* Continuous: *It's always going wrong.* Present Passive: *The system is being changed.* Giving feedback: *really, quite, rather,* etc. Vocabulary: *visit, trip, programme, problem, issue, hassle, making progress, going well, follow up, find out, get back to*	Following up on a project Thanking by email Reporting back
4 Dealing with change	Three years ago, we were taken over by BSK. We now process orders centrally. All the transactions that used to be handled by my team are now handled by the global team based in Frankfurt. There's more pressure than there used to be.	Past tenses, Active and Passive Past time markers: *a year later, the previous year* *used to, be used to, get used to* Vocabulary: *reorganisation, restructuring, business unit, division, department, go bankrupt, go into liquidation, take over, close down, cut back*	Explaining operational changes to a customer Talking about changes during your working life Talking about your company history
5 Culture and values	It was a traditional / progressive company. The workforce was skilled but unmotivated. Working practices have been changing. The management attach a lot of importance to loyalty.	Past tenses, of continuous forms Opposites of adjectives: *friendly / unfriendly,* *honest / dishonest* Vocabulary: *mission, aim, strategy, enterprising, innovative, progressive, bureaucratic, cautious, critical, look after, try out, fit in*	Writing for advice on working practices and values Discussing corporate culture A questionnaire on values at work

UNIT	EXPRESSIONS	LANGUAGE CHECK	PRACTICE
11 Networking	Mary Jones suggested I contact you. I was wondering if I could come and see you. It's a good idea to send an email before you call. It's John Smith; we met in Manheim.	Expressing intentions: *I intend to call Maria.* Etiquette advice: *It's best not to talk too much.* *be supposed / meant to*: *I was meant to send some samples.* Vocabulary: *network, socialise, circulate,* *work colleague, professional contact, business associate,* *custom, convention, guideline,* *keep in contact with, follow up with*	Corporate hospitality packages Writing an invitation to a client Networking tips and practice
12 Security abroad	I have to report a theft. My car's been towed away. There's something wrong with the air conditioning. It won't be working again till after lunch.	Future Continuous tense: *How will you be paying?* Future Perfect tense: *We will have left by then.* Order of adjectives: *a brown leather wallet* Vocabulary: *switch, plug, bulb,* *basin, tap, drain, pipe,* *fused, faulty, broken, dead,* *blocked, cracked, leaking, jammed*	A difficult trip to Torreon (Mexico) Safety guidelines for San Diego (USA) Dealing with travel hassles
13 Salaries, incentives and rewards	What I earn depends on my sales figures. My total package is worth about 90 grand. Directors get a free car; it's a perk that goes with the job. The Board have agreed to an increase of 5%.	Modal verbs, present forms: *would, could, should,* etc. Expressing likelihood: *bound to, likely to* Rates and charges: *time and a half, flat-rate fee* Symbols and numbers: +, -, =, 10K, $7^1/2$ Vocabulary: *reward, benefit, perk, salary, wage, pay rise, raise, increase, put in for, turn down, think over*	A letter about executive rewards Benefit packages (listening realia) A pay review
14 Personal and company finances	Altogether, our running costs amount to $1.7 million. Sales are up from $9.8 million to $10.7 million. We made a profit of $2.2 million on sales of $20.7 million. I had to sell my shares in Unicorn to pay off a debt.	Modal verbs, past forms: *would have, would have been* Spelling rules: *i before e,* except after *c* Use of hyphens: *day-to-day expenses* Vocabulary: *add* Financial terms: *add up to, cut back on, go up / down*	Talking about financial performance Talking about expenditure and assets A news item about Caffè Nero Writing a request for a salary increase An article about the sale of a company
15 Managing credit	I'm calling about our invoice number AK-40 7/AZ. It was passed for payment ten days ago. My card's just been declined. What's going on? How can I protect myself from ID theft?	Advising and suggesting: *I think / don't think you should …,* Modal verbs (criticism / regret): *You ought to have …,* Conditional sentences without *if*: *otherwise, or else* Vocabulary: *credit limit, credit record, credit status,* *due, overdue, due date,* *look into, sort out, pay off*	Handling credit card and mobile phone problems Querying an invoice Writing a message about late payment An article about ID theft

UNIT	EXPRESSIONS	LANGUAGE CHECK	PRACTICE
16 Time management	In this job, you have to be able to work under pressure. It is important to delegate and prioritise. The course showed us how to establish priorities. They gave us tips on running meetings.	More on conditionals without *if*: *or, or else, otherwise* *wish / if only*: *I wish I could …* Reflexive pronouns: *yourself, themselves* Latin expressions: *vice versa* Vocabulary: *planning, prioritising, delegating, workload, paperwork, backlog, problem solving, fire fighting, keep on top of, build up, get through*	Reviewing time management skills Time management questionnaire Organising to go on a training course Tips on running meetings
17 Delivering quality	What we sell is quality and service. It would improve our performance … if we had better procedures for logging faults. We encourage best practice in all areas. The secret is to listen to what your clients say.	More on conditionals (2nd / 3rd conditionals) Alternative sentence structures *prevent* vs. *avoid* Vocabulary: *high / low quality, well / poorly made, very / not very good, really first class, user-friendly, value for money, be above / below / up to standard*	Talking about quality performance Handling compliments and complaints Writing a letter of apology A customer care questionnaire
18 Working practices	Our management style is very informal. We are very customer focused. We have to comply with the regulator's requirements. The main changes have been in the area of technology. There is more competition – the pace is faster.	More on conditionals: *should they, were they to*, etc. Expressions of frequency: *three times a year, very seldom*, etc. Accord, indicating parallels: *X does and so does Y* Terms relating to compliance: *comply with, enforce*, etc. Vocabulary: *flexitime, job sharing, equal opportunities, requirements, guidelines, procedures, industrial / staff relations, do spot cheques, give a good / bad impression*	Talking about dress and behaviour codes Interview with an employee relations manager Article on managing paperwork Questionnaire on company culture
19 Advertising and promotion	The service is promoted over the Internet. We depend a lot on personal recommendation. Do you have a leaflet or something? The price list is printed on the back. We should try a campaign based on radio ads.	Passive verb forms: present, future, past Omissions in clauses: *being the client* vs. *as we are the client*, etc. Vocabulary: *advertising agency / campaign / slogan, focus group, market survey, sponsored link, brochure, leaflet, flyer, junk mail, nuisance calls, spam, highlight, target, put across*	Talking about your advertising Promoting a company / a product Preparing promotional literature An article on spam and nuisance calls
20 Offers and orders	The unit weighs $2^1/_2$ kilos. I'm calling to place an order. We had to put our prices up. We ought to have been informed. Some customers order on-line (in order) to cut costs.	More on passives: continuous, infinitive, *-ing* forms Giving reasons: *because, in order to, so that*, etc. Measurements: dimensions, volume, capacity, etc. Vocabulary: *retail, retailer, wholesale, wholesaler, quantity / trade discount, take someone up on an offer, put prices up / down, place an order*	Taking / placing / confirming an order Product enquires – written and by phone Querying an invoice Dealing with late deliveries

UNIT	EXPRESSIONS	LANGUAGE CHECK	PRACTICE
21 Customer care	It sounds as if the machine is overheating. Do you have a service contract? Call out time is supposed to be two hours. This isn't the result of normal wear and tear. We're very unhappy about the way we're being treated.	Impressions: *seem / look / sound, as if / though,* etc. Cause and effect: *be caused by, the result of,* etc. Complaining: *complain about, be unhappy about,* etc. Vocabulary: *care, concern, support, guarantee, warranty, protection plan, neglect, misuse, wear and tear, refund, replacement, credit note, put customers first, take it back, look into it*	Practice in giving and receiving customer care Managers talk about service they receive Writing a letter of complaint Case practice: returning goods to a shop
22 Home and family	In this picture you can see the house where we live. That's my son; he doesn't look like me at all. We're about 15 minutes from the centre of town. The alarm usually goes off just before 6 o'clock. I drop the children off at school on the way to the station.	Similarities and differences: *similar to, the opposite of,* etc. *each / every / all* Possessive *'s: a friend of my sister's, her parents' house,* etc. Vocabulary: *single, engaged, divorced, mother / father-in-law, half brother / sister, a top-floor apartment, a terraced house, grow up, bring up, move in / out*	Taking about your home and family Listening to people talking about family photos Writing a request for time off A feature on couples in business together
23 Work / life balance	I find it difficult to balance work and domestic commitments. I'm very keen on golf; it's fun and it helps me unwind. I take exercise on a regular basis. I'd much rather eat out than entertain at home. It's far more relaxing and a lot less hassle.	More on comparisons: *far more / less interesting than* Preference: *prefer, would rather, rather than* Agreement: *agree with, accept, in agreement with* Alternative adverb forms: *regularly* vs. *on a regular basis* Non-verbal communication: *Ah, Hey, Oh* Vocabulary: *get together, meet up, come round, take up, give up, be keen on*	Talking about leisure time Interview with a publishing director A questionnaire on work / life balance Article and discussion on taking exercise
24 Getting away	I want to get away for a few days, preferably somewhere warm. The climate is good, although it can be chilly at night. It's best to go before the high season. I have to get back to my office. If you want to travel tomorrow, you'll have to upgrade to business class.	Contrasting ideas: *although, even so, all the same* Giving (holiday) advice: *Remember that ..., I'd advise you to ...* Short form questions: *Where to? How long for? whatever, whoever, whenever* Vocabulary: *travel agent, local rep, stand-by passenger, package holiday, high/off season, fully booked, on stand-by, get away, head for, check in / out*	Organising a holiday People talking about their holidays Sending a greetings message back to colleagues A feature on mini-breaks in New York
25 Politics and business	The government is a coalition of the left and centre. It is difficult to predict who will win the next election. However, the right have a good chance. They announced a new trade agreement on the news. The evidence against privatisation is very clear.	Verbs of reporting: *say, announce, warn,* etc. Contrasts and alternatives: *however, whereas,* etc. Vocabulary: *local / state / federal government, balance of payments, imports, exports, vote for / against, hold a referendum*	Talking about government policies Discussing political / economic issues Considering election possibilities Writing a political / economic briefing on an area

UNIT	EXPRESSIONS	LANGUAGE CHECK	PRACTICE
26 Taxation	How much did we pay in tax last year? Companies are taxed at a rate of 25%. They announced they would cut the rate to 15%. As far as I know, you can reclaim the tax. Our accountant promised she'd file the return the next day.	Reported speech: *asked us if, announced that* Reported speech timeframes: *following day, previous year*, etc. Terms used to qualify statements: *as far as I know, I'm not an expert but*, etc. Vocabulary: *income tax, corporation tax, sales tax, tax liability, tax allowance, tax assessment tax exempt, tax refund, tax free, go in tax, go up / down, fill in a return*	Talking about personal and company tax Dealing with tax queries – examples from a specialist site Tax case studies – reading and listening 'Death and taxes' – an article
27 Legal matters	Our lawyers warned us it wouldn't be worth going to court. Their finance director was convicted of fraud. Why weren't we notified? I thought it was required by law. This document is a mess. We need to add another bullet point.	More on reported speech: advice, commands, questions Making reference: *concerning, with regard to*, etc. Terms related to text layout: *underlined, in brackets*, etc. Vocabulary: *laws, legislation, regulations, a case, a trial, a legal decision, a judge, a jury, a verdict, to go to court, to sue for, to settle out of court*	Talking about legal matters Listening – a journalist talking about medical liability Summarising legal advice Case study – a document on customers' rights
28 Planning	The scheme was planned in three phases. My role is to liaise with the other participants. To start with, I need to make an action plan. There are a number of factors to be taken into account. At the moment we are on schedule.	Indicating sequence: *to start with, in the second stage*, etc. Terms related to structuring ideas / arguments: *for one thing, in addition to that* Gender-free reference: *he or she, they* Tag questions: *You do, don't you?* Vocabulary: *schedule, timetable, deadline, phase, stage, milestone, feasibility study, contingency plan, on target, on schedule, on track, take into account, put forward / back*	Talking about plans and commitments Listening to a project update Writing an outline plan Reading about a major project and assessing it
29 Work in progress	I need an update on the state of play. The project has fallen behind schedule. Do we have a contingency plan? This table shows … / The dotted line indicates … Before I summarise the key points, are there any questions?	Reporting on the state of play: *go according to plan, on / behind schedule* Terms used in presentations Referring to graphs / tables: *This table shows …, As you can see from the dotted line …* Vocabulary: *update, progress check, overview, contingency plan, alternative, plan B, improvement, increase, rise, deduction, decrease, fall, be held up, be let down, chase up*	Giving project updates, discussing progress Listening to reports by project managers Writing a project update Reviewing a company's performance Presenting conclusions
30 Feedback and review	What's your overall assessment? Bearing in mind the circumstances, I thought we did really well. I'm disappointed I didn't meet my targets. To sum up, I'd say you did a good job.	More on giving opinions: *am positive, consider, guess* Terms used in evaluating: *really outstanding, quite disappointing* Summarising: *My overall view …, On the whole …* Indicating context: *Bearing in mind …, Considering …* Vocabulary: *assessment, evaluation, feedback, aim, target, objective, meet targets, put into practice, make progress*	Performance review (self and others) Work style questionnaire Discussing next steps

Introduction

English for Business Life is a four-level course designed for people who need English for their everyday work.

English for Business Life is:

- a course written by authors with a wide experience of teaching English for business in a range of international contexts, countries and cultures
- a course that respects the modern need for flexibility; learners can follow fast, standard or comprehensive tracks through the materials
- a course that follows a progressive and comprehensive grammar syllabus, with the stress on the effective use of grammar for clear communication
- a course that satisfies the requirements of the Common European Framework, BEC and equivalent global testing authorities
- a course that supports the learner in a highly connected modern world.

The Upper Intermediate level of the course consists of:

- a Course Book with a detachable answer key and Business Grammar Guide
- course book listening exercises on CD
- a Self-study Guide packaged with an accompanying audio CD
- a Trainer's Manual.

Learners can follow fast, standard and comprehensive tracks through the material – 45 to 90 hours of work:

- fast track – 45 hours
- standard track – 60 hours
- comprehensive track – 90 hours.

Summary of components

Course book

The Course Book consists of:

- 30 units Intermediate and Upper Intermediate levels (36 units Elementary and Pre-intermediate levels)
- a Glossary of business-related terms
- a Grammar / language index
- audioscripts of all listening activities
- Answers and Business Grammar Guide in a detachable booklet.

Two audio CDs are available as a separate component.

Self-study guide

The Self-study Guide consists of:

- 30 parallel units (36 units Elementary and Pre-intermediate levels)
- material that can be used in support of the course book or as a self-standing resource
- audio CDs containing recordings of core language, pronunciation points and listening exercises
- reinforcement / consolidation exercises
- a grammar / language reference section
- a glossary of business-related terms.

Trainer's manual

The Trainer's Manual consists of:

- notes on exercises and ideas for consolidation / extension work
- a glossary of business-related terms
- notes on business practice
- answers and audioscripts for course book exercises
- progress tests.

Business English exams / testing equivalence

Levels	Common European Framework Level	ALTE	BEC	London Chamber of Commerce (EFB)
Upper intermediate	C1 – C2	4	Higher	Level 3
Intermediate	B2 – C1	3	Vantage	Level 2
Pre-intermediate	B1 – B2	2	Preliminary	Level 1
Elementary	A2 – B1			Preliminary/ Level 1

Useful websites

For more on the European Framework visit www.alte.org

For BEC visit www.cambridgeesol.org/exams/bec.htm

For the 'Business Language Testing Service' visit www.bulats.org

For the London Chamber of Commerce Exams visit www.lccieb.org.uk

For the TOEIC American exams for working people visit www.ets.org/toeic

A range of training situations

English for Business Life presents the language that is essential for doing business in English; it has strong global relevance. Groups that will benefit from using the materials include:

- business schools and colleges
- language schools which offer English for business courses
- company training courses and study programmes
- vocational adult education classes
- schools and colleges which aim to equip their students with the language skills they will need in their working lives.

Upper Intermediate level

The Upper Intermediate level of **English for Business Life** will be appropriate for you if you have studied English for perhaps four to six / seven years at school and / or college. You will probably be able to use the language with a good degree of fluency and will be able to manage in most situations where you need English.

At this level you will probably feel that you need to improve the appropriateness and structural accuracy of the language you use, your listening and writing skills, and your business-related vocabulary. You will also need to develop your knowledge and use of everyday business idiomatic language. This book focuses on helping you to develop these key areas of language.

Content

The materials cover everyday business speaking, listening, reading and writing skills, through a range of guided and free practice and exercises. The aim is to find out what you can do in English within a given theme and then to help you to develop these skills.

Each unit contains at least one listening exercise (core practice) which encapsulates the target language of the unit and others which develop sensitivity to different types of English, in line with the fact that English is used as an international language of communication between speakers of many nationalities.

Each unit also contains a number of study points – grammar and vocabulary. The language reference sections are concerned specifically with helping the learner to use the language accurately for effective and clear communication. There is a glossary of business-related language at the back of the course book.

Flexibility: different tracks through the materials

Fast track: 45 hours (approximately 1.5 hour per unit) involving, for example:

- introductory discussion on the main themes of the unit
- language focus and language notes
- core practice (listening and speaking)
- further appropriate practice activities.

Standard track: 60 hours (approximately 2 hours per unit) involving, for example:

- introductory discussion on the main themes of the unit
- language focus and language notes
- core practice (listening and speaking)
- practice activities (listening, reading, writing and role play)
- study notes and selected exercises from the Self-study Guide.

Comprehensive track: 90 hours (approximately 3 hours per unit) involving, for example:

- introductory discussion on the main themes of the unit
- language focus and language notes
- practice activities (listening, reading, writing and role play)
- detailed study of related Self-study Guide materials.

Some study tips

- Make time for your English studies. Approach them with the same level of commitment that you would any other project in your work or spare time.
- Find the study pattern that works best for you. In our view 'little and often' is more effective than occasional long sessions.
- Keep an organised study file. Make sure that the language that is most relevant to your needs is clearly highlighted.
- Ensure that you relate the language presented in the course back to your area of business or study. If there are terms you need which are not included in the material, consult your trainer, English-speaking colleagues and friends, and make thorough notes.
- Make use of the English-speaking media – web pages, radio, TV, professional journals, magazines and newspapers to follow up your business and leisure interests in English.
- Make use of monolingual and bilingual dictionaries. A number of dictionaries are available on-line, and the 'synonym' and 'thesaurus' keys on your computer are always useful.

Study themes in *English for Business Life*

Upper Intermediate level

- Business travel
- Following up
- Dealing with change
- Culture and values
- Conferences and exhibitions
- Networking
- Delivering quality
- Work / life balance
- Feedback and review

Other levels

Elementary level

- You and your job
- Your company
- Brief exchanges
- Arrangements
- Telephoning

- Business hospitality
- Business trips
- Your working environment
- Enquiring and booking

Pre-intermediate level

- You and your company
- Meeting people
- Time off
- The workplace
- Numbers and figures
- Business travel
- The product
- Arrangements
- Business entertaining
- Sales and selling
- Requesting / supplying information

Intermediate level

- Contacts
- Companies
- Personnel
- Products and services
- Entertaining
- Meetings
- Travel
- Money and finance
- Presentations

The authors

IAN BADGER has extensive experience of developing courses and systems of language training for business. He is a regular speaker at international conferences. He is a partner in Business and Medical English Services, and a director of English4 Ltd (www.english4.com). His publications include *Everyday Business English*, *Everyday Business Writing* (Longman) and *Business English Phrases* (Penguin).

PETE MENZIES is an associate of Pod (Professional and Organisational Development) and founder of Commnet, a dedicated training agency specialising in effective communication for international teams. Awards for his published work include the Duke of Edinburgh ESU Prize and the Gold Medal at the Leipzig Industrial Fair.

UNIT 1 Business travel

1 Core practice

Listening and speaking

Listen to the exchanges (a – d) and mark the statements (part i) true ☐T, false ☐F or unclear ☐U. Then, working with a partner, practise the exchanges indicated in part ii.

a **i** The speakers plan to meet in the middle of June. ☐
   ii Arrange a visit to your company.
b **i** Speaker 1 is in farming. ☐
   ii Talk about the geographical features and weather in your area.
c **i** They are going to call off the meeting. ☐
   ii Practise rescheduling a visit.
d **i** The caller is a valued customer. ☐
   ii Explain to a visitor how to get to your offices from the station or airport.

> **Preparation**
>
> Think about the trips you and your colleagues make, and the people who visit you. What is involved? What communications have to take place for these events to occur? What areas do you need to practise? As part of your preparation, check the Useful Phrases on page 16. If possible, bring examples of related documents to the class – invitations, timetables, alterations, etc.

2 Language check

Refer to the Language Notes on page 16 as you complete the examples below using the choices provided – only one is correct. Then prepare a version of each example that you might use.

1 There is .... money in the budget for gifts but not ....
  a a little / lots of
  b some / much
  c very little / many

2 – Are there .... rooms available next week?
  – Yes, but ....
  a some / a few
  b any / very little
  c any / very few

3 We spend a large .... of money on entertaining.
  a amount
  b bit
  c number

4 The best beaches in the country are only .... kilometres away.
  a some
  b a few
  c few

5 We have .... time to change the arrangements; we have to check in in 20 minutes.
  a none
  b not any
  c no

6 – Do you have any customers who ask you to pay their travel expenses?
  – ....
  a No, none.
  b Yes, a bit.
  c No, not any.

7 It rains .... the time in September – it's the monsoon season.
  a some
  b whole
  c all

8 We have a problem with the arrangement for the 24th. Can we .... it off till the following week?
  a change
  b switch
  c put

9 If you let me know when you are arriving, I'll send a car to pick ....
  a you up
  b up you
  c you

10 Our main production facilities are located .... in an .... area ten kilometres north of the capital.
  a in the centre / rural
  b inland / urban
  c in the mountains / farming

3 Listening

Travel tips

Listen to the speakers giving advice on places they know, and make notes. Then fill in the table.

Travel information mentioned ✓ not mentioned ✗	car hire	public transport	telephone system	accommodation	food	restaurants	night life	the people	hospitality	gifts	conventions	dress / clothing	climate	landscape	currency	prices / cost of living	tipping	doing business	regulations	other
Speaker 1 Country / area																				
Speaker 2 Country / area																				

4 Writing

Confirming a visit

After sending you this email, Felix Bezst calls you. Points you discuss include:

- how to get from the airport to the city centre
- how long the journey takes
- where to stay overnight
- how to get to the Nootex plant in the morning
- who will be at the meeting.

Write an email following the phone call, confirming the main points.

Delete Reply Reply All Forward Compose Mailboxes Get Mail Junk

Subject: Visit 11 march
Attachments: 📎 🖼 brochure

I would like to thank you for agreeing to meet us. We appreciate that you are already talking to a number of possible suppliers. I attach a copy of our latest brochure, which gives further details of the options we can offer you. The new PX 274 system which we discussed on the phone is not in the brochure yet, but you can view it at www.alcamsystems.com/bochure/ px274

We are very much looking forward to meeting you.

Best regards

Felix Bezst

Business Development Manager

Setting up a visit

Read the message from Helga and the information about Norway. Then, working in pairs, draft a reply to Kitty Ruban's queries. Attach the country profile of Norway to your message.

COUNTRY PROFILE

Norway

Road

Taxis: in most cases fares are metered. Taxis can be found at ranks or booked by telephone.

Car hire: available at airports and in most towns, but costly. In general, problems of cost and parking make public transport more practical and convenient. It is also possible to hire bicycles.

Urban

Good public transport systems operate in the main towns. Oslo has bus, rail, metro and tramway services. Tickets have to be purchased in advance. Meters on taxis are obligatory.

Excursions / sightseeing

In summer there is a wide choice of ferry-boat trips on the fjords. In winter skiing is popular in resorts like Lillehammer and Geilow. In the Oslo area the following are popular: the Munch Museum, the Norwegian Folk Museum, the Viking ships, the *Kon-Tiki* Museum, the Norwegian Maritime Museum.

Food and drink

Food: many hotels and restaurants serve lunch from a *koldtbord* (cold table), which typically offers a variety of fish such as smoked salmon, fresh lobster, shrimp; hot dishes are also available.

Quick snacks: open sandwiches topped with meat, fish, cheese and salad are widely available.

Drink: aquavit (schnapps) is a local favourite, but in general alcohol is limited and expensive.

Shopping

Norway has a high standard of living – shops are good but expensive. Tax refunds can be obtained from any of the 2,500 shops carrying the sticker 'Tax free for tourists'. These shops save visitors 10 – 15% of the list price.

Doing business

If invited to a home, a visitor should bring a bunch of flowers for the hostess. Punctuality is expected. People normally shake hands when they meet. Smoking is prohibited in public buildings and on public transport. Do learn a few words of Norwegian – like *'Takk for maten'*, which means 'Thank you'.

Tipping

It is not customary to tip taxi drivers. Waiters expect a tip of no more than 5% of the bill. Porters at airports, railway stations and hotels charge per piece of luggage.

Climate and clothing

Norway is cold in winter but warm and pleasant in spring and summer. By April the days are already long. But the climate is changeable so be prepared for any type of weather. Dress is generally informal.

Kitty Ruban from our Durban office is visiting the new Norwegian plant in February. She wants to know about:
- climate and clothing
- car hire
- culture points / tipping
- shopping.
Could you sort something out? Thanks.
Helga

Adapted from *The World Travel Guide*

LANGUAGE REFERENCE

Language Notes

For further notes on these points, see the accompanying Business Grammar Guide (BGG).

Review of countability

(BGG 10)

• Countable nouns

Nouns we count, e.g. *date*, *trip*, *room option*.

e.g. There are (not) **many** free dates.
We have **a lot of** / **lots of** options.
We have **a few** possible dates.
We have **very few** options in June.
We have **some** difficult choices to make.
We have **a number of** possibilities.
We have **no** plans.
We don't have **any** plans.
Do you have **any** rooms available in July?

• Short answers:

e.g. Yes, (quite) a lot.   No, not (very) many. / Not a lot.
Yes, (quite) a few.   No, (really) very few.
Yes, some.   No, (absolutely) none.

• Uncountable nouns

Nouns we measure, e.g. *hospitality*, *time*, *budget*.

e.g. **Much** of our budget is spent on hospitality.
We spend **lots of** money on entertaining.
We spend **a little** time each morning planning.
We spend **very little** (money) on process analysis.
We have **some** software that breaks the figures down.
We always fix **an amount of** money for training.
We have **no** budget for gifts.
There isn't **any** money in the budget for that.
Do you have **any** money reserved for contingencies?

• Short answers

e.g. Yes, (quite) a lot.   No, not (very) much / not a lot.
Yes, a little / a bit.   No, (really) very little.
Yes, some.   No, (absolutely) none.

Some examples of *all* / *the whole* (BGG 10.3)

all the time = the whole time
all my life = my whole life
all of Norway = the whole of Norway
all of the city = the whole city
all the money = the whole sum of money (not *the whole money*)
all the water = the whole bottle of water (not *the whole water*)

But notice: all the companies (= every company)
whole companies (= entire companies)

Vocabulary

• Words and phrases
(See BGG 24.3 for notes on temperature.)

e.g. rural area, farming community, agricultural region,
industrial region, manufacturing area,
urban environment, built-up area,
a heavily / lightly populated area,
on the coast, in the mountains, in the interior,
in the centre, on the outskirts, in the country,
mountainous, hilly, flat,
twenty-five degrees centigrade / fahrenheit (25°C or 25°F)

• Verbs and verb phrases
e.g. If you tell us when you can visit us, we'll **set** it **up**.
If you fly to Oslo, I'll **pick** you **up** from the airport.
Something has **come up** at this end.
I'm afraid I'm going to have to **call** it **off** / **put** it **off**.

Useful Phrases

We'd be pleased to organise a programme for you.
How's the 12th? Would the 19th suit you better?
I really don't mind. Both dates are OK by me.
Let's make it the 19th then.

There aren't many people here in July; it's holiday time.
Why don't you come in June?
Are there any rooms available in June?
Yes, a few.   Yes, but very few.   No, none.

Where are you in relation to the town centre?
The easiest way is to catch the express bus.
In the Arrivals Hall, follow the signs to the bus station.
On arrival in (Amsterdam), take a taxi to (your hotel).

How do I get to the site?
We'll send a car to pick you up.
There are directions on our website – I'll send you a link.

We're only 15 minutes from the mountains.
The best beaches in the country are just a few kilometres away.
It rains all the time in September.
The temperature at that time of year is over 30 degrees.
You must remember to bring your skiing gear.
Don't forget to bring plenty of warm clothing.

I'm afraid something has come up.
Can we reschedule the meeting for the following week?
Provisionally, let's arrange it for the 27th.
If that doesn't work, we'll have to set up a video conference.

UNIT 2
Representing your company

Have you ever written on a banana in biro? It's crazy but it works like a dream. It flows. It's smooth. It's sensual. A strongly worded You wish all writing could be this way. Sonnets, odes to lilies. You get the urge to write poems; that everything can be letter of complaint is impossible. It makes you realise, that everything can be improved. That even the familiar can be looked at in a new light. And that imagination is more powerful than knowledge. Do you believe in the power of dreams? HONDA

Preparation

This unit is about welcoming visitors, showing them round and explaining what the company does. In this context, you might have to introduce people, discuss arrangements and explain processes. Before class, check the Useful Phrases on page 20. Come prepared to 'represent' your organisation. If possible, bring emails and timetables from past visits to the class.

1 Core practice

Listening and speaking

Listen to the exchanges (a – d) and mark the statements (part i) true ☐T, false ☐F or unclear ☐U. Then, working with a partner, practise the exchanges indicated in part ii.

a i The speaker's company was taken over by the Melox group. ☐
  ii Introduce your organisation in a similar way.

b i The machine is running smoothly. ☐
  ii Talk about a project you are working on at the moment.

c i Mel and Donna have already met. ☐
  ii Practise introducing a visitor to a colleague.

d i The new high-speed processor is not ready to be demonstrated yet. ☐
  ii Practise showing someone round your business.

2 Language check

Refer to the Language Notes on page 20 as you complete the examples below using the choices provided – only one is correct. Then prepare a version of each example that you might use.

1 We're meeting for .... lunch at .... Mariot Hotel on .... June 27th.
  a – / the / –   **b** the / – / the   **c** – / – / –

2 .... frames are made of .... reinforced fibreglass.
  a The / –   **b** The / the   **c** – / –

3 She's .... European representative to .... main Board.
  a an / –   **b** the / the   **c** – / –

4 We .... in all-weather paints.
  a specialise   **b** are concentrating   **c** concentrate

5 The organisation .... three divisions.
  a consists of   **b** is dividing into   **c** is made up

6 This machine .... It .... replaced.
  a isn't working / is being   **b** doesn't work / is   **c** doesn't work / needs

7 This is Annie Petak who .... our catalogue sales.
  a runs normally   **b** is currently running   **c** is being lead

8 Boris called – according to the timetable we .... at 10.00
  a are meeting   **b** sometimes meet   **c** are usually meeting

9 As soon as everyone is here, I'll .... you round the site.
  a go   **b** look   **c** show

10 .... your clothes – the paint is ....
  a Watch / live   **b** Be careful / greasy   **c** Mind / wet

3 | Listening

A tour of the company

Look at the timetable below. Then listen to extracts (1 – 5) from the visit and write the approximate times when the extracts took place.

Extract 1 ...9.15....

Extract 2 ....

Extract 3 ....

Extract 4 ....

Extract 5 ....

Van Breda Footwear	
9.15	Arrival and welcome
9.30	Coffee in boardroom
10.00	Presentation: Introduction to Van Breda
10.30	Tour of plant
11.15	Visit to showroom
12.00	Round-up session in boardroom
12.30	Lunch in staff canteen
2.00	Departure

4 | Writing

An introduction

You are planning to visit an area where you would like to do (more) business. Write a letter introducing your organisation, suggesting a meeting. Enclose brochures and / or other printed information as appropriate.

Useful Language

[John Smith] of … has suggested that I …

Your name was mentioned by …

I am planning to visit …

I would welcome the opportunity to …

We are very interested in …

As you (may) know, we are part of …

We are based in …

We make / specialise in …

We are looking for opportunities to … / outlets for …

in conjunction with …

areas of common interest …

Please do not hesitate to …

I look forward to …

I enclose …

5 | Feature

Company purpose / mission

Read the extracts from the Honda website and answer the questions.

a What is the purpose of this text?
b How effective is it in your view?
c What do you understand by 'glocalized'?
d How do you react to the statement: 'We have taken on the challenge of doing things only Honda could do'?
e How do we know this is an American text?
f Express the following in other words.
  - Honda has been powered by dreams
  - we are realizing that dream
  - we're always ahead of the curve
  - coming up with technologies
  - We have taken on the challenge
  - Honda strives in all its activities

HONDA

MESSAGE

Let's go! We have dreams to pursue!

Since our foundation in 1948, Honda has been powered by dreams. Our initial and ongoing dream is to provide genuine satisfaction to people everywhere. Providing products of the highest quality at a reasonable price, we are realizing that dream one step at a time.

Our mission is to offer products, technologies and services that contribute to society and make people's lives better. That's why we're always ahead of the curve, coming up with technologies that make mobility safer and more environmentally sustainable. We see challenges ahead and are facing them squarely, determined to build a brighter future.

We have taken on the challenge of doing things only Honda could do, creating new value in the form of new products and services that meet the needs of our mobile society and are in harmony with our world.

Through the creation of new value for our customers, the expansion of our glocalized operations, and the development of safety and environmental solutions for future generations, Honda strives in all its activities to be a company whose existence is valued by people around the world.

OVERVIEW

Company name
Honda Motor Co. Ltd.

Head office
2-1-1 Minami Aoyama,
Minato-ku Tokyo 107-8556,
Japan
Tel: +81-(0)3-3423-1111

Established
September 24, 1948
President and CEO
Takeo Fukui

Capital
¥86,067 million

Sales
Consolidated:
¥8,162,600 million
Unconsolidated:
¥3,319,793 million

Total number of employees
Consolidated: 131,600
Unconsolidated: 27,187

Consolidated subsidiaries
317 subsidiaries

Chief products
Motorcycles, automobiles,
power products

From http://world.honda.com/profile/message/

LANGUAGE REFERENCE

Language Notes

For further notes on these points, see the accompanying Business Grammar Guide (BGG).

Review of articles (*a*, *the*, –)

- Examples of *a / an* (the indefinite article) (BGG 9.1)
- e.g. We have **an** interesting programme for you.
  An email arrived for you.
  You need **a** new charger.
  I'm **a** secretary.
  She trained as **an** actuary.

- Examples of *the* (the definite article) (BGG 9.2)
- e.g. Did you give him **the** message?
  Have you read **the** report I gave you yesterday?
  It's **the** biggest software company in Europe.
  the end of the month
  the 22nd of December
  How far are you from **the** airport?

- Examples of *the* in names (BGG 9.2)
- e.g. **the** Finance Department
  the European Union
  the T-Mobile network
  the USA, **the** Middle East
  the Atlantic, **the** Nile, **the** Alps
  the Hilton (hotel), **the** *Times* (newspaper)

- Examples with no *a* or *the* (BGG 9.3)
- e.g. Industry is suffering.
  They manufacture toys.
  Meet me for lunch.
  I'm at work.
  Today's news
  Brown's Hotel
  China's economy

- Examples of no *a* or *the* in names (BGG 9.3)
- e.g. IBM, Daewoo, Nokia, BA, McDonald's
  Charles de Gaulle Airport
  I work in Accounts.
  Independence Day

The Present Simple tense vs. the Present Continuous tense

- Examples of the Present Simple (BGG 1.1)
- e.g. We **specialise** in footwear for children.
  We normally **operate** a three-shift system.
  This gauge **controls** the temperature.
  The sign **says** 'No entry'.
  When **does** the meeting **start**?
  My plane **leaves** at 6.00pm.

- Examples of the Present Continuous (BGG 1.1)
- e.g. Currently we **are producing** over 200 units a day.

Our suppliers **are being** very difficult.
The situation **is getting** better.
We **are planning** to replace it.
The group from KLS **is arriving** after lunch.
While we **are waiting**, I'll tell you a bit about …

Some warnings

- e.g. Be careful – those wires are live.
  Mind your head.
  Watch where you step – the paint is wet.
  Take care – the floor is slippery.
  Watch out! Mind out! Look out!
  slippery, sharp, greasy, wet, fragile, live

Vocabulary

- Words and phrases
- e.g. clear mission, shared vision, corporate values,
  agreed aim, short-term / long-term objectives,
  the manufacturing division, a business unit,
  global responsibility, local function

- Verbs and verb phrases
- e.g. Marco will **show / take** you **round** the plant.
  We are **made up of** two separate companies.
  Could you **run through** the arrangements again?
  John's going to be late – he's **held up** in traffic.

Useful Phrases

I'd like to welcome you to Van Breda and to thank you for coming.
I'm glad you could all make it.

While we are waiting, I'll run through the timetable.
There are a couple of changes to the programme.
The first presentation starts at 10.00.
Jan our MD is joining us later.

Come and meet Dick.
The best person to talk to is Mel.
Have you been introduced?
I'm sorry – I thought you knew each other.
John, this is Meg Kato, head of training at TLK.

We are part of the Levit group of companies.
We are mainly a sales organisation.
The organisation consists of three divisions.
We're in the process of reorganising our manufacturing division.

I'd like to show you round the factory.
Please follow me up the stairs.
I'm afraid this area is closed to visitors.
Mind out! The floor is slippery.

This is what we are working on at the moment.
We're installing a new system which will make it possible for us to turn orders round in four hours.
Is everything clear so far?

UNIT 3 Following up

Preparation

This unit is about the things that happen after a trip – following up on actions agreed, getting back to people with information, reporting and saying thank you. Come prepared to talk about the follow-up you are involved in – after a trip or meeting, etc. Check the Useful Phrases on page 24. If possible, bring a 'thank you' message and a progress report to class.

1 Core practice

Listening and speaking

Listen to the exchanges (a – d) and mark the statements (part i) true $\boxed{T}$, false $\boxed{F}$ or unclear $\boxed{U}$. Then, working with a partner, practise the exchanges indicated in part ii.

a i Ron Lomax hasn't received the samples. □
  ii Leave a voicemail following up on work that is overdue.
b i They agreed to talk in ten minutes. □
  ii Call someone to give them information you found out for them.
c i The folder was left in the reception area. □
  ii You think you left something behind – call and check.
d i The caller is a sales rep. □
  ii Call to thank someone for their hospitality.

2 Language check

Refer to the Language Notes on page 24 as you complete the examples below using the choices provided – only one is correct. Then prepare a version of each example that you might use.

1 I .... if you could help me?
  a wonder
  b am wondering
  c am thinking
2 They are having .... in the factory today.
  a new security system
  b a lot of problems
  c a new foreman
3 Is anything .... about the missing money?
  a doing
  b being done
  c to do
4 The site doesn't .... us.
  a belong to
  b owned by
  c belong

5 They .... the access codes.
  a keep changing
  b are keeping changing
  c keep to change
6 She .... for new ways of presenting the information.
  a always is looking
  b always looks
  c is always looking
7 I .... it was a very successful visit.
  a am believing
  b think
  c am thinking
8 The question-and-answer session at the end was ....
  a slightly good
  b really disappointing
  c slightly excellent

9 I thought the arrangements weren't .... good enough.
  a quite
  b fairly
  c rather
10 Could you get .... to me with the figures as soon as possible, please?
  a round
  b on
  c back

3 | Application

Following up on a project

1 Using realia and case material, work in pairs or threes to decide on a simple project. Agree the key milestones and who is doing what.
2 Write an email summarising the meeting and listing the action points.
3 Progress chase: the person responsible for coordinating the project calls to check on progress. Discuss any slippage and decide how to handle it.
4 Prepare an email summarising the points agreed in the phone call.

4 | Writing

A 'thank you' message

1 What is your opinion of this letter? For example, is it too long, should it have a heading, etc.?
2 Rewrite it as an email. Add a subject at the beginning. Aim to be shorter and simpler.

T. Sven
Montorex AB
Stockholm
Sweden

Dear Tom

Once again, I am in your debt for the kind hospitality extended to our group on our visit last week.

Mr Smithson was very impressed with the versatility and size of your plant, and he believes, as I do, that a two-way partnership will be possible. This will, of course, depend on the forthcoming trials, but I have great confidence in your abilities.

Please pass on my thanks to Simo and Jan, especially for the skiing lesson. As I am sure you remember, it was a first for me, but a very enjoyable first. The weekend was very memorable.

I look forward to returning your hospitality here in Madrid soon. As promised, I will take you for a tour of our tapas bars. Better late than never! Let's hope that we can celebrate the beginning of a successful business relationship.

With kind regards

Antonio Milagros

Sr Antonio Milagros

Mismanagement of company funds

1 Read the report by the finance director of Yukon Tours, a holiday travel company based in Vancouver. It is a month since you received the report, and you need an update on the situation. In pairs, go through the contents and write the questions you would like answered.

e.g. Did Ray Felli supply the missing information by 21 February as required?

REPORT

To: Donna Yang
From: Peter Baska
Date: 19 February 2…
Subject: Canadian trip

The purpose of the trip was to review the management of the company bank account by the local personnel.

Current position

The account is funded by Yukon Tours. Local expenditure is reimbursed on the basis of evidence forwarded from the Vancouver office. Our area manager, Ray Felli, is assisted in the preparation of this information by a local part-time accountant.

Cheques are drawn in Canadian dollars by local personnel for the staff salaries, together with a series of cheques for expenses such as social security tax, rent, cleaning, accountant's fees. The latter cheques are not supported by documents / vouchers. They are cashed either to pay suppliers direct, or to be deposited into the personal bank account of Ray Felli to be drawn on when payment in cash is required.

Findings

I spent one and a half days reviewing the bank account. Although I was able to establish and verify the deposits, I was unable to support withdrawals from the account by vouchers or documents. Further, the whereabouts of the US$7,000 advanced by Head Office to set up the account is not apparent.

Ray has been requested to forward details of the movement of company funds via his personal account by 21 February – he requires the assistance of the part-time accountant for this task.

Despite the picture the above suggests, I do not feel that there has been any intentional mismanagement or appropriation of company funds. It seems more likely that the situation is the result of the manager's inability to control the flow of company funds effectively. The ability of the part-time accountant is also questionable – a simple cash book is not maintained.

Recommendations

i The Vancouver office to issue cheques on the 15th of each month for the following items: salaries, social security taxes, income tax, rent, cleaning, accounting, motor leases. A reimbursement cheque / deposit to be paid into the account to cover these items.

ii The Vancouver office to introduce a standard petty cash system for small day-to-day expenses.

iii Yukon Tours to review the status and number of local staff.

2 Listen to the author of the report giving an update on the situation, and make notes. Then mark your questions as follows: answered [✓], half answered [¹/₂], not referred to [✗].

LANGUAGE REFERENCE

Language Notes

For further notes on these points, see the accompanying Business Grammar Guide (BGG).

More on Present tenses (BGG 1.1)

- Verbs normally used in the Simple form

e.g. I **gather** your trip went well.
I (do not) **feel** / **think** / **agree** (that) …
We **hear** / **understand** / **believe** (that) …
As far as I **know** …
I **wonder** why they did that.
Everything **depends** on …

- Where the Continuous form has a different meaning

e.g. When **are you thinking** of leaving?
We**'re seeing** Milo this evening.
We **are having** problems.

- Where you can use either form

e.g. He **doesn't feel** / **isn't feeling** well.
They **hope** / **are hoping** to complete tomorrow.
We **look forward** / **are looking** forward to seeing you again.

- Special uses

e.g. It **is always going** wrong.
They **keep changing** the date.

Some present passive forms (BGG 4)

- Simple

e.g. The site **is owned** by DLK Holdings.
The manager **is assisted** by a part-time accountant.

- Continuous

e.g. The system **is being changed**.
Are these figures **being checked** by anyone?

- Infinitive

e.g. The report is going **to be circulated**.
When is the account going **to be paid**?

Giving feedback: examples of *really*, *quite*, *rather*, etc. (BGG 14.4)

e.g. It was **really** good.
The arrangements were **not quite** up to standard.
I thought it was **fairly** dull / **rather** boring.
I have to say we were **slightly** / **a bit** disappointed.
Frankly, I was **pretty** dissatisfied.
It was **absolutely** first class.

Vocabulary

- Words and phrases

e.g. a useful / valuable trip, an exhausting / pointless visit,
a stimulating / relevant / well-planned programme,
a number of problems, one of two issues,
a serious set-back, a few minor hassles

- Verbs and verb phrases

e.g. We need to **follow up on** those enquiries.
You asked me to **find out** how things are going.
Could you **let me know** when the work will be ready?
How soon can you **get back to** me with the samples?
I'm afraid I can't **get hold of** the documents you want till Monday.
How are you **getting on with** the B60 project?
We are **making good progress**.
It's **progressing well**.

Useful Phrases

How are you progressing with the X50 project?
How you getting on? How is it going?
I managed to get hold of the figures you wanted.
I understand you don't need the brochures.

I'm just following up on the samples you were going to send me.
Have you been able to send them yet?
As far I know, Guido is finding out about it.
Could you ask him to let me know what's happening?

You asked me to find out about the timetable.
The system is being upgraded.
They keep changing it.
It is always going wrong.
I'm afraid I am having problems getting the details.

I thought everything went pretty well.
I have to say I was a bit disappointed.
I felt the presentations were rather boring.
I thought the organisation was absolutely first class.

I'm pretty sure I left some papers behind.
They were in a green folder, marked 'Liaison'.
Nothing has been handed in.
I'll let you know if anything turns up.

I'm just calling to thank you for organising such an interesting visit.
You're very welcome – it was a pleasure.
We're glad you could make it.
We are looking forward to seeing you again soon.

UNIT 4 Dealing with change

1 Core practice

Listening and speaking

Listen to the exchanges (a – d) and mark the statements (part i) true ☐T☐, false ☐F☐ or unclear ☐U☐. Then, working with a partner, practise the exchanges indicated in part ii.

a i The catalogue was delayed because a new range of products had to be included. ☐

  ii Talk about a job where the objective changed.

b i The new MD was an internal appointment. ☐

  ii Talk about staff changes in your area.

c i The R&D department at Head Office has been closed down. ☐

  ii Talk about a recent reorganisation.

d i The local team has been made redundant. ☐

  ii Practise explaining a restructuring to a customer.

Preparation

The focus here is on change through historical development, reorganisation and takeover. Come prepared to talk about changes in your organisation. Check the Useful Phrases on page 28. If possible, bring to the class documents relating to change programmes you have been involved in.

2 Language check

Refer to the Language Notes on page 28 as you complete the examples below using the choices provided – only one is correct. Then prepare a version of each example that you might use.

1 By the following year, the new CEO ....
  a was appointed
  b has been appointed
  c had been appointed

2 She .... her new job till this July.
  a hasn't started
  b hadn't started
  c didn't start

3 They .... 20,000 units so far this week.
  a have produced
  b produced
  c had produced

4 I .... for Trovit for three years when I was in the States.
  a was working
  b worked
  c used to work

5 This .... in Mexico, but now we make it ourselves.
  a was made
  b used to be made
  c has been made

6 .... our product range was very limited.
  a To begin
  b First
  c Initially

7 We .... two reorganisations before we were taken over.
  a have already
  b had already
  c had already had

8 After the company .... , the assets were sold off.
  a bankrupted
  b went bankrupt
  c liquidation

9 We were hit by the recession, and had to cut .... on our investment programme.
  a back
  b off
  c through

10 As soon as we had .... the new structure, they introduced another change programme.
  a got used to
  b been used to
  c used to

3 | Listening

Changes during working life

Mark Jarvis works in aircraft manufacturing. Here he talks about the changes that have taken place during his working life.

1 Listen and list the changes he refers to.
   e.g. When he started work 22 years ago, there was no direct dial out.
2 List the changes that have occurred in your working life.
   e.g. It is much easier to work abroad than it used to be.

4 | Writing

Liaising with customers

1 Think of a change you have been involved in. Imagine it is happening now and write an email to a key customer (internal or external) explaining the change. In your message, you might do the following – as appropriate.
   • Outline the change.
   • Indicate the benefits.
   • Describe your new role.
   • Indicate who will be responsible for what in future.
   • Reassure the customer.
   • Offer to answer questions.
2 Now working in pairs, practise the phone call that might follow the email.

Read and discuss the case study. What lessons relating to change does it have:

- for your company (or one you know)
- for you personally?

Saving **BIG** BLUE

In the nineties, computer giant IBM was suffering in a rapidly changing market.
It took an outsider to see how its fortunes could be reversed.

ON THE SLIDE

For decades, IBM dominated the computer industry, enjoying spectacular financial success. By the late 1980s, however, things were changing. The company had severely underestimated the opportunity that personal computers represented, and when it did enter the PC market, it made a key strategic mistake by allowing Microsoft to retain rights to DOS, the operating system it had developed for the IBM PC.

That was not IBM's only problem. Cheap clones in the hardware market had eroded profits in PCs, too. Moreover, sales of mainframes had dramatically declined. By the end of 1994, the company had racked up $15bn in cumulative losses over the previous three years.

A SAVIOUR ARRIVES

It was around this time that an outsider called Lou Gerstner took charge. The essence of his strategy was simple yet profound. He realised that with the industry exploding in all directions, new users, devices and platforms were being added all the time. This made the integration

Lou Gerstner (above) shifted IBM's focus from products to applications. His non-IBM background helped bring objectivity to the situation.

of all these technologies a major problem for business customers. IBM, with its vast knowledge of hardware and software, was eminently positioned to provide the solution.

While Gerstner was convinced that his strategy of becoming an integrator was the only viable alternative, he knew that would entail an enormous organisational revolution. IBM had always established standards rather than

adapting to them, and its thousands of highly qualified employees considered the idea of altering their technologies to suit competitors' products anathema.

THE TURNAROUND

Gerstner's accomplishment lay in changing the strategy, culture and organisation of IBM.

At the strategic level, IBM became a services company. Culturally, Gerstner radically altered the inward-looking philosophy of the company to one that embraced competitors' products.

At the organisational level, IBM consolidated its dispersed software competence and rewrote much of its software to make it 'cross platform'. It recruited and trained about 5,000 new software sales specialists who could sell this software, which would help integrate different platforms for the customer.

By the year 2000, IBM had achieved a dramatic reversal in fortunes. From a loss of $8.1bn in 1992, it produced a profit of $8.1bn in 2000. And the trend has continued since then.

Adapted from *Business Life Magazine*

LANGUAGE REFERENCE

Language Notes

For further notes on these points, see the accompanying Business Grammar Guide (BGG).

Past tenses

Active (BGG 1.2, 1.3, 1.4, 1.5)
- The Past Simple (*We did it.*)
e.g. We **changed** the system last year.

- The Present Perfect (*We have done it.*)
e.g. We **have** recently **changed** the system.

- The Past Perfect (*We had done it.*)
e.g. We **had** already **changed** the system before the takeover.

- The Past Continuous (*We were doing it.*)
e.g. We **were thinking** of changing the system, but there was no budget.

Passive (BGG 4)
- The Past Simple (*It was done.*)
e.g. The system **was changed** last year.

- The Present Perfect (*It has been done.*)
e.g. The system **has** already **been changed** three times.

- The Past Perfect (*It had been done.*)
e.g. The system **had been changed** by the time I arrived.

- The Past Continuous (*It was being done.*)
e.g. The system **was being changed** when I left.

used to / to be used to / to get used to (BGG 1.6)
- *used to*
e.g. Our head office **used to be** in Madrid, but they moved it to Finland last year.

- *to be used to*
e.g. I'm not **used to living** in Northern Europe.

- *to get used to*
e.g. I can't **get used to** the cold climate.

Some past time markers
- Establishing a time
e.g. **26 years ago**
    during the 90s

- Referring to the first period / phase
e.g. **originally / initially**
    to begin with

- Indicating a later time
e.g. **a year / several years later**
    a week / few weeks after that

- Indicating an earlier time
e.g. **a week / two weeks earlier**
    two months before that / prior to that

- Indicating the same time
e.g. **While** they were developing …, they had to …,
    At the same time as she was working on …, she was trying to …

- Contrasting two past times
e.g. **After** he read the report, he fired the Financial Controller.
    Having seen the figures, we decided not to buy the company.

Vocabulary

- Words and phrases
e.g. reorganisation, restructuring, rationalisation,
    relocate, downsize,
    outsource, offshore,
    business unit, retail division, HR department,
    front office, middle office, back office,
    go bankrupt, go into liquidation, go broke / bust

- Verbs and verb phrases
e.g. They were **taken over** by Sinwung two years ago.
    The Saõ Paulo plant was **closed down** in 2002.
    We had to **cut back** on R&D because we were losing money.
    In the late 90s we nearly **went out of business**.
    We have **set up** a new sales company in Tunisia.
    The old processing plant was **sold off**.
    It was **taken over** by Alcam.

Useful Phrases

The company was founded 20 years ago.
In the early days we were based in Seattle.
Three years ago we were taken over by BSK.
Recently, we switched to local suppliers.
In the last year or so, we've been doing a lot of business in APAC.

John became head of my business unit.
It was an internal appointment.
The CEO retired three months ago.
A woman called Dena Stroe took over from him.
She used to work in Compliance.
In the new structure, I have a reporting line to John and a dotted line to Dena.

We now process orders centrally.
We no longer handle the work locally.
The work was outsourced to BLK.
I am no longer involved on a day-to-day basis.

Magda is now in charge.
You should send your queries to her.
But do feel free to contact me if there are problems.

All the transactions that used to be handled by my team are now handled by the global team based in Frankfurt.
There should be no difference in the day-to-day running of your account.

What are the main changes?
What difference has reorganisation made?
We have to do the same job with fewer resources.
There's more pressure than there used to be.

UNIT 5 Culture and values

1 | Core practice

Listening and speaking

Listen to exchanges (a – d) and mark the statements (part i) true ☐T☐, false ☐F☐ or unclear ☐U☐. Then, working with a partner, practise the exchanges indicated in part ii.

a i For 18 months the management has been 'living in the past'. ☐
  ii Talk about a time when a new boss changed the working atmosphere.

b i The speaker was fired because he didn't fit in. ☐
  ii Talk about a situation where somebody didn't fit in.

c i The company places great emphasis on employees taking responsibility for their own work. ☐
  ii Practise talking about the culture in your organisation.

d i Before this job, the speaker had been working with state-of-the-art equipment. ☐
  ii Practise talking about a situation where you have 'foreign' management.

> **Preparation**
>
> In this unit you can practise talking about company culture and values, and where the organisation is going – its mission. Come prepared to talk about your organisation in these areas. Before class, check the Useful Phrases on page 32. If possible, bring to the lesson related brochures and web pages.

2 | Language check

Refer to the Language Notes on page 32 as you complete the examples below using the choices provided – only one is correct. Then prepare a version of each example that you might use.

1 The new management were trying to introduce a more enterprising culture, but it ....
  a had been working
  b wasn't working
  c hasn't been working

2 The company .... investing in new equipment so standards are rising.
  a was
  b had been
  c has been

3 We called as soon as we heard, but they .... a decision.
  a had already made
  b already made
  c had already been making

4 I .... working with automated systems for years, so I didn't need to retrain.
  a have been
  b had been
  c wasn't

5 I had been having a hard time at work ....
  a recently
  b for several months now
  c even before that

6 The problem is that the company isn't very ....
  a well run
  b badly run
  c poorly run

7 Several of their factories are ....
  a dismotivated
  b overstaffed
  c inorganised

8 It's difficult to make a comparison because the company is non- ....
  a profitable
  b profit-making
  c public

9 He had to leave because he didn't .... in with the culture.
  a fit
  b get
  c turn

10 The new team are willing to put .... with poor quality control, so the level of defects has been going ....
  a up / down
  b down / up
  c up / up

3 | Writing

Panasonic's values

The image opposite is a bookmark distributed by Panasonic introducing its Basic Business Philosophy.

1 Rewrite 'Values' and 'Actions' as full statements.
   e.g. Seek to make a contribution to society.
2 Write a list that shows your top ten values.

4 | Listening

Working abroad

1 A British manager talks about her recent transfer to a Dutch subsidiary. Listen and answer the questions.
   a In general, how does she feel about the move?
   b How well is she integrating into the company?
   c What does her new job involve?
   d Why has she had to learn Dutch?
   e What is the relationship between the British and the Dutch factory?
   f Are there any drawbacks?
2 You have a new job with a company in another country. Write an email to the company asking for advice (e.g. on cultural differences, domestic considerations, climate, etc.). Use the Useful Phrases on page 133 as necessary.

Basic Business Philosophy

MISSION

Basic Management Objective

VALUES

- Contribution to Society
- Fairness & Honesty
- Cooperation and team spirit
- Untiring effort for improvement
- Courtesy and humility
- Adaptability
- Gratitude

ACTIONS

- The customer first in practice
- Profit as a measure of contribution
- Autonomous management
- Co-existence and mutual prosperity
- Management by all with collective wisdom
- Fair competition
- People before products

Mission

Values   Actions

Courtesy at work

1 Answer the questionnaire. Unless otherwise instructed, tick only one answer for each question. The scoring is on page 133 – do you agree with it?

How well do you treat colleagues?

1 What hours do you expect those below you to work?
a Longer hours than you. ☐
b The same as you. ☐
c Shorter hours than you. ☐

2 Alone in the office, you take a phone call which isn't for you. What do you do?
a Explain, and ask the caller to ring again. ☐
b Explain, and take a message. ☐
c Explain, and take a message only if it is for someone more senior. ☐

3 Someone has made a major blunder. What do you do?
a Publicly criticise them to teach them and others a lesson. ☐
b Have a word with them in private. ☐
c Discuss privately what went wrong, and how to avoid a repetition. ☐
d Have a word with them in private with the door open. ☐

4 Which of these facts do you know about your closest colleague?
(Tick all that apply. Add a bonus of 4 points if you have thanked them with feeling five times in the last week.)
a Correct spelling of their name. ☐
b Age and birthday. ☐
c Names and ages of children / partner. ☐
d Favourite hobby. ☐

5 You are chief executive and your company is in a major upheaval. What do you do?
a Let those outside the boardroom discover what they can from the press. ☐
b Keep everyone briefed as far as possible, and explain press comment. ☐
c Talk to the staff once it hits the press. ☐
d Talk to all the management, but only once it hits the press. ☐

6 How are meetings arranged?
a To suit your convenience. ☐
b As far as possible to suit the work and private commitments of everyone involved. ☐
c As far as possible to suit the work commitments of everyone involved. ☐

7 What do you do to introduce newcomers?
(Tick all that apply. Add a bonus of 4 points if colleagues are briefed on newcomers.)
a Have them shown around by their boss and introduced to key colleagues. ☐
b Give them a list of the names and positions of senior personnel. ☐
c Give them a list of the names and positions of immediate colleagues. ☐
d Give them documentation on company structure. ☐
e Tell them the hours or work, arrangements for breaks, payment of expenses, etc. ☐
f Explain who to ask for information. ☐

8 What is your view on the issue of opening doors?
a Everyone should open their own. ☐
b Everyone should open doors for all, regardless of sex or need. ☐
c Men should open doors for women. ☐
d People should open doors for all if it will be helpful and welcome. ☐

9 Which view do you hold on manners to the opposite sex at work?
a The opposite sex should be treated with special courtesy. ☐
b Either sex should be treated equally. ☐

10 Which of the following have you done to equals or juniors?
(Tick all that apply.)
a Shouted at them. ☐
b Made remarks about them within their hearing. ☐
c Asked them to make a coffee or tea when it's not their job. ☐

Adapted from *Intercity*

2 In the area of courtesy, discuss the standards you expect and practise in the following areas.

- Customer relations and customer service.
- Working atmosphere, relations between colleagues.
- Management style.
- Written communication, email conventions.

LANGUAGE REFERENCE

Language Notes

For further notes on these points, see the accompanying Business Grammar Guide (BGG).

More on Past tenses: continuous forms

(BGG 1.2 – 1.5)

• Past

Simple:	I **worked** for a Japanese company for three years.
Continuous:	I **was working** for a Japanese company at that time.

• Present Perfect

Simple:	I **have worked** for a German company twice in my life.
Continuous:	I **have been working** for a German company for the last two months.

• Past Perfect

Simple:	I **had worked** for an American company before that, so I could already speak English.
Continuous:	I **had been working** for an American company for several years before I started to learn English.

The simple form communicates the facts of the matter. The continuous form indicates that the situation lasted over a period of time.

The opposite of adjectives (BGG 13.2)

• *un-* is the most common negative prefix.

e.g. friendly / **un**friendly
motivated / **un**motivated
reliable / **un**reliable
businesslike / **un**businesslike

• Notice also these negative prefixes: *in-, im-, ir, il-, dis-*.

e.g. effective / **in**effective
practical / **im**practical
responsible / **irr**esponsible
legal / **ill**egal
organised / **dis**organised

• Other examples.

well / badly (poorly):	well-run / badly run, well-treated / badly treated
over / under:	overstaffed / understaffed, overpaid / underpaid
high / low:	high quality / low quality, high level / low level
non-:	profit-making / non-profit-making, interactive / non-interactive

Vocabulary

• Words and phrases

e.g. enterprising, innovative, progressive, cutting-edge, supportive, encouraging, positive, bureaucratic, cautious, traditional, old-fashioned, critical, negative, demotivating, average, standard, middle-of-the-road, staff turnover, head count, absenteism

• Verbs and verb phrases

e.g. They **look after** their workers very well.
The management won't **put up with** low quality work.
It's a very progressive company; they are willing to **try out** new ideas.
She was very well-qualified, but she didn't **fit in**.
The manager **attaches** a lot of **importance** to loyalty.
In this company, if you work hard, you will **get on**.
They are always willing to **try out** new ideas.

Useful Phrases

I used to work for a company in the UK.
It was a very traditional organisation.
The culture was very old-fashioned.
They weren't interested in innovation.

The workforce was skilled but unmotivated.
Junior staff were very badly treated.
Staff turnover was high.
The main aim was to avoid risk.

I've been working here for three months.
When I first started, it all seemed a bit strange.
I had never worked for a Japanese company before.
Previously, I had been working with manual systems.

When I first started, the department was much bigger.
We used to check the machines by hand.
The technology involved has changed completely.
The equipment had to be upgraded.

We've been learning new skills.
The company has been investing a fortune in training.
Our working practices are changing.
It is a very competitive environment.

The atmosphere is extremely businesslike.
We work together as a team.
There are good bonus and incentive schemes.
The management attach a lot of importance to loyalty.
We're all highly motivated.

UNIT 6 Environmental issues

1 Core practice

Listening and speaking

Listen to exchanges (a – d) and answer the questions in part i. Then, working with a partner, practise the exchanges indicated in part ii.

a i Do the speakers agree? What do they agree?
  ii Identify the environmental issue that you feel is most important.
b i What are they arguing about?
  ii Discuss an environmental issue that concerns you.
c i Why is the company moving over to an environmental procurement policy?
  ii Discuss a change you have made for environmental reasons.
d i Is the speaker in favour of recent environmental legislation?
  ii Give an example where green legislation has affected you or your work.

Preparation

What is your personal position on the main environmental issues? How do they impact your company? Before class, check the Useful Phrases on page 36. If possible, bring documents relating to your company's green strategies. Come prepared to speak about your organisation's policies in this area.

2 Language check

Refer to the Language Notes on page 36 as you complete the examples below using the choices provided – only one is correct. Then prepare a version of each example that you might use.

1 Do you .... with the new guidelines?
  a accept
  b follow
  c go along
2 As far as .... , illegal dumping is the main problem.
  a I'm concerned
  b I think
  c my view is
3 How do the new regulations .... your business?
  a affect
  b effect
  c inject
4 Radioactive waste is .... dangerous.
  a fairly
  b completely
  c extremely
5 It is .... possible to develop alternative .... but it is expensive.
  a technically / energy sources
  b politically / declining resources
  c environmentally / green issues

6 The last report indicates that the .... of marine pollution is rising.
  a total
  b number
  c level
7 47% of our products are made from .... materials.
  a organic
  b green
  c biodegradable
8 We send most of our waste products to the new .... plant.
  a recycled
  b recycling
  c dumping

9 We don't accept that the recent oil .... were unavoidable.
  a dumpings
  b spillages
  c emissions
10 If current trends continue, our natural gas supplies will .... in ten years.
  a run out
  b use up
  c get rid of

3 | Reading

Radioactive waste

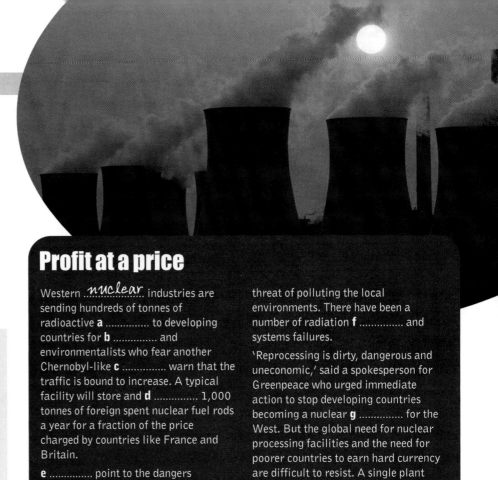

1 Fill in the gaps in the text using terms from the box below. Is the tone of the article approving, critical or neutral?

2 What is your view of nuclear power?
  • What are the benefits?
  • What are the costs?
  • What are the options for economies that do not have oil or hydro power?

► atmosphere	► biodegradable
► conservation	► disaster
► disposal	► dump
► emissions	► energy
► environmentalists	► green
► landfill	► leakages
► nuclear ✓	► organic
► polluted	► radioactive
► recycle	► reprocessing
► spillages	► waste

Profit at a price

Western *nuclear* industries are sending hundreds of tonnes of radioactive **a** .... to developing countries for **b** .... and environmentalists who fear another Chernobyl-like **c** .... warn that the traffic is bound to increase. A typical facility will store and **d** .... 1,000 tonnes of foreign spent nuclear fuel rods a year for a fraction of the price charged by countries like France and Britain.

e .... point to the dangers involved in transporting the radioactive material long distances, and to the threat of polluting the local environments. There have been a number of radiation **f** .... and systems failures.

'Reprocessing is dirty, dangerous and uneconomic,' said a spokesperson for Greenpeace who urged immediate action to stop developing countries becoming a nuclear **g** .... for the West. But the global need for nuclear processing facilities and the need for poorer countries to earn hard currency are difficult to resist. A single plant can create 5,000 jobs and earn nearly $2 billion a year.

4 | Writing

A complaint from the public

The environmental complaint form below has been forwarded to you from your company's website. Working in pairs, draft a response.

ENVIRONMENTAL COMPLAINT FORM

Complete the following form to report a complaint regarding air quality, odours, noise, water pollution, illegal dumping and chemical spills.

Type of complaint

☐ Noise
☑ Odour
☑ Air quality
☐ Water pollution
☐ Chemical spill (includes oil)
☐ Other

Description of complaint

At 11.00am this morning I noticed that one of the chimneys on your Zone 26 site was producing clouds of yellow smoke. This continued for about 11 minutes. There was a strong chemical smell that lasted for about an hour. Later, my car and the windows of my apartment were covered in a fine yellow dust. I would like to know what caused the yellow smoke, whether it is dangerous and if it is likely to happen again.

Address where alleged offence occurred

Your Zone 26 site

SUBMIT   CANCEL

Partner A: Your information is opposite. It is your job to reply to complaints of this kind. Work with **Partner B** who has the necessary technical knowledge to draft a response.

Partner B: Your information is on page 133.

5 Case study

The Body Shop

1 A representative of The Body Shop talks about the company's environmental policies. Which of the following areas are covered?
   a The company's environmental audit programme.
   b The key features of the company's 'green' policies.
   c The company's approach to packaging.
   d The benefits to the company of these policies.
2 In pairs discuss the issues featured in this download from the company's website. Then answer the following questions.
   • Would you describe yourself as environmentally friendly?
   • Have you ever taken part in an environmental audit? Should they be standard procedure?
   • Does your company support any of the strategies listed on The Body Shop homepage?
   • To what extent is environmental performance a competitive issue in your business?

AGAINST ANIMAL TESTING
We consider testing products or ingredients on animals to be morally and scientifically indefensible.

SUPPORT COMMUNITY TRADE
We support small producer communities around the world who supply us with accessories and natural ingredients.

ACTIVE SELF-ESTEEM
We know that you're unique, and we'll always treat you like an individual.
We like you just the way you are.

DEFEND HUMAN RIGHTS
We believe that it is the responsibility of every individual to actively support those who have human rights denied to them.

PROTECT OUR PLANET
We believe that a business has the responsibility to protect the environment in which it operates, locally and globally.

LANGUAGE REFERENCE

Language Notes

For further notes on these points, see the accompanying Business Grammar Guide (BGG).

Some terms used in discussion (BGG 21.2, 21.3)

- Giving opinions
e.g. I think / believe / guess …
    In my view … / From my point of view …
    As far as I'm concerned …
    I would have thought (that) …
    Do you realise … ?

- Asking opinions
e.g. What do you think of …
    What is your view / opinion of …
    Are you saying that …
    I'm not sure what you are saying – do you mean … ?
    Do you agree / think that … ?

- Agreeing
e.g. I (absolutely) agree with what you're saying.
    I think you're right when you say …
    I agree up to a point / on the whole.
    I accept that, but …
    I see what you mean / take your point, but …

- Disagreeing
e.g. (I'm afraid) I can't go along with …
    That doesn't follow.
    You must remember … / Don't forget …
    On the other hand …
    That's just not true / so / the case.

- Making reference
e.g. That's very similar to John's example.
    It's the same as the case you mentioned earlier.
    Our situation is very different from yours.
    In a disaster like this …
    In situations like that …

Adverbs in phrases (BGG 14.4)

- Adverbs can modify strength
e.g. **extremely** dangerous
    completely untrue
    highly unpopular
    really interesting
    reasonably cheap

- Adverbs can modify meaning
e.g. **environmentally** friendly
    technically developed
    economically viable
    theoretically possible
    politically correct

Level / volume / amount of …, etc.

e.g. the **level of** pollution
    the **volume of** business
    the **amount of** time
    the **quantity of** oil
    the **degree of** confusion
    the **number of** regulations

Vocabulary

- Words and phrases
e.g. alternative technologies, green issues, sustainable policies, pollution, dumping, spillage, waste, global warming, declining resources, green issues, organic farming, population control, biodegradable products, bottle bank, recycling plant, landfill site, incineration plant

- Verbs and verb phrases
e.g. Our natural resources are being **used up** at an alarming rate.
    Our oil supplies will **run out** in the next 15 years.
    The old reactors are all being **phased out** / **shut down** / **decommissioned**.
    It is very difficult to **get rid of** nuclear waste.
    It costs millions to **clean up** after a major oil spillage.

Useful Phrases

What impact are green issues having on your business?
Customers are worried about the environmental impact of the products they buy.
People ask questions about our environmental practices.
Environmental performance is a competitive issue.

We are running out of landfill sites.
We now recycle our waste.
We used to throw it away.
The cost of waste disposal is so high that recycling is economically viable.

How are the new laws affecting you?
laws   regulations   guidelines
They are adding to our costs.
Something has to be done about pollution.
The level of air pollution is rising.
But in our view the cost of compliance is too high.

Alternative sources of energy are very important.
They say that existing supplies will run out in 20 years' time.
We can't rely on green technologies to fill the gap.
We believe that conservation is the key.

I don't accept that we have an energy problem.
There are many alternative sources.
How do you feel about nuclear energy?
What about the environmental costs?
We need a source of renewable energy.

UNIT 7 Recruitment and training

1 Core practice

Listening and speaking

Listen to the exchanges (a – d) and mark the statements (part i)
true ☐T☐, false ☐F☐ or unclear ☐U☐. Then, working with a partner,
practise the exchanges indicated in part ii.

a i They use specialised job-search sites for all vacancies. ☐
  ii Talk about how you recruit new staff.

b i The recruitment manager didn't receive the
    applicant's emails. ☐
  ii Practise calling a company and asking about a job
    advertisement you have seen.

c i The speaker studied banking at college. ☐
  ii In pairs, compare how you got your first job.

d i The training manager is going to organise a course
    that will meet the caller's needs. ☐
  ii Practise calling the training department to ask about
    a course you need.

Preparation

This unit is about finding new
staff, training existing staff and
personal development
planning. How did you get your
job? How do you maintain your
development? Before the
lesson check the Useful
Phrases on page 40. If possible,
bring a job advertisement, an
application form and training
information to class.

2 Language check

Refer to the Language Notes on page 40 as you complete the
examples below using the choices provided – only one is correct.
Then prepare a version of each example that you might use.

1 I have spoken to everyone ....
is coming to the interview.
  a whom
  b –
  c who

2 I have received confirmations
from everyone .... name is on
the shortlist.
  a which
  b whose
  c who

3 This is the RF292 file, in ....
we keep a record of all the
courses our people go on.
  a that
  b where
  c which

4 Buz Morter, ... , will be
present at the interviews.
  a who is head of the section
  b head of the section
  c head of section

5 Is this the new software
.... we talked about
yesterday?
  a –
  b of which
  c about which

6 It was your training
manager ....
  a I sent the CV
  b I sent the CV to
  c whom I sent the CV

7 I have mislaid my notebook,
.... are highly
confidential.
  a which contents
  b whose contents
  c the contents of which

8 I was afraid that if I applied for
the job I would be turned ....
  a down
  b out
  c off

9 Unfortunately, I didn't ....
on very well at the interview.
  a make
  b take
  c get

10 What kind of person are they
looking .... ?
  a after
  b into
  c for

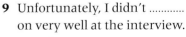

3 Listening

Training

1 Listen to the speakers talking about the training they have received, and make notes. Then tick the categories they refer to.
2 What training do you have? Are there any courses you want to go on? Compare notes with a partner.

Acquiring skills and experience	**Speakers: 1**	**2**
• General business knowledge, e.g. health and safety, trade affairs	☐	☐
• Technical skills, basic knowledge needed to carry out specific tasks	☐	☐
• Development of core skills through on-the-job training	☐	☐
• Knowledge of related functions, e.g. finance and marketing	☐	☐
• Business-related skills, e.g. communication, decisions-making, negotiating	☐	☐
• People-related skills, e.g. leadership, motivation, team building, delegation	☐	☐

From *The Manager's Handbook*

4 Writing

Application letter

Imagine you are applying for a job. In the advertisement you were asked to write a letter to accompany your resumé (CV). Read the notes below and write the letter.

A good application letter contains the following elements.

1 How you learned about the vacancy (unless you're applying 'blind').
2 A brief statement as to why you are interested in the job and why you believe you qualify for it.
3 A request for a personal interview.
4 Information about where you can be reached.

From *The McGraw-Hill Handbook of Business Letters*

Personal development planning

Read the step-by-step guide. Then, working in pairs, talk to your partner about his / her development needs, and fill in the planner. There is a completed sample on page 133, which you can use as a model.

Using the personal development planner

STEP 1: Fill in the focus areas, e.g. time management, networking, technical skills. Make sure you focus on your primary needs.

STEP 2: Think about where you are. Fill in how you are performing now in the second column. Think of the feedback you have received.

STEP 3: Think about your objectives. In the third column, record the level of performance or skill you want to achieve.

STEP 4: Think about any action you need to take. What are you going to do to achieve the goals listed in your plan? Record your action points in this column.

STEP 5: Think about timing. In this column record the dates you will start and finish, then put the dates in your diary!

Personal development planner

	Focus area	Where now	Objective
1			
2			
3			

	Actions	Timing
1		
2		
3		

Adapted from uncommon-knowledge.co.uk

LANGUAGE REFERENCE

Language Notes

For further notes on these points, see the accompanying Business Grammar Guide (BGG).

Relative clauses (BGG 16)

- Defining clauses – people (no commas)

e.g. The person **who** / **that** interviewed me came from Cape Town.
  I have written to all the people **who** / **that** applied for the job.
  Seja Bulow is the person **who** / **that** / – we appointed.
  Are you the person **whose** car broke down?

- Defining clauses – things and places (no commas)

e.g. This is the data storage system **which** / **that** / – we use to track applications.
  Is this the report **which** / **that** / – you sent?
  Did you include the three references **which** / **that** / – they asked for?
  This is the office **where** they interviewed me.

- Non-defining clauses – people (commas needed)

e.g. I have sent a text to Tiu Haize, **who is** the person I'm dealing with.
  Tiu Haize, **who is** the recruitment manager, is handling the matter.
  Tiu Haize, **who** I have run through the details with, is going to sort it out.
  We have a staff of 12, **all of whom** are fully qualified.

- Non-defining clauses – things and places (commas needed)

e.g. We liked the new training equipment, **which** we have all tested, but it's too expensive.
  BZ Training, **which** runs most of our courses, is based in Zurich.
  Room G3, **where** all the big meetings are held, is just along here.

- Prepositions in relative clauses

Notice you can say the following.

Standard: The people I worked **with** in Cape Town were very friendly.

Formal: The people **with whom** I worked in Cape Town were very friendly.

- Other examples

That's the person I had my interview **with**.
That's the person **with whom** I had my interview.
This is the address I sent the application **to**.
This is the address **to which** I sent the application.

Vocabulary

- Words and phrases

e.g. first / second degree, postgraduate qualification, professional diploma, over-qualified, under-qualified, continuing education, ongoing development, continuous improvement, school leaver, job applicant, personal background, employment history, recruitment agency, head-hunter

- Verbs and verb phrases

e.g. We only **shortlisted** two candidates **for** the job.
  How did you **get on** at the interview? Did it go well?
  Your application form needs to **be in** by Monday.
  I applied for the job but I was **turned down**.
  Have your **filled in** your PDP (personal development plan)?
  You should **go through** the form with your manager.
  I need to **update** my CV (curriculum vitae).

Useful Phrases

I joined the company straight from school.
Most of my training has been on the job.
I qualified in chemical engineering at Berlin University.
I have a degree in Business Studies.

We get most of our people through job-search sites.
We get a large number of unsolicited applications.
We make very little use of recruitment agencies.
We also post vacancies on our website.

I'm ringing about your advert for a product manager.
Could you give me some further details?
What kind of person are you looking for?
Could you tell me something about yourself?

Have you filled in your PDP (personal development plan)?
You haven't put anything in the final column.
You need to decide your action steps.
How are you going to improve your performance?
Do you want me to go through the form with you?

I'd like to go on a documentation course.
Is there one you could recommend?
There's nothing advertised on the web page.
Can I go on the waiting list?

I was very happy with the course.
I was disappointed.
The course didn't really stretch us.
The course was very demanding.

UNIT 8 Staff relations

1 Core practice

Listening and speaking

Listen to the exchanges (a – d) and
mark the statements (part i) true
[T], false [F] or unclear [U]. Then,
working with a partner, practise the
exchanges indicated in part ii.

a i The atmosphere in the
factory has always been
bad. ☐

   ii Talk about a work
environment where there
are problems. Give details.

b i The new production
manager is a member of
the Workers' Council. ☐

   ii Talk about a situation
where a new manager has
improved team morale.

c i The man will get paid for
the time off. ☐

   ii Practise requesting time off.

d i The person representing
the company accepts the
proposals. ☐

   ii Practise asking for an
increase in benefits.

Preparation

This unit is about the balance in the workplace between staff and management and the
relationship between managers and unions. Come ready to talk about staff relations in your
organisation. Check the Useful Phrases on page 44. If possible, bring related articles or
reports to class.

2 Language check

Refer to the Language Notes on page 44 as you complete the examples
below using the choices provided – only one is correct. Then prepare a
version of each example that you might use.

1 We are .... for a 10% increase.
  a wanting
  b suggesting
  c looking

2 Would you be .... to
.... a settlement of 2.5%?
  a willing / know
  b prepared / consider
  c happy / meet

3 We had .... mind a figure
.... 5%.
  a on / by
  b at / to
  c in / of

4 Your revised offer .... fair.
  a means
  b plays
  c sounds

5 .... sacked him, they
found they couldn't find a
replacement.
  a As they hadn't
  b Having
  c Not having

6 .... a non-unionised
company, we have a no-strike
agreement.
  a As being
  b For
  c Being

7 The local trade union is
represented by a very effective
....
  a shop steward
  b shop worker
  c trade steward

8 Management relations with the
.... are excellent.
  a workforce
  b work team
  c labourers

9 The latest dispute has been sent
for outside ....
  a discussion
  b arbitrating
  c arbitration

10 We are working .... a
very difficult timetable.
  a up
  b to
  c off

3 | Listening

Getting on with your boss

Read the 'do's' and 'don'ts' of getting on with your boss. Do you agree with the points made? Would you add others? Listen to the two speakers. Which of the *do's* particularly applies to Speaker 1? Which of the *don'ts* applies to Speaker 2?

4 | Writing

Manager review

Read the text below. How does your boss compare with the profiles presented? Using ideas from the text, write a brief review of your manager's performance.

- What are his / her good points?
- What are the areas where he / she could improve?

Do's and don'ts

DON'T wait for a bad situation to get better. It won't, so act now.

DON'T criticise your boss behind his / her back; it's unprofessional.

DON'T be sarcastic and don't find fault with everything; it's immature.

DON'T be scared of confronting your boss with your problems. Honesty is always the best policy.

DO believe in yourself. If you don't, who will?

DO pay attention to timing. Asking your boss for a meeting when he's / she's rushing off to an important meeting won't work.

DO get your facts right. Presenting him / her with the wrong information will only cause irritation.

From Helena Jaworski, The Harding Syndication

How to spot the boss from hell

BY OLIVER FINEGOLD

The Good Boss Company consultancy group surveyed 1,000 workers and found nearly one in four classed their boss as 'bad' or 'dreadful'.

More than two-thirds said they had been bullied or publicly humiliated. Others were set unachievable deadlines and made to feel worthless and angry. Key findings include the following.

- Six out of ten people with a bad boss have looked for a new job.
- Almost 70% of workers often criticise their boss to colleagues.
- Only 1% are made to feel proud and wanted.
- Bad bosses mean more absenteeism. More than a third of staff admitted to 'sickies'.
- Staff have some sympathy with their tormentors. Almost half say their bosses haven't had enough training.

But report authors Andrea Gregory and Lisa Smale said simply being more willing to listen, support and develop their teams would motivate them to do a better job and reduce anger and frustration.

THE WORST ...

1. Leave things to the last minute.
2. Provide little or no direction.
3. Go for easy, quick-fix solutions.
4. Keep changing decisions.
5. Are stressed by a lack of organisational skills.
6. Disregard work / life balance.
7. Are poor at identifying problems.
8. Provide no career options.
9. Over-commit the team.
10. Delegate difficult and unpleasant tasks.

AND THE BEST ...

1. Defend the team when necessary.
2. Do not let personal life affect work.
3. Give credit where it's due.
4. Support career development.
5. Always support team members.
6. Are cheerful and positive.
7. Are gently persuasive.
8. Challenge decisions with which they disagree.
9. Face up to difficulties.
10. Have reasonable expectations.

From *The Evening Standard*

Job satisfaction

1 Complete the questionnaire. The scoring is on page 133.

HOW CONTENT ARE
YOU IN YOUR JOB

John Nicholson is a leading expert on running businesses and getting the best from people who work in them. To him this depends crucially on managers having the right relationship with those working for them, and those people in turn having a healthy attitude to their jobs and to themselves. When diagnosing business problems and attempting to put them right, he often uses questionnaires.

		True	False
1	If I won the lottery, I certainly wouldn't carry on working where I am now.	☐	☐
2	The most important things that happen to me involve work.	☐	☐
3	I'm always looking for ways to do my job more effectively.	☐	☐
4	When I get into difficulty at work, there's no one I can turn to for help.	☐	☐
5	Even if another employer offered me a lot of money, I would not seriously think of changing my present job.	☐	☐
6	In all honesty, I couldn't advise a friend to join my company.	☐	☐
7	I often find myself looking back on a day's work with a sense of a job well done.	☐	☐
8	I am too embarrassed to tell people who I work for.	☐	☐
9	If I had my life over again, I would choose to do the job I'm doing.	☐	☐
10	It makes me unhappy when my work is not up to its usual standard.	☐	☐

From *How Do You Manage?* by John Nicholson

2 Work in pairs.
  a Compare scores and discuss the interpretation offered. Do you agree with it?
  b In the area of employee satisfaction, are the circumstances in your organisation satisfactory?
  c Where relevant, compare your experiences in the following areas.
    • Job security, lay-offs.
    • Terms of employment, full-time staff, contract staff.
    • Benefits, pension plans, health insurance, maternity leave.
    • Disputes, industrial unrest, strikes, pickets, arbitration.
    • Productivity agreements, no-strike deals, flexible working.

LANGUAGE REFERENCE

Language Notes

For further notes on these points, see the accompanying Business Grammar Guide (BGG).

Some language for making and countering demands

- Proposing

e.g. We have in mind something in the region of 10%.
Would you be prepared to consider an offer of 10%?
We would like to suggest 10%.
We are looking for a 10% increase.
Does that sound fair to you?

- Accepting

e.g. That's more or less what we had in mind.
I think that's reasonable.
That sounds fair.
We would be willing to accept that.
I am sure that we can agree to that.

- Rejecting

e.g. That's not what we had in mind.
I'm afraid we can't meet these terms.
Our people are very unlikely to accept.
I'm afraid that's out of the question.
Your demands are totally unrealistic / unacceptable.

Linking ideas (BGG 8.1)

- Cause

e.g. I can't get a job **because** I'm not a member of the union.
As / Since I'm not a member of the union, I can't get a job.
Not being a member of the union, I can't get a job.
I can't comment **because** I haven't seen the report.
As / Since I haven't seen the report, I can't comment.
Having not / Not having seen the report, I can't comment.

- Time

e.g. They changed their minds **when** they had signed the agreement.
After signing the agreement, they changed their minds.

Having signed the agreement, they changed their minds.
We went to a restaurant **when we had finished** the meeting.
After finishing the meeting, we went to the restaurant.
Having finished our meeting, we went to a restaurant.

Vocabulary

- Words and phrases

e.g. reward / benefit package, fringe benefits, no-strike agreement, binding agreement, industrial dispute / action, sympathy strike, 24-hour stoppage, work to rule, overtime ban, job cuts, pay freeze, voluntary redundancy, natural wastage, sack, fire, terminate

- Verbs and verb phrases

e.g. We hope that the problem will **work** itself **out**.
I am **working on** the problem at the moment.
We are **working under** a lot of pressure.
We have to **work to** very tight deadlines.
Some staff **worked through** the stoppage.

Useful Phrases

The firm encourages good relations between management and staff.
The workforce feel that they have a real stake in the company.

Many disputes are pay-related.
Compulsory redundancy has been a major issue.
There have been a number of stoppages.
In my view the bosses are out of touch.
The shop stewards have too much power.

There's a 'them and us' mentality.
Relations have deteriorated since the job cuts.
The atmosphere has improved since the new CEO took over.
We have a no-strike agreement.
Any disputes go to arbitration.

Have you had a chance to consider our proposals?
What's your reaction to our revised offer?
We feel the terms need to be improved.
We're doing what we can to meet your demands.

We will need to look at your proposals in detail.
I'm afraid we can't meet your demands in full.
We're prepared to meet you half way.
I'm afraid it's the best I can do.

Leave it with me … I'll see what I can do.

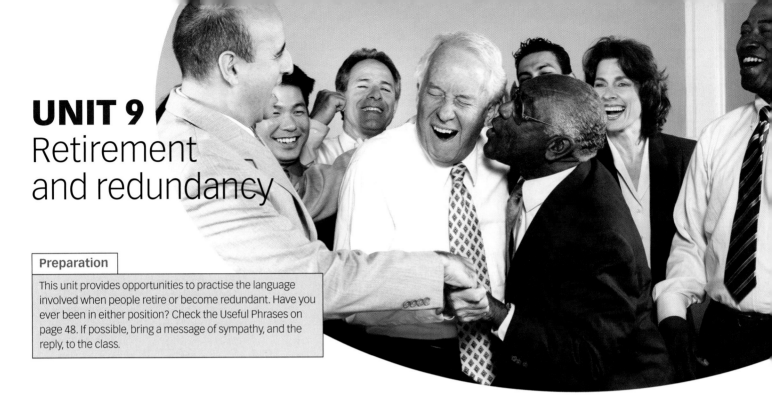

UNIT 9
Retirement and redundancy

Preparation

This unit provides opportunities to practise the language involved when people retire or become redundant. Have you ever been in either position? Check the Useful Phrases on page 48. If possible, bring a message of sympathy, and the reply, to the class.

1 Core practice

Listening and speaking

Listen to the exchanges (a – d) and mark the statements (part i) true T, false F or unclear U. Then, working with a partner, practise the exchanges indicated in part ii.

a **i** They laid off two people. ☐
   ii Talk about a time when people in your area lost their jobs.

b **i** Paul has been made redundant. ☐
   ii Practise delivering a farewell massage to someone who is leaving.

c **i** The second speaker is under 65. ☐
   ii Practise comparing retirement ages and pension entitlements.

d **i** They think he'll get another job soon. ☐
   ii Practise expressing sympathy to someone who has lost his / her job.

2 Language check

Refer to the Language Notes on page 48 as you complete the examples below using the choices provided – only one is correct. Then prepare a version of each example that you might use.

1 I can't get used to .... to work any more.
  a not go
  b not to go
  c not going

2 I won't miss .... back from work on dark evenings.
  a to commute
  b commute
  c commuting

3 I appear .... the only person who isn't looking forward ....
  a be / leaving
  b to be / to leaving
  c being / to leave

4 After .... I set up my own business.
  a I leave
  b leave
  c leaving

5 I'm really sorry .... you are leaving.
  a hearing
  b to hear
  c hear

6 When they closed the plant, everyone was .... redundant.
  a taken
  b fired
  c made

7 There is no work; all of the operators have been laid ....
  a up
  b on
  c off

8 When the chairman retired he was given a .... handshake.
  a golden
  b silver
  c firm

9 I don't know how to .... the news to everyone.
  a tell
  b make
  c break

10 I'm afraid there is something I have to ....
  a speak
  b say
  c tell

3 | Listening

Retirement

1 Listen to two people talking about retirement, and make notes. Then tick the points below they refer to.

Preoccupations and concerns	Speakers: 1	2
• Getting another job, working part time	☐	☐
• Starting a business, working for themselves	☐	☐
• Taking a holiday, having a rest	☐	☐
• Having time for their interests, personal schemes	☐	☐
• Earning enough, making ends meet	☐	☐
• Moving to a better / warmer area	☐	☐
• Pensions, lump-sum payments	☐	☐
• Getting bored, missing work	☐	☐

4 | Writing

A letter of regret

1 What is your view of this enquiry? What is the policy in your company? What advice would you give the writer? See Sue Nickson's reply on page 134.

2 A colleague of yours is being made redundant. Write a letter expressing regret – see the Useful Language on page 134.

Sue Nickson is a partner and head of employment law at Hammonds

the **JOB CLINIC**

I am about to be made redundant, but my employer is offering only the statutory redundancy payment, even though previous employees in the same situation have received more.

Is it true that an employer who has previously offered more generous redundancy terms will be in breach of contract if the same policy is not applied to subsequent redundancies?

From *Financial Mail on Sunday*

Losing a job

1 Work in pairs.

Partner A: Read the article about Inge Timperley below and prepare to recount the information to your partner.

Partner B: Read the article about Nick Filleul on page 134 and prepare to recount the information to **Partner A**.

Just six months into a new job as a marketing executive, Inge Timperley, 26, was made redundant. 'You start thinking you're to blame and that maybe there's something wrong with you – you doubt yourself a bit,' she says. 'A lot of other people had already been made redundant, but I kept thinking it wouldn't be me because I hadn't been with the company for long.

'Then my boss called me into the office, on the Friday – the typical situation. He said he was dreadfully sorry but, unfortunately, the company wasn't doing very well and they couldn't keep me on after that day. He didn't beat about the bush, which was just as well, and was very apologetic, but I wasn't really listening.

'I let him say what he wanted and, as soon as he looked like he'd finished, I just got up and left. I went and packed my stuff. Everybody else kept on working, except a friend of mine who helped me carry everything out of the building. She had known beforehand but couldn't tell me. I was very upset and initially shocked.

'It was a bit embarrassing telling my parents' friends, but it wasn't as though I had been sacked. I've since found out that another 30 to 40 people were made redundant after me and that the atmosphere there is now dreadful – I was lucky to leave when I did.'

Two weeks ago, a month after being made redundant, Inge began a new job as an assistant researcher for a City bank.

Facing redundancy: what happens next?

Adapted from The Evening Standard

2 In pairs, practise recounting news which you have recently seen, heard or read.

> ### Useful Language
>
> **Speaker:** I read in the paper that she had been sacked.
> Did you read about the guy who was made redundant?
> It says / Apparently, he / she was very upset.
> They told him / her that …
> He / she had to …
>
> **Listener:** What happened? / When did it happen?
> That's terrible. / How awful.
> He / She must be … / must have been …
> The same thing happened to (a friend of mine).
> Did you hear about …?

LANGUAGE REFERENCE

Language Notes

For further notes on these points, see the accompanying Business Grammar Guide (BGG).

Infinitive and -ing form (BGG 6)

- Examples of verbs + -ing (BGG 6.3, 6.4)

e.g. I want to keep **working** as long as possible.
He's spending a lot of time **planning** my next step.
She really regrets **losing** her job.
I miss **working** regularly.
They don't mind **doing** overtime.
We will enjoy **not working** for a while.

- Examples of verbs + infinitive (BGG 6.1, 6.2)

e.g. Do you happen **to remember** when she retired?
We seem **to be losing** our best people.
I was very sorry **to hear** you are leaving.
I forgot **to thank** you for your message.
I didn't dare **(to) tell you**.
Can you help me **(to) buy** a leaving present?

- Examples of verbs + -ing or infinitive (BGG 6.3, 6.4)

Difference in meaning

e.g. Did you remember **to send** the redundancy notices?
Do you remember **sending** the redundancy notices?
We have tried **introducing** new working methods.
We have tried **to introduce** new working methods.

No significant difference in meaning

e.g. I like **to start** work early in the mornings.
I like **starting** work early in the mornings.
I prefer **to travel** by train.
I prefer **travelling** by train.

- Examples of prepositions + verb (BGG 6.4)

e.g. Are you very interested **in working** part time?
I'm not very keen **on working** on my own.
She's fed up **with working** so far from home.
We're no good **at networking**.
They set up my own business **after leaving** the company.
Do you always make some notes **before phoning** a customer?

Some expressions of regret and shock

e.g. I'm sorry to have to tell you …
I'm very sorry to hear you are leaving.
I don't know what to say.
It must have been a shock.
How did you break the news?
I thought that they took it very well.

Vocabulary

- Words and phrases

e.g. pension scheme, lump-sum payment, golden handshake, unemployment benefit, legal entitlement, early retirement, voluntary / compulsory redundancy, natural wastage, unemployed, temporarily out-of-work, laid off

- Verbs and verb phrases

e.g. When we lost the Cabex account, we **laid off** 400 people.
There wasn't enough work, so we had to **let** them **go**.
Many of the older staff **took early retirement**.
We had to **make** the rest **redundant**.
Sometimes it is difficult to **break** the **news**.
I was **given** one month's **notice** – the statutory minimum.

Useful Phrases

We have never had any redundancies in our company.
We have never made anyone redundant.
We had to lay people off in the summer.
It was a great shock for everyone.

I am very sorry to hear that you are leaving.
I was terribly sorry to hear that you have lost your job.
I hope that you find something soon.
It must have been a shock.

The company operates its own pension scheme.
I have opted out of the scheme.
I'll get a state pension when I retire.
How much do you contribute?

I'm planning to retire in three years' time.
I'm looking forward to having some free time.
I don't like working on my own.
I try not to think about retiring.
Are you interested in working part time?

It is possible to take early retirement in our company.
They have reduced numbers by a system of 'natural wastage'.
Do you lose your pension entitlement if you leave early?

I would like to wish you a happy retirement.
Good luck for the future.
All the best. Keep in touch!
Come and see us.

UNIT 10 Conferences and exhibitions

1 Core practice

Listening and speaking

Listen to the exchanges (a – d) and mark the statements (part i) true ☐T☐, false ☐F☐ or unclear ☐U☐. Then, working with a partner, practise the exchanges indicated in part ii.

a i The second speaker is a customer. ☐
  ii Call a customer and invite him / her to visit your exhibition stand.

b i The first speaker is one of the conference organisers. ☐
  ii Have a similar conversation with a guest speaker at a conference you are organising.

c i The visitors to the stand are thinking of ordering a Solvex B. ☐
  ii Practise talking to a customer who is using a competitor's products or services, and is looking for alternatives.

d i The visitor has no real intention of buying an upgrade. ☐
  ii Practise talking to visitors to your stand about upgrades.

> **Preparation**
>
> In this unit you can practise the language you need at conferences and exhibitions – on a stand, meeting people, booking tickets. Come prepared to talk about one event you have been involved in, as a visitor or a provider. When preparing refer to the Useful Phrases on page 52. If possible, bring documents relating to a conference or exhibition you have been involved in.

2 Language check

Refer to the Language Notes on page 52 as you complete the examples below using the choices provided – only one is correct. Then prepare a version of each example that you might use.

1 We .... to introduce the upgrades at the New York motor show.
  a will plan
  b are planning
  c are going to plan

2 It's very cloudy. I am sure it ....
  a is going to rain
  b is raining
  c rains

3 Thanks for calling. .... get the registration file.
  a I just
  b I'm just going
  c I'll just

4 What time .... your workshop start?
  a does
  b will
  c is going to

5 I .... you a link to the programme if you give me your address.
  a am sending
  b will send
  c send

6 When .... for lunch? We could meet ....
  a do you stop / out
  b will you stop / together
  c are you stopping / up

7 The flight carrying the equipment for our stand .... at 5 o'clock?
  a due to arrive
  b is due in
  c due

8 The session in the main hall on Internet selling .... start.
  a is about to be
  b is about to
  c is about

9 How long is the conference going .... ?
  a for on
  b for
  c on for

10 If you have .... , you need .... pass.
  a a stand / an exhibitor's
  b a workshop / an organiser's
  c a display / a visitor's

3 | Listening

Internet marketing

Listen to Pete Ubanez calling the reservations number after receiving this mailout, then tick the points in the text mentioned in the call.

TICKET #U5Y-CDT-M

TICKET ADMITS TWO

→ Why Start a Website?

→ Getting Ready to Sell on the Internet?

→ What Computer Skills Do You Need?

→ Search Engine Techniques

→ How to Capture Your Local Market

→ What others are Selling Online?

→ Search Strategies

→ ... And much much more!

Reserve Your Place At This Exclusive Full Day Internet Marketing Conference

For: P. Ubanez and guest

Confirm before Friday, 14 October
Saturday, 15 October

8.30am Registration
9.00am Presentations and workshops
6.00pm End

Intermark Floris Hotel
114 Jarvis Square
Toronto, Ontario
M5B 2C1
Canada

Make your reservations now by calling
06-000-326-687
intermark.com/toronto

4 | Application

A trade exhibition

Practise presenting information about your products or services. Prepare to run a stand at a trade exhibition. Decide on the business sector and what you are exhibiting. Agree what the main questions might be.

Group A: You are running the stand. Review the tips below for making the day go smoothly. Prepare to meet the public.

Group B: You are the public – representatives from various companies who visit this stand. Your information is on page 134.

On the day: HOT TIPS

Ten tips for making the day go smoothly.

- Find out what time the venue is available for setting up your stand, and get there early.
- Check that all the equipment works before you go 'live'.
- Give everyone on your stand a badge identifying who they are and the name of your company.
- Have plenty of helpers on the stand during the day. Don't rely on one or two people – they'll get tired and won't be able to keep up their enthusiasm.
- Make sure the helpers are well briefed. Give them a means of recording queries they need more help to answer.

- Give enough time to each visitor to arrange appointments, and enable them to put their questions.
- Take breaks away from the stand. Don't drink coffee or eat food when you're on duty.
- Don't spend time talking to your colleagues. Visitors will be put off if they have to interrupt you.
- Have plenty of promotional materials to hand out.
- Don't put customers off by demanding too much detail now; you can collect that later.

From businesslink.gov.uk

Coordinating a visit

Read the message forwarded by Jason Crevich to his assistant, and the related documents. Then draft a reply to Sonia Liddi with the information she needs.

File	Edit	View	Tools	Message	Help

Create Mail · Send/Recv · Addresses · Find

Could you please reply to Sonia Liddi on my behalf? Please give her my apologies and say that I can't meet her, but we'll send a company car. Please include details of her flight on to Damascus on the 27th. And could you check that we've booked the hotel for her, and give her the details.

Thanks.

JC

From Sonia Liddi
Date 9 October
To jcrevich@metcalmholdings.com
Subject The Odex Conference, Cairo

Dear Jason

At last, I can confirm that I am available for the presentations at the Odex Conference. I will be arriving in Cairo on 24 November by Euroair (flight no. EK 173), ETA 19.50 your time.

Do you have details of the Damascus flight yet? Will I be staying at the Menhar, as last time? Could you let me know as soon as you have the information? I need to leave contact details with my people here.

The Odex Conference, 25 November, 10.30

Guest Speaker Sonia Liddi, Head of Compliance at EGD Banking, will be speaking on 'Compliance in the Global Workplace'.

(Main hall)

TELEPHONE MESSAGE

They have made a flight booking for Sonia Liddi – 27 November departing Cairo for Damascus at 12.30 on Arab Air, flight number AA312, arriving Damascus 15.20 local time.

The Menhar Hotel has reserved a single for three nights starting 24 November in the name of Liddi.

They will email the e-booking details.

LANGUAGE REFERENCE

Language Notes

For further notes on these points, see the accompanying Business Grammar Guide (BGG).

Future tenses (BGG 2)

• Future with *will* for deciding and confirming (BGG 2.2)

e.g. **I'll call** you back in five minutes.

I'll see you at the exhibition tomorrow.

– **Will you be** at the reception at 6.30?

– Yes, **I will**. / No, **I won't**.

• Future with *going to* for intentions and plans, and weather forecasting (BGG 2.2)

e.g. The conference is **going to be** in Rome next year.

I'm afraid I'm not **going to be able** to meet you next week.

What are we **going to do**?

It's very cold. I think it's **going to snow**.

• Future with Present Continuous for personal plans and arrangements (BGG 2.1)

e.g. What **are you doing** this evening?

Nothing – **I'm staying** in.

I'm leaving at 6 o'clock this evening.

What time **are we starting** tomorrow?

• Future with Present Simple for scheduled events (BGG 2.1)

e.g. When **does** your workshop **finish**?

My train **leaves** at 7 o'clock tomorrow evening.

Does it leave from Platform 4?

Yes, **it does**. / No, **it doesn't**.

• *is due (to be)* (BGG 2.6)

e.g. The lecture **is due to start** in five minutes.

= It is scheduled to start in five minutes.

When **is** Maria **due back**? We're very busy.

= When is Maria scheduled to get back?

What time **is** your flight **due (in)**?

= What time is your flight scheduled to arrive?

Vocabulary

• Words and phrases

e.g. trade fair, agricultural show, conference venue, lecture hall, seminar room, exhibition stand, display area, market stall, promotional material, printed handout, keynote lecture, open session, workshop, exhibitor's pass, exhibition guide

• Verbs and verb phrases

e.g. Why don't you **come over** and visit our stand?

Let's **meet up** during the exhibition?

The organisers are going to **take the** speakers **out** to dinner.

How long is the lecture **going on** for?

Will it be possible to **try** the upgrades **out**?

The session on Internet selling **is about** to start.

Useful Phrases

I'll be in Prague next week for the Focus 49 exhibition.
Why don't we meet up?
How long does it go on?
It starts on Monday and ends on Friday.
I'll leave a pass for you at the information desk.

We saw your display – it's very impressive.
We're thinking of changing our machines.
We are looking to see what is available.
Would you like to come and sit down?
It's quieter – we can talk without being disturbed.

I'm a user – I have one of your products.
I'd like to know what upgrades are available.
I'd like to upgrade to the latest model.
We have it on display at the back of the stand.
Can we try it out?
If you leave your details, I'll get our technical people to call you.

When is your workshop?
It is due to start in five minutes.
The session on Internet selling is about to start.
Let me know if you need anything.
My pager number is on the back of your pass.
The organisers would like to take the speakers out to dinner.
I'd like that very much.

What time are we starting tomorrow?
I'll see you in the morning.
My train leaves at 7 o'clock in the evening.
The conference is going to be in Rome next year.

UNIT 11 Networking

1 Core practice

Listening and speaking

Listen to the exchanges (a – d) and mark the statements (part i) true T, false F or unclear U. Then, working with a partner, practise the exchanges indicated in part ii.

a i The second speaker has only agreed to meet because he knows Silke Ollek. ☐

ii Practise introducing yourself to someone a colleague has suggested you contact.

b i Both speakers are nuclear service engineers. ☐

ii Practise starting a conversation with someone you don't know. Ask for their card.

c i Juanita Curtiz is a personal friend of the second speaker. ☐

ii Practise asking for advice about someone you are going to meet.

d i Gerry Atailer didn't send the details he promised. ☐

ii Practise following up on an introduction.

Preparation

Networking is one of the skills all professionals need. Come prepared to talk about your experience of developing contacts. You can prepare by looking at the Useful Phrases on page 56. If possible, bring to the class messages you have sent introducing yourself to new contacts, or following up on a first meeting.

2 Language check

Refer to the Language Notes on page 56 as you complete the examples below using the choices provided – only one is correct. Then prepare a version of each example that you might use.

1 When are you .... up the contacts you made?
a intending follow
b plan following
c going to follow

2 We are .... make the same mistake again.
a not determined to
b determined not to
c determined to not

3 I suggest .... about the local customs before the event.
a find out
b to find out
c you find out

4 Can you advise me? ....
I wear a .... ?
a Could / evening dress
b Should / black tie
c Will / dinner jacket

5 Just to .... you, you will be .... to say a few words in Arabic.
a help / meant
b mention / asked
c warn / expected

6 I was .... call her and arrange a meeting but I forgot.
a meant to
b expected
c supposed

7 Are they .... us to take our shoes off? What is the .... ?
a meaning / custom
b expecting / convention
c supposed / rule

8 I think we'd better .... – it was nice .... to you.
a mix / socialising
b network / meeting
c circulate / talking

9 We work .... – he's a ....
a together / business colleague
b hard / important contact
c as a team / associate

10 How do you keep .... contact .... your business associates?
a on / for
b in / with
c at / to

3 | Listening

Corporate hospitality

Listen to an excerpt from a radio interview with the head of an EU corporate hospitality and event association. Your company is considering offering corporate hospitality in Europe. You have been asked to circulate notes on the points highlighted on the right. Make rough notes as you listen, then write a summary of your notes.

What are:
- the main benefits of this kind of promotion?
- the range and type of events available?
- maximum and minimum costs?

4 | Writing

An invitation

Working in pairs or groups, choose between the events featured, then draft a letter of invitation to send to favoured customers. See page 134 for Useful Phrases.

Monaco Formula 1 Grand Prix:
May (weekend)

The ultimate corporate entertaining event. Your clients will really know what you think of them if they receive an invitation to Monte Carlo for Grand Prix weekend. Style, glamour and celebrity are everywhere and the racing usually serves up a few crashes on the tight and winding streets of Monte Carlo. All in all, an unforgettable weekend for your guests. And the evening entertainment is second to none. Not cheap at up to £6,000 per person for the weekend, this is the treat for your high value clients.

Ambiance: ✪ ✪ ✪ ✪

Beautiful weather, sophisticated surroundings and thrills on the race track – what more can you ask for?

Quality time: ✪ ✪ ✪

With qualifying on Saturday and race day on Sunday, there's plenty of opportunity to build those key relationships.

Overall rating: ✪ ✪ ✪ ✪

Wimbledon:
June to July (two weeks)

Still the most popular of all the corporate hospitality events. Suitable for just about everybody, particularly if the prized Centre Court seats are on offer – this guarantees a 100% turnout. Can be slightly tiresome if your tented accommodation is on the other side of the road in the canvas 'village', as guests have to step through mud if it is wet, or hordes of teenagers if it is sunny. The cost with good seats can be £1,000 per head on ordinary days, but can rise to a hefty £4,000 per head for men's finals.

Ambience: ✪ ✪ ✪

English summer weather often as poor as the performance of its tennis stars; can be disappointing.

Quality time: ✪ ✪

If the sun shines, forget it; the tent will suddenly empty and only refill properly at tea. Talking while watching is strictly forbidden. Rain can be very welcome, but expect grumpy guests.

Overall rating: ✪ ✪ ✪ ✪

Networking tips

1 Read the networking tips. Do you agree with them? What advice would you give on networking / developing contacts? With the group, brainstorm tips you would add.

Networking tips

ROCHESTER NETWORK
making connections

What is networking?

Whether you network to find a new job, to develop your current career, to explore new career options, to obtain referrals and sales leads, or simply to broaden your professional horizons, it is important to focus on networking as an exchange of information and experience.

In any industry, networking helps you to make connections in a personal way, build relationships and explore mutual benefits. It is a skill set no serious professional can be without in the 21st century.

How to network

- Start with a purpose. It does you no good to attend any networking functions unless you define your objectives. Why are you there?
- Wear your name tag on the right side to provide an easy sight-line when shaking hands.
- Have an effective handshake. This may appear obvious, but you have probably been on the receiving end of at least one 'bone-crusher' and one 'limp fish'.
- Be sure to introduce yourself!
- Say your name clearly – e.g. 'Hello, my name is Juanita Curtiz. It's a pleasure to meet you.'

- Use an 'elevator' speech: describe who you are or what you do in a few sentences.
- When appropriate offer a business card, and ask the other person for his / hers.
- Start with small talk.
- Don't stay too long in one place. After eight to ten minutes, excuse yourself with a pleasantry such as: 'It was nice meeting you ...'
- Let preparation and practice be your guide. Spend some time planning topics you might talk about.
- Once the event is over, be sure to follow up with the people you've met.

From Rochester Network

2 Prepare your 'elevator' speech – a brief statement of who you are and what you do. Then deliver it to the group.

3 Select a networking opportunity you might take advantage of, decide the context and details, and then practise it in pairs.

Networking opportunities

- Call someone you met on a plane.
- Call someone you met at a conference who said: 'Call me sometime.'
- Call someone who a colleague has suggested you contact.
- Introduce yourself to the person next to you on a plane or train, and start a conversation.
- Call someone who gave you their card a while ago – they work in an area that is now important to you and your team.
- Approach someone at a social event.

LANGUAGE REFERENCE

Language Notes

For further notes on these points, see the accompanying Business Grammar Guide (BGG).

Expressing intentions (BGG 21.1, 2.2)

• Present

e.g. I am (not) going to call the people I met at the conference.

I am (not) planning to contact Moira.

I (don't) intend to follow up the contacts I made as soon as possible.

I am determined to get through to the decision makers.

• Past (BGG 1.4)

e.g. I was (not) going to call the people I met at the conference.

I was (not) planning to contact Moira.

I intended (didn't intend) to follow up the contacts I made.

I was determined to get through to the decision makers.

Etiquette (BGG 21.1)

• Questions

e.g. Should I wear a jacket?

Do I need to take a gift?

Would you advise me to wear evening dress?

Ought I to reply in writing?

Will I be expected to know the local customs?

• Advice

e.g. It's a good idea to send a 'thank you' note.

I suggest you learn a few words of Chinese.

It's best not to talk too much.

Remember not to sit down before your host.

It's not a rule, it's more a guideline.

• Warnings

e.g. Can I give you a word of advice?

Just to warn you that you will be expected to make a speech.

If I were you, I wouldn't discuss politics.

It would be better if you didn't mention the war.

Whatever you do, don't discuss religion.

be supposed to / be meant to (BGG 20.1)

e.g. She is supposed / meant to be in Chicago by 5 o'clock. (But her plane is late.)

Were you meant / supposed to arrange the meeting? (Why didn't you do it?)

I was meant / supposed to send him some samples. (But I didn't do it.)

We're not supposed / meant to smoke in this building. (But we do.)

Vocabulary

• Words and phrases

e.g. a professional relationship, a valued contact, a valuable connection, to network, to circulate, to mix, to make connections, to build relationships, to explore mututal benefits, to explore common interests, to make small talk, dinner jacket, evening dress, tuxedo, black tie

• Verbs and verb phrases

e.g. Do you **network with** the other passengers when you are travelling?

How can I **make contact with** the people who matter?

It is important to **keep in contact with** your network, but it takes time.

I'm afraid I **lost contact with** him when he changed jobs.

Why don't we **get together** / **meet up**?

After an event, make sure you **follow up** (with) the people you've met.

Useful Phrases

May I introduce myself?
I wanted to say 'hello'.
Mary Jones suggested I contact you.
I believe you know Fred White.
How do you know Fred?
We work together – we're colleagues.

It's good to meet you.
I was wondering if I could come and see you sometime.
Do you have a card?
These are my details.

Well, I think we should circulate.
It was nice meeting you.

What can you tell me about Liz Brown?
Any points I should watch out for?
She is really into sailing.
Don't discuss politics.
What's the best way to make contact with her?
It would be a good idea to send an email before you call.
Can I mention your name?

It's John Smith – we met in Manheim.
Do you remember – we talked about anti-corrosion techniques.
You asked me to call you.
I remember – you were supposed to send me some samples.
Yes, that's why I'm calling.
Would it be possible to meet up?

UNIT 12 Security abroad

Listening and speaking

Listen to the exchanges (a – d) and mark the statements (part i) true ☐T☐, false ☐F☐ or unclear ☐U☐. Then, working with a partner, practise the exchanges indicated in part ii.

a i The visitor is going to be overcharged. ☐
  ii Practise buying something in a foreign shop when you don't have the local currency and they don't accept credit cards.
b i The staff shortages are causing delays. ☐
  ii Practise finding out what has happened to your baggage.
c i The wallet was taken from the mini safe. ☐
  ii Practise reporting a theft to hotel security.
d i The car was parked in a 'No Parking' area. ☐
  ii Practise locating your car when it has been towed away.

Preparation

This unit looks at security when travelling abroad – possible problems and the language you need to deal with them. Think of your own experience. What could go wrong? Come prepared to talk about your experience. As you prepare, look at the Useful Phrases on page 60. If possible, bring to class a message related to a specific issue.

2 Language check

Refer to the Language Notes on page 60 as you complete the examples below using the choices provided – only one is correct. Then prepare a version of each example that you might use.

1 Sorry about the delays. Your luggage .... through very soon.
  a comes
  b will be coming
  c will have come
2 The network is down and .... again till tomorrow.
  a doesn't work
  b isn't working
  c won't be working
3 I .... by the time the police arrive. You will have to speak to them.
  a will have left
  b will be leaving
  c am leaving

4 .... the air conditioning by tomorrow?
  a Have you fixed
  b Will you be fixing
  c Will you have fixed
5 It's a .... briefcase; I think I left it in the lobby.
  a leather large black
  b large black leather
  c black leather large
6 When I tried the hotel's .... connection my laptop crashed.
  a secure high-speed Internet
  b high-speed secure Internet
  c secure Internet high-speed
7 The water won't drain away. The sink is ....
  a leaking
  b blocked
  c jammed

8 The safe has a .... lock.
  a cracked
  b fused
  c faulty
9 There is something wrong .... my remote control. Could you have a look .... it?
  a with / at
  b for / into
  c in / over
10 My car's been towed .... and I don't know when I'm going to get it ....
  a in / out
  b up / down
  c away / back

3 | Listening

A difficult trip

While working on the *Lonely Planet Travel Guide to Mexico*, Paul Talley visited Torreon. Listen to his description of the trip and answer the questions.

a Where had he come from?
b Did the journey go smoothly?
c What kind of place is Torreon?
d What's the weather like there?
e How was he feeling when he arrived at the hotel?
f What went wrong when he tried to check in?
g Did things get better?

4 | Application

Travel hassles

On the right is a list of common difficulties reported by business travellers. Discuss the list. Is it complete? Add any hassles you feel are missing. Which are most common? Which are hardest to handle? Identify the one you find the biggest challenge and practise it in pairs. Before you begin:

- agree the details with your partner
- prepare the language you need.

Common travel difficulties

- Baggage: loss, non-arrival
- Travel delays: late arrival, missed connections
- Facilities: closing times, facilities being closed when you need them
- Hustlers: people pushing goods, services, other forms of 'help'
- Security: theft from hotel rooms
- Parking: fines and penalties
- Heath factors: quality of the drinking water
- Service disputes, especially tipping
- Payment: credit card security, overcharging, wrong change
- Connectivity: Internet connections that don't work
- Mobility: poor mobile phone coverage
- Equipment: shower, TV, air-conditioning not working

5 | Feature

Safety guidelines

1 Read the extract from a brochure for tourists. In pairs discuss the suggestions.
Are some points more important than others?

WELCOME TO SAN DIEGO, AMERICA'S MOST HOSPITABLE CITY

It is our hope that during your stay you experience all the many sights and attractions this beautiful city has to offer. The suggestions and hints in this brochure should help to ensure that your visit to San Diego is a safe one.

- Use travellers cheques and credit cards. Keep a record of their serial numbers in a separate and safe place in case they are lost or stolen.

- Carry only the cash you will need and in small denominations.

- Be aware of your surroundings and never discuss your plans or the amount of money you are carrying.

- If you must carry large sums of money, do not display it openly.

- Carry your purse close to your body and your wallet in your front pocket.

- Keep track of your plane, train or bus tickets; they are as good as cash.

- Photocopy all documents – including passport, credit cards and tickets – before leaving home, and store copies in the hotel safe.

- Never pick up hitchhikers.

- Leave un-essential non-travel papers such as local credit cards and irreplaceable photos at home.

- If your car breaks down, turn on your flashers and raise the hood. If you must abandon your car, park safely and keep all passengers together. Freeway boxes are spaced one half mile apart.

From the San Diego Visitor Safety brochure

2 A colleague is about to visit San Diego. Forward the guidelines with a covering message.
Draw attention to the points that you believe are key; add others if necessary.

See Useful Phrases page 135.

LANGUAGE REFERENCE

Language Notes

For further notes on these points, see the accompanying Business Grammar Guide (BGG).

Future Continuous tense (BGG 2.3)

e.g. How **will you be paying**?

I'm afraid the lift **won't be working** till after lunch.

Will you be using the shower in the next hour?

We definitely **won't be going** back there!

Future Perfect tense (BGG 2.4)

e.g. I **will have left** by then; I have a meeting.

I will be back at 6.00pm. **Will you have fixed** it by then?

Will you have finished your investigation before I leave?

They won't have completed the report by then, so they will email it.

Order of adjectives (BGG 13.1)

e.g. a brown leather wallet

a white plastic light switch

a large comfortable hotel room

a brand-new green Range Rover

Nouns as adjectives (BGG 11.1)

e.g. hotel guest / room

lobby area

door handle

TV remote control

bathroom window

Internet connection

Vocabulary

• Words and phrases

e.g. a missed flight connection, a delayed flight, lost baggage,

mobile phone coverage, no connection,

to overcharge, to short change, to demand a tip,

to receive a parking fine, to be towed away, to be clamped,

stolen from my room, taken from my bag,

a jammed lock, a faulty switch, a cracked basin, a leaking tap

• Verbs and verb phrases

e.g. There's something **wrong with** the air conditioning in my room.

Could you send someone **to have a look at** it?

We **were** completely **out of** cash / petrol.

My car **was towed away** / **taken away**.

When will I **get** my car / passport **back**.

Useful Phrases

Is there any sign of our luggage yet?

We've been waiting for half an hour.

I'm sorry, the baggage handlers are on strike.

It will be coming through quite soon.

How much do you usually tip?

About 100 baht – more if you think the service is good.

I'm sorry, this is all I have.

The safe in my room won't open; it's jammed.

There's something wrong with the air-conditioning.

Could someone come and have a look at it?

It won't be working again till after lunch.

I have to report a theft.

It's a brown leather wallet.

It was stolen while I was having a shower.

The police will be here in half an hour.

But I will have left by then.

I am afraid we do not accept credit cards.

I am sorry, but your card has been declined.

I'm completely out of cash and the banks are shut.

My car has been towed away.

Do you know where it was taken?

It doesn't say 'No Parking'.

How much will I have to pay to get it back?

I don't believe it. That's terrible.

UNIT 13 Salaries, incentives and rewards

Preparation

Here you will look at ways of talking about pay and remuneration – the financial rewards and non-financial benefits you receive. When do you talk about these things? How much do you use English? Come prepared to talk about the conventions in your area. Prepare by looking at the Useful Phrases on page 64. If possible, bring a job description and details of the related remuneration to the class.

1 Core practice

Listening and speaking

Listen to the exchanges (a – d) and mark the statements (part i) true ⊤, false ⨍ or unclear Ⓤ. Then, working with a partner, practise the exchanges indicated in part ii.

a i The crèche is subsidised.
  ii Talk about items in your reward package.

b i The speaker receives all sorts of executive perks.
  ii Talk about any perks you receive.

c i The speaker doesn't get paid for overtime.
  ii Talk about your main financial benefits.

d i The manager supports the pay demand.
  ii Practise following up on your manager's promise of a raise.

2 Language check

Refer to the Language Notes on page 64 as you complete the examples below using the choices provided – only one is correct. Then prepare a version of each example that you might use.

1 With a bit of luck, we .... have a response .... the weekend.
  a must / before
  b would / at
  c should / by

2 She .... be getting an increase .... salary – she's only been here two months!
  a can't / in
  b might not / for
  c wouldn't / with

3 They are .... to accept the terms .... the end; it's in their own interests.
  a likely / by
  b bound / in
  c unlikely / at

4 Overtime is .... after six and .... after nine.
  a time and a half / twice

  b one and a half times / double time
  c time and a half / double time

5 Senior executives get more .... than ordinary staff members; it goes with the job.
  a benefit package
  b perks
  c awards

6 We get .... of 3% if we meet our sales ....
  a a discount / budgets
  b a payment / goals
  c an incentive bonus / targets

7 .... pay .... deductions for the technical grades is in the region of $5,500 per month.
  a Gross / before
  b Gross / after
  c Net / before

8 Only .... said they were satisfied with their terms of employment.
  a five to one
  b one in five
  c two out of ten

9 Think .... and call me when you have decided.
  a over it
  b it over
  c it about

10 The committee suggested that we split the difference, so we .... for 3.5%, ... to July.
  a signed / dated
  b accepted / scheduled
  c settled / backdated

Benefits packages

Listen to the two speakers talking about the remuneration they receive, and make notes. Then answer the questions.

a What is the first speaker's benefits package? Please summarise.
b How is the second speaker rewarded?
c Do the speakers receive any benefits that are performance related?
d Does either of them receive any perks?

4 | Writing

Executive rewards

a What is the tone of the article on the right – critical, supportive or neutral?
b What is your view of exit packages for senior executives?
c Find phrases in the text that mean the same as the following: *overpaid executive, in the news, vote, non-repeatable*
d You are a shareholder in the company. Write a message to the company secretary either supporting the rewards offered to the retiring chief executive, or criticising them. See the Useful Phrases on page 135.

I won't talk about pay says fat cat

Lavish rewards for the retiring chief executive were in the spotlight at the annual meeting of Motim Financial Services last week.

John Fu is being given US$120,000, a US$20,000 car and a part-time job.

The meeting included the company's first poll on executive pay. Some 10% of voting members rejected the board's policy, a response thought to have been prompted by Fu's one-off leaving presents.

The highly unusual payments come on top of his generous US$325,000 pay. As a non-executive director, Fu, 58, will earn US$32,000 a year for working a few days a month.

Fu will benefit from magnificent pension entitlements estimated by Molteck Financial Services to have a value of US$3.5 million. Mr Fu attacks the figure as 'ludicrous', but refuses to give an accurate assessment. 'To have details of my pay and pension discussed in this way is embarrassing,' he says.

At the meeting, chairman Charles Maefield insisted that all directors, including Fu, were 'unequivocally independent'. This is despite the fact that Fu was chief executive for 19 years. Maefield said that under Fu, assets had grown substantially and costs fell for 13 years running.

5 | Application

A pay review

1 Which of the items listed do you receive? What would you expect to be in the reward package of the following people?
- An executive director in your company
- A politician
- An airline pilot
- An IT support manager

Elements of a reward package

- basic pay / salary
- bonus
- incentives (commission)
- performance-related pay
- overtime
- shift pay
- allowances (clothing, travel, etc.)
- subsistence
- childcare facilities
- holidays
- pension (including company contributions)
- private health insurance
- long-term disability insurance
- life insurance
- company car
- fuel for private mileage
- health club membership
- social club facilities
- sick pay
- training and development
- mentoring and coaching
- share options
- share of profits

From businesshr

2 Consider the factors below, then take part in an informal pay / salary review. Working in pairs, agree the business context and enough detail to practise the interaction.

Partner A: You are the manager. Talk to **Partner B** about his / her pay / salary claim. Use the agreed details of the case in your responses. Decide whether to support, reject or postpone **Partner B**'s requests in line with your view of the business requirements. Use the Useful Phrases to help you.

Partner B: Your information is on page 135.

Factors to think about before the meeting

- What is the current business environment? Increasing pay will have an impact on costs. Can the company afford this? What are the sales and profit forecasts?

- How does this pay review relate to existing agreements with other groups in the business? Do you have to maintain parity between certain teams?

- Is there a formal negotiating structure in the company? For example, if you make an award here, will you have to offer it to similar grades across the company?

- How do your pay scales compare with the competition? Is there a danger of competitors poaching your staff?

- How do your benefits compare? Do they enable you to remain competitive in your labour market?

Useful Phrases for Partner A

Awards have to be approved by the Board.
If you put your request in writing, I'll see what I can do.
I'm afraid this is not a good time.
A pay demand is very unlikely to succeed at the moment.
I'll put your request before the board, but I don't hold out much hope.
They are likely to link the increase to a productivity agreement.
They are unlikely to accept your demands in full.
5% is well above the going rate.
They might be willing to make a special merit award in your case.

LANGUAGE REFERENCE

Language Notes

For further notes on these points, see the accompanying Business Grammar Guide (BGG).

Modal verbs, Present forms (BGG 7)

The modal verbs are: *can, could, will, would, shall, should, may, might, must, ought to, have to*

- Simple

e.g. We **should have** a response by Friday.
They **might want** to interview you.
This **can't be** their final offer.

- Continuous

e.g. They **must be thinking** it over.
We **ought to be planning** our next step.
I **might be looking** for a new job next week!

- Passive

e.g. **Couldn't** the meeting **be delayed**?
Awards **have to be approved** by the Board.
They **might be persuaded** to reconsider.

Expressing likelihood (BGG 2.5)

e.g. They are **sure / bound** to reject the claim.
They are **very likely** to link the increase to a productivity agreement.
They **will probably** offer you an improved package.
They **may / might** impose conditions.
They **should** agree to your request in the end.
They **are unlikely** to accept your demands in full.
They **definitely won't** agree to that!

Rates, fees, charges

- Rates

e.g. I receive / get **time and a half** after six o'clock.
The **call-out rate** is $50 an hour, plus sales tax.

- Fees

e.g. They charge **a flat-rate fee** of $2,000 a day, plus expenses.
The **fee** does not include tax.

- Charges

e.g. We **charge** 50 cents a minute, double at weekends.
There is a **surcharge** of 10% on late payments.

Numbers (BGG 24.2)

10K = ten thousand, ten grand
$7\frac{1}{2}m$ = seven and a half million
$1.7bn = one point seven billion dollars
65.3% = sixty-five point three per cent
3:1 = a ratio of three to one
gross = before deductions
net = after deductions

Symbols (BGG 24.2)

+ = plus / and
− = minus / less, or dash / hyphen
× = times / multiplied by
÷ = divided by / by
= = equals

Vocabulary

- Words and phrases

e.g. reward, remuneration, benefit,
non-financial benefit, perk,
gross / net earnings, take-home pay,
time and a half, double time,
call-out rate, flat rate fee, commission, bonus,
discount, surcharge, overtime,
annual pay rise, performance-related increase

- Verbs and verb phrases

e.g. They **put in for** a rise of 5%, backdated to 1st January.
Could you **put** your request **in** writing.
The board **turned** you / your request **down**.
I'll **put** your request **before** the board but I don't **hold out** much hope.
Who does it have to be **signed off** by?
I need time to **think** it **over**.
They **settled for** 3%.

Useful Phrases

I work a 35-hour week.
With overtime it comes to about 43 hours.
My basic salary is quite low.
What I earn depends on my (sales) figures.
I get an incentive bonus of 2.5%.
My total package is worth in the region of 90 grand.

Everyone gets 21 days paid holiday.
I have the use of the crèche, which is subsidised.
We get a 10% discount on all company products.
We normally receive a New Year's bonus.
It's usually one week's pay.
Directors get a free car.
It's a perk that goes with the job.

When would be a good time to do my pay review?
I feel the company should recognise contributions like this.
It is easy to feel undervalued in these circumstances.
I agree, but this is a bad time.
A pay demand is very unlikely to succeed at this time.
So what would you suggest I do?
You ought to be thinking about your next step.

Taking into account the cost of living / the rate of inflation / your contribution to the bottom line, the Board have agreed to an increase of 5%.

UNIT 14 Personal and company finances

1 Core practice

Listening and speaking

Listen to the exchanges (a – d) and mark the statements (part i) true ⊤, false ⊏ or unclear ⊔. Then, working with a partner, practise the exchanges indicated in part ii.

a i The company is in a healthy financial position.
  ii Practise talking about your company's financial performance.
b i The speaker's family spends about $1,500 a month on essentials like food clothing, heating, etc.
  ii Practise talking generally about your domestic expenditure.
c i House prices have been stable.
  ii Practise talking generally about your personal assets.
d i A move into franchising has brought about a significant increase in turnover.
  ii Practise talking about the financial impact of a new development in your business.

> **Preparation**
>
> In this unit you will look at the everyday language of financial performance, personal and corporate. When and where do you talk about profits, liabilities and expenditure? As you prepare, look at the Useful Phrases on page 68. If possible, bring some accounts, yours or your company's, to the class.

2 Language check

Refer to the Language Notes on page 68 as you complete the examples below using the choices provided – only one is correct. Then prepare a version of each example that you might use.

1 These spread sheets .... delivered by special messenger, while we were out.
  a might have been
  b must be
  c can't have
2 I don't understand these fuel costs. .... the tank have .... ?
  a Can / be leaking
  b Could / been leaking
  c Could / been leaked
3 The accounts .... have been audited yet; year end was only last week.
  a ought
  b won't
  c mustn't
4 Our main overhead cost is ....
  a running costs
  b raw materials
  c head office salaries

5 .... on developing new sites rose by 17% in the period.
  a Expenditure
  b Earnings
  c Outgoings
6 According to these figures, your .... from investments was higher than your salary.
  a turnover
  b asset value
  c income
7 We find that child care and school fees .... to about $18,000 a year.
  a add
  b amount
  c account
8 We have to cut .... entertainment allowances; they are .... by 27%.
  a back on / up
  b back / over
  c – / high

9 This payment of .... represents a ....
  a twenty two million / one-off redundancy cost
  b twenty-two million / one-off redundancy cost
  c twenty-two million / one off redundancy cost
10 .... was low because we had suffered the biggest .... in our history; .... were down and we could not meet our ....
  a Confidence / losses / receipts liabilities
  b Confidence / loses / reciepts liabilitys
  c Confidance / losses / receipts liabilitys

3 | Listening

Caffè Nero

Listen to the news item about the Caffè Nero chain of coffee houses. What is the relevance of these figures?

a 5.9 ....

b 7.5 ....

c 25 ....

d 34 ....

e 52 ....

f 230 ....

4 | Writing

A salary increase

You have talked to your boss about a pay rise (practised in Unit 13). Your boss has asked you to put your request in writing. Read the notes on the right, then write your request. See the Useful Phrases on page 135.

- Before asking for a rise, review how well your department and company are doing. Is your manager complaining about cutbacks? Right timing is essential.

- Prepare a statement of your accomplishments. List your results. Give specific examples with percentages, numbers, facts and figures. If possible, make before-and-after comparisons.

- Present your goals for the next quarter. Rather than explaining your need for a rise as a personal issue – for example, 'My husband lost his job' – present it in a business framework. Explain how others with similar responsibilities are paid. If you can, show industry research.

- Never present your request for a rise as a demand or threat. That makes you an adversary. Instead, you could say: 'I've accomplished more than expected [show accomplishments], and I plan to do even more next quarter [show goals]. How do you think the company would feel about paying me X euros per month?'

- Finally, wait until your manager is on a personal high, and don't expect a decision overnight.

From CareerLab.com

The sale of a company

1 Read the article.

Bengal Bites Bonanza!

RAGI ANGSHUMAN, founder of upmarket snacks maker Bengal Bites, today became a multi-millionaire, selling his StraitSnax company to Logan Foods. Logan Foods is paying SG$150 million (US$88.5 million).

Angshuman, as 32% shareholder, will receive about SGD$48 million (US$28.33 million) of that. 'I'll get half in cash and the rest in shares,' he says.

Angshuman began Bengal Bites 11 years ago. Backed by an investment group, which owns 28% of the company, Angshuman and three colleagues set up their snack group in Singapore.

Ragi Angshuman's trio of friends will also do nicely out of today's deal; between them they stand to make around SG$50 million (US$29.5 million).

So what is the secret of Bengal Bites' success? 'We happened to tap

Ragi Angshuman

into a vein of the market which was waiting to be exploited – that is adult snacks,' says Angshuman.

The group's best-known snack is tortilla chips. But it also makes a range of titbits, from Punjab Mix to Mexican corn chips. He and the others create the new products by visiting faraway places and tracking down snacks on the street. 'Most of them are genuine village receipes,' he says.

This financial year, Bengal Bites expects to produce a turnover of SG$150 million (US$88.54 million) and profits of around SG$12 million (US$7.1 million). 'Our margins are at the top end of the food industry but they are not spectacular,' says Angshuman.

StraitSnax has been looking for a buyer since last year when it decided it lacked the resources to expand as quickly as it wanted. Now the intention is to move into Europe, Australia and the US.

Angshuman wants to double turnover in the next three years. StraitSnax already employs 330 people in Singapore. That should increase significantly if all goes to plan.

Key financial information

- SS bought by LF with US$ 150m.
- RA will recieve $48m because he founded the company.
- His friends / colleags are making more (SG$ 50m each).
- Turnover this year SG$ 88m, profit million SG$ 7m.
- Wanted a buyer because of resources to expand.
- RA wants to double turn over in three years' time
- 330 employed Singapore people to increase significantly.

2 A colleague gives you these notes to check. Correct the errors and omissions including the spelling mistakes. Discuss the notes in pairs. Do they cover the main points?

Revise the information so that it accurately summarises the terms of the deal.

LANGUAGE REFERENCE

Language Notes

For further notes on these points, see the accompanying Business Grammar Guide (BGG).

Review of modal verbs, past forms (BGG 7)

The modal verbs are: *can, could, will, would, shall, should, may, might, must, ought to, have to*

- Simple

e.g. I **must have made** a mistake, but I can't see where.

We **should have brought** a copy of the accounts.

They **can't have spent** $18,000 on flowers!

What **would** you **have done**?

- Continuous

e.g. We **should have been selling** 12,000 units a week.

You **can't have been using** 3,000 litres a day!

Could the payments **have been going** into the wrong account?

We **must have been spending** more on entertaining than we thought.

- Passive

e.g. These accounts **ought to have been audited**.

How could the money **have been 'mislaid'**?

The job **wouldn't have been completed** on time if we hadn't cut corners; you **could have been fired**!

Hyphens, some uses (BGG 24.6)

- Some common expressions

e.g. multi-million, fast-food, ex-boss, twenty-five

- Some compound adjectives

e.g. day-to-day expenses, long-term debts one-off costs, fifty-dollar bill

Spelling rules

See Business Grammar Guide Section 24.5.

Personal and company finances

- Vocabulary

See also the Glossary page 158.

- assets / asset value: total value of assets with a life of more than one accounting period (e.g. computers, buildings, vehicles)
- balance: sum remaining (on an account)
- balance sheet: a statement of assets and liabilities
- capital costs: money spent on fixed assets (property, etc.)
- current liabilities: debts that may be repayable within 12 months (e.g. bank overdraft)
- depreciation: provision to write off the cost of a fixed asset (e.g. a machine)

- dividend: share of profit paid to shareholders
- earnings: money earned / total earnings
- expenditure: any money spent
- fixed assets: assets used in production (buildings, etc.)
- fixed costs: costs that do not vary with sales (e.g. rent)
- investment: money spent with a view to a return in the future
- outgoings: any money spent
- overheads: costs not directly related to producing goods / services (e.g. directors' salaries)
- profit and loss account: a statement of income and expenditure
- receipts: any money received
- running costs: money spent running an organisation / car, etc.
- surplus: income less all deductions
- turnover: total sales

- Verbs and verb phrases

e.g. These three items **add up to / come to / amount to** $47,000 in all.

Sales in the first quarter **are up / down** by $9 million.

Imports **account for / make up** 25% of our production costs.

We had to **cut back on** the R&D budget.

A customer **went into liquidation**; we had to **write off** the debt.

Our household expenses **went up / down** (by) 20% last year.

I sold some shares to **pay off** a debt.

We are finding it difficult to **keep** our day-to-day expenses **down**.

Would you like me to **break** the figures **down**?

Useful Phrases

Our main overhead is the site cost – that includes rent, insurance, building maintenance, etc.

Our fixed costs come to about 40,000 per month in total.

That includes depreciation charges of 3.5 thousand.

Altogether our running costs amount to 1.7 million.

Can you give us a breakdown of this figure?

I should have brought a copy of the accounts.

My fixed outgoings include the usual things – mortgage, fixed taxes, insurance premiums, and so on.

I suppose the biggest item is my pension.

As a rough guide, I'd say our day-to-day living expenses come to about 3,000 per month, on average.

We must have been spending more on entertaining than we thought.

In the year, I exchanged my old Peugeot for an up-to-date model.

I had to sell my shares in Unicorn to pay off some debts.

On the plus side, I own some land which has gone up in value.

I got the promotion I was hoping for, which I'm pleased about.

On the work front, the outlook is very satisfactory.

Over the last year, we performed well in respect of our core activities – we met our sales targets in key markets.

Sales are up from $9.8 million last time, to $10.7 million.

Results are more or less in line with forecasts.

We made a profit of 2.2 million on sales of 20.7 million.

UNIT 15 Managing credit

1 Core practice

Listening and speaking

Listen to the exchanges (a – d) and mark the statements (part i) true $\boxed{T}$, false $\boxed{F}$ or unclear $\boxed{U}$. Then, working with a partner, practise the exchanges indicated in part ii.

a **i** The invoice has been paid. □
   ii Practise taking a call from someone chasing an unpaid invoice.

b **i** The phone belongs to the speaker. □
   ii Practise dealing with a mobile phone operator who has put a bar on your phone in error.

c **i** The card has been cloned. □
   ii Practise calling a credit card company and talking about theft from your account.

d **i** The speaker is going to register with an anti-fraud agency. □
   ii Discuss ways of preventing ID theft.

Preparation

This unit explores corporate and personal credit management. What language do you need when your credit card is stolen or you find someone is withdrawing funds from your account? In preparation, look at the Useful Phrases on page 72. If possible, come prepared to talk about an example of credit fraud.

2 Language check

Refer to the Language Notes on page 72 as you complete the examples below using the choices provided – only one is correct. Then prepare a version of each example that you might use.

1 You .... have kept us informed then we .... have known what was going on.
  a ought / could
  b should / would
  c must / would

2 I would advise you .... any promises you can't keep.
  a not to make
  b don't make
  c not making

3 I .... that you protect yourself .... ID theft.
  a suggest / for
  b advise / against
  c recommend / from

4 I think .... have warned them .... advance about the overlimit charges.
  a you need / with
  b you should / in
  c we would / to

5 We must settle the account today, ... get the discount.
  a or else we'll
  b if not we'll
  c otherwise we won't

6 We'll give you a refund .... you return the goods.
  a as long as
  b as well as
  c as far as

7 How soon can you pay .... the balance .... your account?
  a back / with
  b off / on
  c for / in

8 They could .... your credit .... and reduce your credit ....
  a downgrade / status / limit
  b upgrade / record / card
  c degrade / payment / control

9 I didn't realise the account was .... Leave it .... me – I'll sort it ....
  a due / with / in
  b due date / for / down
  c overdue / to / out

10 They have put a .... on my phone – could you .... out what the problem is.
  a stop / sort
  b bar / find
  c ban / look

3 | Listening

Querying an invoice

Listen to the speaker, who has been to a conference and is now querying an invoice which the organisers have sent to him. Answer the questions.

a What is the problem?
b Where is the invoice reference number?
c What is John Mars going to do?
d How did John Mars handle the situation? Aggressively? Diplomatically?
e What would you expect the outcome to be?

4 | Writing

Late payment

1 Work in pairs. Do either **a** or **b**.
   a Phone a customer and ask for payment of an overdue invoice. You will need to establish the background to the case – how overdue the invoice is, the relationship between the customer and the supplier.
   b Phone a supplier and explain that you would like to delay payment of an invoice because of a short-term cashflow problem. As with task **a**, you will need to establish the background to the case.
2 Send a message confirming what was agreed over the phone.

> **Useful Language**
>
> … following our phone call …
> … I would like to confirm / summarise …
> … a short-term problem …
> … send a duplicate invoice …
> … pay by return …
> … resume deliveries as soon as we receive your payment …
> … extend the period of credit …
> … payment should now reach you / us by …
> … return to normal terms of trading …
> … can I stress …?
> … a one-off arrangement …
> … thank you for your cooperation …
> … I would like to thank you for your understanding …

1 Read the text and discuss it. Have you or anyone you know experienced ID theft?
2 Work in pairs.
   Partner A: Having read the article, you want advice. How can you protect yourself? How can you reduce the risk? You call **Partner B**.
   Partner B: Your information is on page 135.

A name and address: it's all ID thieves need

By **Helen Loveless**

Cases of ID theft have soared more than eightfold in the past five years. Last year, 126,000 cases were reported in the UK at an estimated cost to the economy of £1.3 billion.

All criminals need is the name and address of their victim. With those bare details, a surprising amount of information can be found legitimately.

Once information is gathered – particularly alongside further details obtained illegally – fraudsters rack up debts in their victim's name.

ID thieves have a number of ways of stealing data. They have been known to scavenge through rubbish bins for personal documents and information.

'Phishing' is the name given to another form of information theft where fraudsters send emails purporting to come from a genuine company, typically a bank.

Customers are asked to verify details by clicking on a link that takes them to a bogus website. Once they have the information, criminals use it to pose as their victims and apply for credit.

Another problem is that personal data, stored on countless marketing databases, is routinely traded with barely any checks on buyers.

CPP, an international company that provides anti-fraud services, is concerned. Spokesman Owen Roberts says: 'Protecting yourself against identity theft goes beyond shredding documents. A name and address is enough to carry out most types of ID theft.'

Cifas, the UK fraud prevention service, runs Protective Registration. Consumers can register their address for £11.75 (€17.35) a year, and then with every application for credit in their name, companies have to carry out extra checks.

Identity theft is sometimes viewed as a victimless crime because banks and card companies cover customers' losses. But the consequences can be distressing.

Anne Kemble, 48, became a victim after applying for a storecard in a sports shop. A card sent out in her name was intercepted by criminals.

The first Anne and her businessman husband John, 52, knew about it was when a statement addressed to Anne arrived in the post claiming that she owed £1,000.

Anne was horrified, but this fraud was just the beginning because the criminals went on to apply for credit from many other sources using the personal details from the stolen card.

Anne discovered the extent of the fraud when she rang Cifas. Fortunately, none of the applications was successful, but her credit record could have been damaged if she had not checked.

'I felt awful knowing criminals had all my personal information,' she says. 'I won't ever apply for storecards again. I have since bought a shredder and signed up to the Cifas anti-fraud register. But I still worry that it could happen again.'

LANGUAGE REFERENCE

Language Notes

For further notes on these points, see the accompanying Business Grammar Guide (BGG).

Advising, suggesting, etc. (BGG 7.4, 21.1)

- Positive

e.g. You need to get a shredder.
You must register with an anti-fraud agency.
I think you should call the company and explain the situation.
I (would) advise you to put forward a realistic payment plan.
I (would) suggest / recommend that you protect yourself from ID theft.

- Negative

e.g. You don't need to shred everything.
You mustn't forget to check your file regularly.
I don't think you should call them at lunch time.
I (would) advise you not to make unrealistic promises.
I (would) suggest / recommend that you don't throw credit card receipts in the rubbish.

Modal verbs: expressing criticism / regret
(BGG 7.8)

e.g. You **ought to have kept** us informed.
You **must have known** there was a problem.
It **would have made** a big difference.
It **could have caused** an accident.
I'm sorry, **we should have let** you know.
I **would have**, but I couldn't get hold of you.

Conditional sentences without *if*: applying pressure (BGG 3.5, 3.6)

e.g. You must settle the account by the 21st **otherwise** / **or else** we'll withdraw your credit status.
They must clear the balance within 14 days; **if not** we'll have to stop supplying them.
We will take no further action **provided** / **as long as** we receive settlement in full by the 15th.
We will accept part-payment **on condition that** you clear the balance within 14 days.

Vocabulary

- Words and phrases

e.g. There's an **overlimit fee** of €50 on accounts that exceed the agreed **credit limit**.
We charge a **late payment fee** when accounts are not settled by the **due date**.
Late payment may affect your **credit record**.
We may **downgrade** your **credit status** and reduce your credit limit.

- Verbs and verb phrases

e.g. I'm afraid we **are** a bit **behind** with our paperwork.
How soon can you **pay off** the balance?
I'll **look into** it and **call** you **back**.
Leave it to me; I'll **sort** it **out**.
My card's been declined; I'd like to know what's **going on**.
Your account is **overdue**.
Payment was **due** last week.

Useful Phrases

I'm calling about our invoice number AK-40 7/AZ for €450.
According to our records, the goods were delivered on time.
When can we expect to receive payment?
We charge 5% on overdue accounts.

It was passed for payment ten days ago.
You should have received our payment by now.
Apparently there's a query on this invoice.
I'm sorry about this; I'll look into it and call you back.
You'll get the money by the 10th without fail.

This account is overdue and the phone is barred.
It's a company phone. What should I do?
The only thing I can suggest is that you make a payment and sort it out with your accounts people later.
I hope this isn't going to affect my credit record.

My card's just been declined – I'd like to know what's going on.
There have been some unusual transactions on your account.
Your card has been blocked automatically.
So what do I have to do?
You should call our fraud line as soon as possible.

How can I protect myself from ID theft?
There are a number of things you can do to reduce the risk.
You need to use a shredder.
You must put your name on the anti-fraud register.

UNIT 16 Time management

1 | Core practice

Listening and speaking

Listen to the exchanges (a – d) and mark the statements (part i) true $\boxed{T}$, false $\boxed{F}$ or unclear $\boxed{U}$. Then, working with a partner, practise the exchanges indicated in part ii.

a i The speaker didn't learn anything new. □
  ii Practise talking about a training course you've been on recently.
b i The job is a nightmare – the speaker is under a lot of pressure. □
  ii Practise talking about the pressure in your job.
c i The job is overrunning because the spec was changed. □
  ii Practise asking for more time to finish a job.
d i The manager has enough in his training budget to cover the cost of the course. □
  ii Practise persuading your manager to let you go on a course.

Preparation

In his unit, the focus moves to time management and running meetings – and the language involved in both. Come prepared to talk about how you manage your time. You can prepare by looking at the Useful Phrases on page 76. If possible, bring to the class documents relating to a training course you have been on.

2 | Language check

Refer to the Language Notes on page 76 as you complete the examples below using the choices provided – only one is correct. Then prepare a version of each example that you might use.

1 I .... do the course .... the company funds it.
  a can't / if
  b can / unless
  c can / as long as
2 .... we don't finish everything now, we'll meet again tomorrow.
  a On the condition that
  b In the case of
  c In the event that
3 .... she didn't waste so much time, I'd give her a job.
  a Providing
  b If only
  c When
4 I wish there .... less pressure to cope with in my new job.
  a was
  b had been
  c would be

5 We should be able to get .... the .... in an hour.
  a over / meeting
  b through / agenda
  c to / deadline
6 I can .... you when .... under pressure and ....
  a cover for / I'm / versus
  b cover for / you're / vice versa
  c delegate to / I'm / pro rata
7 The programme teaches .... how to organise ....
  a people / themselves
  b you / oneself
  c staff / ourselves

8 If you're not organised, the .... will get on top of ....
  a paperwork / you
  b backlog / yourself
  c workload / it
9 If possible I'd like some time .... to .... a course.
  a of / attend
  b away / go for
  c off / go on
10 If you have a / an .... assistant, it can .... a lot of pressure .... you.
  a demanding / get / on
  b good / put / off
  c efficient / take / off

3 | Listening

Meetings

1 In pairs, go through the tips on the right for running a successful meeting. Add, delete or amend points until you feel the list is satisfactory.

2 Listen to an interview with John Farrer, MD of Pod, a management training organisation, and make notes. Then tick the points that he refers to.

> **Running time-efficient meetings**
> - Make sure everyone is informed of time and place.
> - Ensure the facilities are right (size of room, enough chairs, etc.).
> - Allow enough time for your agenda.
> - Restrict the numbers present.
> - Distribute copies of working documents in advance.
> - Circulate a clear agenda in advance.
> - Make sure the person in the chair has experience.
> - Stick to the agenda.
> - Make arrangements for calls to be held.
> - Take and circulate clear minutes of the meeting.

4 | Writing

Allocating your time

Match the charts below with the texts. Compare yourself with the models given.
Then prepare a pie chart showing how you allocate your time, and write an accompanying text.

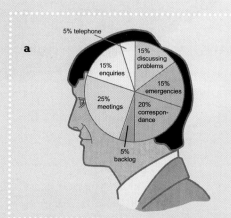

a
- 5% telephone
- 15% discussing problems
- 15% enquiries
- 15% emergencies
- 25% meetings
- 20% correspondance
- 5% backlog

1 This effective manager delegates correspondence to subordinates and deals with major issues in person or by telephone. His meetings are well planned: he attends only the key parts, leaving the rest to staff, and can often fit in two meetings where a busy colleague has not completed one. He is popular with customers and suppliers because he spends time getting to know them, and his reading makes him knowledgeable about the industry. He does not merely discuss problems, he solves them. He always seems to have time.

2 This busy manager's life is not planned. Perhaps that is why he is busy. His use of time indicates an entirely responsive approach to his job, with more time devoted to administration than customer service. The high level of emergency is indicative of serious problems. (Peter Drucker states in *The Effective Executive* that well-run organisations do not have crises.) This manager should ask: 'What am I here to do? Do I delegate enough? If I allowed more time for planning, would those emergencies go away?'

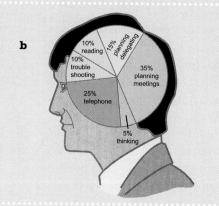

b
- 10% reading
- 15% planning delegating
- 10% trouble shooting
- 35% planning meetings
- 25% telephone
- 5% thinking

From The Manager's Handbook

A course for managers

1 Read the advertisement, and discuss it with a partner. Answer the questions, and make a note of your queries.

2 Now call for further information, e.g. cost, availability, duration.

Partner A: You are the potential customer.

Partner B: You represent TMI. Your information is on page 136.

Say 'YES' too often and you probably need TIME MANAGER

Other people's demands, or their problems, can make you less effective as a manager. But not if you have Time Manager.

A unique training programme and planning system, Time Manager helps you to build on your major strength – achieving results.

Over two stimulating days, it gives you a new framework in which to sharpen your skills – for example, in setting objectives, developing strategies, implementing projects, controlling tasks, measuring performance, people management.

As you might expect, too, the programme guides you on effective time management. And you receive full support. We offer an optional 'tune-up' day, free updates and a telephone hotline.

Over a million managers now use Time Manager. If, like them, you want to reach your goals, contact us. You'll get some pretty positive answers.

	YES	NO
Do you have trouble completing jobs through frequent interruptions?	☐	☐
Do you find it difficult to turn work away?	☐	☐
Do you feel obliged to work excessively long hours?	☐	☐
Does your colleagues' lack of organisation sometimes put your job on the line?	☐	☐
Are you ever frustrated by poor communications?	☐	☐
Do you routinely spend weekends working, rather than with your family?	☐	☐
Have you ever cancelled a holiday because of work?	☐	☐

TMI

LANGUAGE REFERENCE

Language Notes

For further notes on these points, see the accompanying Business Grammar Guide (BGG).

More on conditionals without *if* (BGG 3.5, 3.6)

- *or, or else, otherwise*

e.g. Do it now **or / or else / otherwise** it will never get done.

= If you don't do it now, it will never get done.

- *unless, without*

e.g. We won't improve **unless** we make changes.

… **without** making changes.

= We won't improve if we don't make changes.

- *providing / as long as / on condition that*

e.g. The company will pay the fees **providing / as long as / on condition that** the course adds value.

= The company will pay the fees, if the course adds value.

- *in the event that*

e.g. **In the event that** we don't reach a decision, we'll have to vote on it.

= If we don't reach a decision, we'll have to vote on it.

- *in the event of / in the case of*

e.g. **In the event of / In the case of** a deadlock, the chair has the casting vote.

= If there's a deadlock, the chair has the casting vote.

wish / if only (BGG 3.2, 3.4)

- Present

e.g. I wish / If only I **was better** organised.

I wish / If only there **wasn't** so much to do.

I wish / If only we **had more** time.

I wish / If only it **wasn't raining**.

- Past

e.g. I wish / If only I **had been better** organised.

I wish / If only there **hadn't been** so much to do.

I wish / If only we**'d had** more time.

I wish / If only the sun **had been shining**.

Latin expressions (BGG 24.4)

e.g. Could you send me a copy of the **agenda**?

The **data** is stored on this disk.

We must consider all the **pros** and **cons**.

Profits are distributed to shareholders **pro rata**.

I help her when she's busy, and **vice versa**.

We are flying **via** New York.

Italy **versus** Brazil should be a good game.

Reflexive pronouns (BGG 12.2)

e.g. The course helps you to organise **yourself** more effectively.

Some people find it difficult to motivate **themselves**.

The secret is not to overcommit **oneself**.

We often tell **ourselves** things that aren't true.

I have to clean my office **myself**.

Vocabulary

- Words and phrases

e.g. workflow planning, prioritising, delegating, workload, paperwork, backlog, problem solving, trouble shooting, firefighting

- Verbs and verb phrases

e.g. The secret is not to let a backlog **build up**.

It's important **to keep on top of** the paperwork.

A lot of our time **is taken up with** meetings.

We normally **get through** the agenda in about an hour.

Poor time management **puts pressure on** everyone.

I'd like to **go on** a course.

Who will **cover for** you while you are away?

Ask HR to **check** it **out**.

Useful Phrases

In this job, you have to be able to work under pressure.
It's very demanding – things can get pretty busy.
It's important to delegate and prioritise.

The phone takes up a lot of time.
I have an assistant who handles routine matters.
I find it difficult to cope with interruptions.
Sometimes I wish there was less pressure.

I'm having trouble meeting the deadline.
I'm afraid the work won't be ready in time.
We've having one or two problems.
Could we reschedule the meeting?

I'd like to attend a course – it would benefit my work.
Time management is a key skill.
I can't do it unless I can take time off.
Ask HR to check it out – especially the cost.
The cost will come out of the department's training budget.
What's your schedule like at the moment?
It's OK by me, providing you can get someone to cover for you.

The course showed us how to establish priorities.
It taught us ways of dealing with stress.
It focused on ways of improving one's performance.
They stressed the importance of to-do lists.
They gave us tips for running meetings.
It helped me to handle my workload.

UNIT 17 Delivering quality

1 Core practice

Listening and speaking

Listen to the exchanges (a – d) and mark the statements (part i) true $\boxed{T}$, false $\boxed{F}$ or unclear $\boxed{U}$. Then, working with a partner, practise the exchanges indicated in part ii.

a i Customers insist on a quality certificate because it guarantees quality.
  ii Do you have quality certification? Practise discussing the benefits. ☐

b i The company cannot compete on price.
  ii Do you sell on price or quality? Practise explaining your company's strategy. ☐

c i They offer excellent back up.
  ii Practise describing key features of what you offer. ☐

d i If they'd had more time they would have re-run the job.
  ii Practise talking about a case that went wrong, and what you learned. ☐

Preparation

This unit is about quality performance and control. Does your company encourage customer focus, internally and externally? Come prepared to talk about the situation in your organisation. You can prepare by looking at the Useful Phrases on page 80. If possible, bring to the class a complimentary message and a complaint received from customers.

2 Language check

Refer to the Language Notes on page 80 as you complete the examples below using the choices provided – only one is correct. Then prepare a version of each example that you might use.

1 If we .... about the scheme we .... to join.
  a knew / would apply
  b had known / would apply
  c had known / would have applied

2 Their products are very shoddy; .... on special offer, ... would buy them.
  a even if they were / nobody
  b if they weren't / someone
  c if they were / everyone

3 Does everyone have a manual? ...., there are some spare ones.
  a If so
  b If not
  c If only

4 – We are applying for a grant to finance some ....
  – .... you don't get it?
  a customer needs / Supposing
  b areas of weakness / As long as
  c performance improvements / What if

5 If .... wasn't .... your help, ... would have lost the order.
  a she / with / she
  b it / for / we
  c I / under / you

6 .... provide .... top quality service.
  a What we / is
  b It is we / the
  c We who / a really

7 We succeed by offering .... quality and ....
  a rock bottom / attention to detail
  b really / best practice
  c top / value for money

8 We are committed ....
  a to raise standards
  b to delivering quality
  c reducing errors

9 We try .... people working late because quality tends ....
  a to avoid / to be down
  b to encourage / to fall short
  c to prevent / to drop

10 We have a manual which .... our standard .... procedures.
  a points out / quality
  b sets out / operating
  c passes on / quality control

3 | Listening

Handling technical complaints

1 What is the procedure in your organisation for handling complaints?
2 Listen to an interview with a technical service assistant in the engineering business, and check these notes. Mark them true $\boxed{\text{T}}$, false $\boxed{\text{F}}$ or not given $\boxed{\text{N}}$.

  a The technical service assistant also deals with some non-technical complaints. ☐

  b The company employs a fairly large number of graduates. ☐

  c He cannot issue credit notes without the authority of his boss. ☐

  d The speaker is proud of his technical background. ☐

  e Most complaints are caused by problems inherent in the machines. ☐

  f Most technical complaints have to be passed on to the R&D department. ☐

4 | Writing

Responding to feedback

1 What do you think of the advice below? Does it apply to your work environment?
2 Refer to a letter of complaint you or a member of the group brought to class, and write a response.

Writing a letter of apology

TIMING	Write the apology letter as soon as possible.
ACTIONS	Rather than focusing on the damage you have caused, write about things you will do to rectify the situation.
BRIEF	Keep your apology letter short and to the point.
SINCERITY	No one wants to read overly dramatic language. Choose your words carefully, and express yourself clearly and simply.
TONE	Your apology letter should be considerate and respectful. Remember, you are trying to rebuild a damaged relationship.
BLAME	Take full responsibility for what you have done.
FOLLOW UP	Try to set up a time when you can apologise in person, then back up your apology with considerate behaviour in the future.

From WriteExpress

5 | Feature

Customer care

1 Read the advertisement. Summarise what the IOCC does and the services it offers.
2 Discuss your experience of customer care. Which companies have high standards? Which do not? How could the IOCC help them?

INSTITUTE OF CUSTOMER CARE (IOCC)

Go Chart

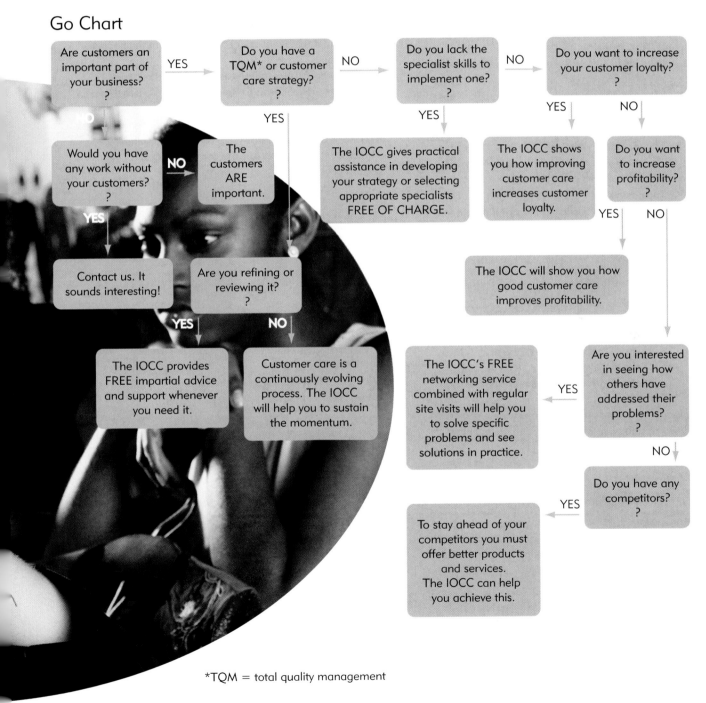

Are customers an important part of your business? — YES → Do you have a TQM* or customer care strategy? — NO → Do you lack the specialist skills to implement one? — NO → Do you want to increase your customer loyalty?

Are customers an important part of your business? NO ↓

Would you have any work without your customers?

NO → The customers ARE important.

YES ↓

Contact us. It sounds interesting!

Do you have a TQM* or customer care strategy? YES ↓

Are you refining or reviewing it?

YES ↓ The IOCC provides FREE impartial advice and support whenever you need it.

NO ↓ Customer care is a continuously evolving process. The IOCC will help you to sustain the momentum.

Do you lack the specialist skills to implement one? YES ↓ The IOCC gives practical assistance in developing your strategy or selecting appropriate specialists FREE OF CHARGE.

Do you want to increase your customer loyalty? YES ↓ The IOCC shows you how improving customer care increases customer loyalty.

NO ↓ Do you want to increase profitability?

YES ↓ The IOCC will show you how good customer care improves profitability.

NO ↓ Are you interested in seeing how others have addressed their problems?

YES → The IOCC's FREE networking service combined with regular site visits will help you to solve specific problems and see solutions in practice.

NO ↓ Do you have any competitors?

YES → To stay ahead of your competitors you must offer better products and services. The IOCC can help you achieve this.

*TQM = total quality management

LANGUAGE REFERENCE

Language Notes

For further notes on these points, see the accompanying Business Grammar Guide (BGG).

More on conditionals (BGG 3)

• Second Conditional (BGG 3.2)

e.g. **If I had** a free hand, **I'd streamline** the whole system.

If we weren't certificated, nobody **would use** us.

If their products **were** better **made**, they **wouldn't get** so many complaints.

• Third Conditional (BGG 3.4)

e.g. If **we hadn't raised** standards, **we'd have gone** out of business.

We **would have** delivered better quality if **we had spent** more on training.

If **I'd known** the risks, I **wouldn't have** done it.

• Some other forms (BGG 3.5, 3.6)

e.g. I wouldn't do it, **even if** you paid me.

What if I offered you $1 million?

Supposing I offered you $2 million?

Do they have a quality certificate? **If not**, we can't use them.

Are you busy? **If so**, I'll call back later.

If it wasn't for you, I wouldn't be working here.

Alternative sentence structures (BGG 19.1)

e.g. 1 We sell on quality and service.

It is quality and service that we sell on.

The thing we sell on is quality and service.

e.g. 2 You need to speak to the manager.

It's the manager (that) you need to speak to.

The person you need to speak to is the manager.

e.g. 3 We achieve our goals because we work hard.

It is because we work hard that we achieve our goals.

The reason we achieve our goals is that we work hard.

prevent vs. avoid (BGG 20.3)

• prevent

The best way to **prevent** bottlenecks is to plan ahead.

We try to **prevent** people working without a break.

The sprinklers **prevented** the fire from spreading.

• avoid

They **avoided** the recession by offering top quality products.

We **avoid** having meetings in the evening because people are tired.

I normally travel early to **avoid** the rush hour.

Vocabulary

• Words and phrases

Adjective + noun: high / low quality, excellent / shoddy workmanship, good / poor aftersales support, complete rubbish

Adverb + past participle: well / poorly made, neatly / sloppily finished, brilliantly / atrociously designed, completely overpriced

Intensifier + adjective: very / not very impressive, really first class, extremely disappointing, absolutely awful

Phrases: attention to detail, best practice, customer focus, state-of-the-art, user-friendly, value for money, cutting edge

• Verbs and verb phrases

e.g. It's important that feedback gets **passed on** to the people concerned.

We encourage all our staff to **take pride in** their work.

By the time errors **come to light**, it's often too late to deal with them.

What we are offering **falls short** of our clients' requirements.

This work **is above** / **below** / **up to** our usual standard.

The quality manual **sets out** the company's quality control procedures.

Useful Phrases

What we sell is quality and service.

We attach great importance to our customers' needs.

The company is committed to raising standards.

raising standards   improving quality   reducing errors

We need to update our system for dealing with returned goods.

It would improve our performance if we had better procedures for logging faults.

It would help us to identify areas of weakness.

We encourage best practice in all areas.

Our experience is that customers insist on quality certification.

Some won't deal with you if you don't have it.

A quality certificate shows that you have good systems in place, and that they're working properly.

It's good from a marketing point of view.

It would undermine our position if we didn't have it.

We have a problem with lack of communication between departments.

Each department records complaints separately.

The system needs to be centralised, and made more efficient.

Quality suffers because nobody knows what is going on.

I'd streamline our internal information systems.

We're selling against a product called Softcell.

It's cheaper, but we believe we're more cost effective.

The secret is to listen to what your clients say.

It's usually not a question of better or worse, but what fits the client's requirements.

UNIT 18 Working practices

1 Core practice

Listening and speaking

Listen to the exchanges (a – d) and mark the statements (part i) true ☐T☐, false ☐F☐ or unclear ☐U☐. Then, working with a partner, practise the exchanges indicated in part ii.

a i A member of staff has recently lost their job because a customer complained. ☐
 ii Practise talking about the attitude to customers in your organisation.
b i The regulations require that there are regular fire evacuation drills. ☐
 ii Practise talking about health and safety procedures in your office.
c i The woman wears jeans to work. ☐
 ii Practise talking about dress and behaviour codes in your organisation.
d i The main changes have been in communication and connectivity. ☐
 ii Practise talking about the way working practices have changed.

> **Preparation**
>
> Think about times when you have to describe or discuss the working practices in your organisation. Here we look at attitudes to customers, compliance, dress and behaviour codes, and how practices are changing. Come prepared to talk about working practices in your organisation. You can prepare by looking at the Useful Phrases on page 84. If possible, bring to class samples of regulations or guidelines that apply in your area of work.

2 Language check

Refer to the Language Notes on page 84 as you complete the examples below using the choices provided – only one is correct. Then prepare a version of each example that you might use.

1 .... a spot check, we .... be in serious trouble because we aren't complying .... the regulations.
 a If the inspectors do / would / to
 b Would the inspector / are / for
 c Should the inspectors do / will / with

2 Visitors to the site are .... to wear hard hats .... there is an accident.
 a required / in case
 b supposed / if
 c allowed / when

3 We have a dress- .... policy. You can wear what you like as long as it looks professional. .... I wear a suit.
 a up / So often
 b code / More often
 c down / More often than not

4 Only on Wednesdays .... time to check the balances. We're supposed to check them ....
 a there is / weekly
 b there isn't / from time to time
 c is there / daily

5 We have a .... agreement with the union, and .... do a number of firms in this sector.
 a no-go / as
 b no-strike / so
 c no-claim / also

6 Exco maintains minimum staff levels. Therefore they .... the payroll in house – .... does their associate company, for the same reasons.
 a don't do / and neither
 b do / and so
 c do / as

7 Health and Safety is part of Karen's job. She .... that the guidelines and procedures are ....
 a enforces / followed
 b ensures / applied
 c controls / observed

8 Is it against the .... to read private emails? We need to find out – there are severe .... for breaking the rules.
 a legislation / prices
 b legal / fines
 c law / penalties

9 It's .... company – if you don't pull your .... , you're out!
 a a traditional / work
 b a progressive / rank
 c an ambitious / weight

10 Our switchboard people let us .... badly. They make a very bad ....
 a down / impression
 b off / sense
 c go / point

3 | Listening

An Employee Relations Manager

Listen to the interview with the Employee Relations Manager of a large French company. Then draft a summary for your boss, who is interested in these areas:

- the company's management style
- relations with the trade unions.

4 | Reading

Dealing with paperwork

1 Select eight of the statistics in the article below and indicate whether they coincide with your experiences: yes Y, no N or don't know D.

e.g.   1   We spend 45 minutes a day looking for information.   N

2   We spend two hours a week filing.   Y

3   85% of information filed will never be used again.   D

2 In respect of each of the three rules of paper management, write briefly what you actually do.

e.g. Rule 1: *I deal with most paperwork after two or three days.*

File those papers under waste basket

There's too much paper in your in-tray – on average 40 hours' worth, according to a recent study.

Nor will you be surprised to know that we spend 45 minutes a day looking for information and two hours a week filing it (even though 85% will never be used again and 45% is already filed elsewhere).

According to a recent survey by office supplier Avery, 43% of office workers had more than 16 items awaiting attention, 85% had a pile of stuff to read that they hadn't got round to, and 35% couldn't remember the last time they saw the bottom of their in-tray.

The costs associated with this accumulation of paper are colossal. Paper breeds costs: in cabinets to keep it in, people to sort, file and carry it around, and finally more paper to tell people where it is and what it's for. Computers make matters worse since most companies now keep everything twice as a hard copy and as an electronic file.

People with cluttered desks work longer and less effectively because they get distracted, can't remember where they put things, lurch from job to job, panic, procrastinate and end up stressed.

You wouldn't think it to judge from most people's desks but the principles of paper management are well established.

Work on one project at a time, prioritise and handle each piece of paper just once. Then follow these rules.

- **Rule 1:** Deal with each piece of paper as soon as possible.
- **Rule 2:** Make one of four possible choices about every item – act on it, pass it to someone else to act on, file it, or bin it. There should be a heavy bias towards the last. Riccardo Semler, the boss of Semco, asks himself: 'What is the worst thing that could happen if I throw this away?'
- **Rule 3:** The hardest to obey – just do it. Many companies have an annual 'Clear your desk' day.

Adapted from *The Observer*

Company culture

In pairs complete the questionnaire. The scoring is on page 136. Do you agree with the analysis?
Discuss your company's practices in this area. Make a list of strengths and weaknesses.

How well are contacts and clients treated in your company?

Unless otherwise stated, tick the answer that most closely applies.

1   The telephone is the front line of a company's contact with the world. How polite is your company's front line? Which of the following does your switchboard operator do?
  a   Say good morning or good afternoon to each caller.
  b   Give the name of the company clearly.
  c   Always sound as if he or she is trying to help the caller, not stop them getting through.
  d   Give the name of the person to whom the caller is being connected if they've asked for someone by position rather than name.
  e   If there's no reply from an extension, respond quickly and offer to connect the caller to someone else or take a message.

Tick every option that applies. (Check your answers by ringing your switchboard in another name.)

2   If someone leaves a message, how does the person who has been rung normally respond?
  a   Returns the call the same day.
  b   Just returns the call another day.
  c   Asks a secretary to ring and apologise if it is impossible to ring back the same day, then rings the next day.

3   Out of the office hours, which message does your answering machine give?
  a   Explains the company hours and offers to take messages of an unlimited length.
  b   Says the company is closed and gives the hours when callers can call again.
  c   Says a message can be left but fails to give the working hours.
  d   There is no answer message: callers have no advice or support.

4   On which of the following are staff told to offer to brief those visiting the company?
  a   The exact location of the company.
  b   Transport, such as nearest station or distance from the station.
  c   Parking facilities nearby.
  d   Staff only brief those who ask or are important.

Tick all that apply.

5   Companies, like people, only get one chance to make a good first impression. If someone has an appointment, how is that person treated?
  a   Always seen at the time.
  b   Sometimes seen slightly later but given an explanation for the delay and something to drink while waiting.
  c   Just left waiting.
  d   Treatment depends on how important they are.

6   Offering hospitality is more than polite, it's a winning ploy: someone who accepts hospitality subconsciously feels like a guest with obligations to good behaviour. What are visitors to your company offered?
  a   Coffee or tea if it's coffee or tea time – but given no choice of which they have.
  b   Offered nothing unless company members are feeling like something themselves.
  c   Given a choice of tea, coffee or water immediately.
  d   It depends on their importance.

7   To whom are visitors introduced?
  a   All those they encounter, including relevant secretaries.
  b   Only executives they encounter.
  c   Nobody except the key person they have come to meet.

8   When a visitor leaves what does the key executive do?
  a   Asks a junior to show the visitor out.
  b   Walks to the lift or front door with the visitor themselves.

9   When arranging a business drink or lunch, what do your people do?
  a   Choose the time and place to suit your company's location and hours.
  b   Make arrangements to suit the client's convenience.
  c   Compromise between a and b.

10 Dale Carnegie said: 'A person's name is to that person the sweetest and most important sound in any language.' When speaking to clients or naming them in letters, on conference labels and so on, are all concerned briefed to ensure the name and title are correct – and as they like to be addressed?
  a   Sometimes.
  b   Always.
  c   No briefing is ever given on this.
  d   They are spelt correctly but it's company policy to call everyone by their first names.

Adapted from *Enquire Within Modern Etiquette*

LANGUAGE REFERENCE

Language Notes

For further notes on these points, see the accompanying Business Grammar Guide (BGG).

More on conditionals (BGG 3.5)

- *If you should* vs. *Should you*

e.g. If **you should change** your mind, give me a call.
Should you change your mind, give me a call.

- *If they were to* vs. *Were they to*

e.g. If **they were to enforce** the regulations, several firms would go out of business.
Were they to enforce the regulations, several firms would go out of business.

- *If we had* vs. *Had we*

e.g. If **we had known** about the problem, we would have sorted it out.
Had we known about the problem, we would have sorted it out.

- *if* vs. *in case*

e.g. I never argue **if** a customer complains.
I'm never rude on the phone **in case** it's a customer.

Expressions of frequency (BGG 14.5, 19.2)

- Some examples

e.g. We have to report **monthly** / **on a regular basis**.
The regulations are updated **from time to time**.
Every so often we get a call from Head Office – **more often than not** late on Friday.
I buy a lottery ticket **now and then**, but I **hardly ever** win.

- Some inversions

e.g. **Only** when there is a major problem **do we** stop the line.
Only on one occasion **did I** get a reply.
Very seldom do they give you a second chance.
Never have I heard such nonsense.

Accord (indicating parallels) (BGG 18.4)

e.g. 1 We put a lot of emphasis on team building
… and so do our competitors.
… and our competitors do too.
… and the same is true of our competitors.
… as do our competitors.

e.g. 2 The managers are not worried about the new legislation, neither / nor are the staff.
… and the staff aren't either.
… and it's the same with the staff.
… and the same is true of the staff.

Terms relating to compliance

e.g. We have to comply with the regulator's requirements.
We have to make sure we are in compliance.
The compliance manager has to ensure the regulations are applied.
We are required (by law) to …
It's against the law to … / It's illegal to …
They are (not) strictly enforced.
There are severe penalties for breaking the rules.

Vocabulary

- Words and phrases

e.g. flexitime, job sharing, equal opportunities, job rotation, cross training, flexible working, job description, job opportunity, standard procedure, operational guidelines, work incentives, job satisfaction, leading by example, clock watching, dress codes, dress-down Friday

- Verbs and verb phrases

e.g. The inspectors **do spot checks** from time to time.
The procedures **are in place** but everyone ignores them
Reception **lets us down badly** – they're so unhelpful.
Our switchboard **makes a good** / **bad impression**.

Useful Phrases

Our management style is very informal.
informal   traditional   progressive
The emphasis is on what works.
We are having to adapt to the demand for flexitime, as are our competitors.
We don't like the new legislation, and neither do they.

We are very customer focused.
Were one of our customers to complain, the people responsible would probably lose their jobs.

Our switchboard lets us down badly.
They make a bad impression.
Had we known about the problem, we would have sorted it out.

Health and Safety comes under Compliance.
It's part of the Building Manager's job.
He has to ensure the regulations are being applied properly.
We have to comply with the regulator's requirements.

The regulations are updated every so often.
Who checks if they are being applied?
The inspectors do spot checks from time to time.
Very seldom do they give you a second chance.

I used to have an administrative assistant.
Now, we work online and handle our own filing.
The main changes have been in the area of technology.
There is more competition – the pace is faster.

UNIT 19 Advertising and promotion

Preparation

Being able to promote yourself, your team and your products is a key skill. When and how do you do these things? Come prepared to talk about the ways your organisation or your team promotes itself. You can prepare by looking at the Useful Phrases on page 88. If possible, bring to the class a sample of promotional literature relating to your activities.

1 Core practice

Listening and speaking

Listen to the exchanges (a – d) and mark the statements (part i) true ☐T☐, false ☐F☐ or unclear ☐U☐. Then, working with a partner, practise the exchanges indicated in part ii.

a i The client has seen the report from the focus groups. ☐
  ii Discuss a possible advertising campaign for your organisation.
b i The speaker refers to three types of literature. ☐
  ii Practise talking about the promotional literature your company uses.
c i Brand advertising in upmarket magazines doesn't work for them. ☐
  ii Practise talking about the different ways in which your organisation promotes itself.
d i The competitor's products are more expensive. ☐
  ii Practise responding to an enquiry about a service or product you provide.

2 Language check

Refer to the Language Notes on page 88 as you complete the examples below using the choices provided – only one is correct. Then prepare a version of each example that you might use.

1 If the ad .... shown on TV, we would have had less ....
   a was / response
   b wasn't / reaction
   c hadn't been / exposure

2 They .... told that the brief .... going to be changed.
   a should have been / was
   b should have been / is
   c should be / was

3 The service .... the Internet. The company pays for a number of sponsored ....
   a is promoted over / links
   b promotes on / attachments
   c was promoted through / connections

4 We .... targeted by .... mailers and .... callers. We used to be called about 40 times a day.
   a are / spam / junk
   b were / junk / nuisance
   c would be / nuisance / spam

5 .... the .... Director, it is my job to keep the client happy.
   a To be / Customer
   b As / Account
   c By being / Company

6 .... all the details, I can now begin work on ideas for the new corporate ....
   a Having heard / brochure
   b Now I have heard / market research
   c Hearing / image

7 .... young people, the .... need to look right.
   a If aimed for / leaflets
   b If it is aimed on / flyers
   c Aimed at / posters

8 The client wants us to come .... some .... ideas.
   a to / new
   b into / promotional
   c up with / fresh

9 Hameed was the account manager .... the 'Tip-top' ....
   a behind / campaign
   b behind with / advertising
   c with / promotion

10 What .... are you trying to .... across?
   a slogan / push
   b message / put
   c advertising / get

3 | Listening

Advertising slogans

Listen and choose an advertising slogan that fits the product described, then write a slogan for the products / services you offer.

a (Speaker 1) ....
b (Speaker 2) ....
c (Speaker 3) ....

Two years free credit

Bargains! 25% off all items

Unbeatable value

AS SEEN ON TV

Three weeks free trial, and no strings attached

Running costs worth pushing for

You know it makes sense

THE OPPORTUNITY OF A LIFETIME

Guaranteed FREE from CFCs

A friendly welcome for all the family

Not tested on animals

HURRY WHILE STOCKS LASTS

The right solution at the right price

Never knowingly undersold

PROBABLY THE BEST IN THE WORLD

Buy two, get one free

GUARANTEED FULL SATISFACTION OR YOUR MONEY BACK

4 | Writing

Promotional literature

Write a possible brief for the people who prepared this advertisement. Make clear what the company does and the main selling points.

Useful Language

… Phoenix specialises in …

… we offer …

… customers can choose from …

… we undertake to complete all work within …

… a 12-month warranty

… recently we have expanded our service to include …

PHOENIX

Seating (Manufacturing Renovations) Ltd

Specialists in Office Furniture, Seating, Suites, Antiques, etc.
7 Vastern Road, Vancouver BC RG00 400, Canada

IMPROVE YOUR OFFICE IMAGE AND ENVIRONMENT TO THE HIGHEST STANDARD WITHOUT SPENDING A FORTUNE!

Let us renovate your existing furniture!

We offer:

- Low costs
- 100% tax relief
- Free collection and delivery
- Free on-site quotations
- Latest flame-retardant foams and materials

- Unlimited choice of materials and colour
- 12 months' warranty
- First-class after-sales service.

New!
We manufacture a wide range of new furniture and can supply reputable brand names at competitive prices.

**Call us now on
(001) 604 459 5535
www.pho-enix.com/renovations**

Spam and junk

1 Read the newspaper article, then answer these questions.

   a What is the main point of the article?
   b What is the good news?
   c What is the bad news?
   d How much spam and junk mail do you receive? How many nuisance calls?
   e Why do spam and nuisance calls happen?
   f How can you stop them?

2 Working with the rest of the group, prepare a list of 'do's' and 'don'ts' to help people like Christine Chivers.

Christine finds peace for £400

Marketing callers were making Christine Chivers' life such a misery that she paid £400 to get them off her back.

Christine, who runs a patchwork and quilting business in Cambridgeshire, was bombarded with calls from companies selling magazine advertising.

'It was a nightmare; I would invariably be rung when I was very busy and the sales people often tried to convince me I had already spoken to them,' she says.

'A common ruse was to say some of the money I would pay would go to charities.' Christine eventually registered with the free Telephone Preference Service and the volume of calls decreased but she was still receiving a considerable number – probably because she was already on a number of companies' lists.

'It got to the point where I was having problems picking up the phone at home as well as at work,' says Christine.

She has now paid OptOutUK about £400 to take her off these lists and she is satisfied with the results.

But she continues to receive junk mail – and about 30 spam emails a day.

From *Sunday Express*

LANGUAGE REFERENCE

Language Notes

For further notes on these points, see the accompanying Business Grammar Guide (BGG).

A review of passive forms (BGG 4.1)

• Present / Future

e.g. The campaign **is based on** radio advertisements.
Nothing **can be done** till the budget is agreed.
Do you know where these ads **are going to be shown**?
Will the design work **be finished** by Tuesday?
I think the poster **ought to be redesigned**.
The market research **won't have been done** by Tuesday.

• Past

e.g. The artwork **has** just **been completed**.
She **was targeted** by junk mailers and spammers.
If the ads **hadn't been shown on TV**, we would have had less exposure.
The poster **had to be redesigned**.
We **should have been told**.

Omissions in clauses (BGG 19.3)

e.g. 1 **If it is handled** properly, the campaign will work.
If handled properly, the campaign will work.
Handled properly, the campaign will work.

e.g. 2 **When you consider** the work that's involved …
Considering the work involved, their fees seem …

e.g. 3 **Now we have changed** agencies, we should see …
Having changed agencies, we should see …

e.g. 4 **As we are** the client, we have the final say.
As / Being the client, we have the final say.

e.g. 5 I enclose a copy of the contract, **as we agreed**.
I enclose a copy of the contract, **as agreed**.

Vocabulary

• Some advertising terms
an advertising agency
an advertising campaign
an account director / manager
direct mail advertising
classified advertising
the medium (radio, TV, the Internet, etc.)
the company image
a message, a slogan
a focus group, a market survey
a sponsored link
market research
upmarket / downmarket

• Some advertising literature
a leaflet   a poster
a brochure   a coupon
an insert   a catalogue
a flyer   a mail order catalogue

• Some problems
junk mail, nuisance calls, spam

• Verbs and verb phrases
e.g. This agency **has a good track record**.
The poster needs **to highlight** the key points.
The campaign **was targeted at** the ABC1 market.
What message do you want **to put across**?
We need **to come up with** some fresh ideas.
Lynn **was behind** the Guinness campaign.

Useful Phrases

The service is promoted over the Internet.
The company pays for a number of sponsored links.
Do you get much spam?
junk mail   nuisance calls
Are you targeted by nuisance callers?

We also use a mail order catalogue.
We tried a corporate advertising campaign but it wasn't worth the £200,000 we spent on it.
The feedback we got from focus groups was not encouraging.
We want to create an image of reliability and technical excellence.

We have a glossy brochure that promotes the company as a whole.
And there are a number of product brochures, which highlight product details.
Our products are aimed at low-income consumers.
The message is that when you buy this, you're buying style.

This leaflet tells you about the company.
Could you tell me a little about your micro pumps?
Do you have a sample I can see?
The specifications are on this sheet.
The price list is on the back.

Our research indicates that there is a large potential market for your product among young people.
Why don't we do a campaign based on radio ads?
Properly handled the campaign could be very successful.

UNIT 20 Offers and orders

Preparation

Offers and orders are central to many aspects of business. The language involved has relevance beyond procurement and sales. You can prepare for the lesson by looking at the Useful Phrases on page 92 and by relating them to your own communication needs. If possible, bring to the class some recent emails relating to offers and orders.

1 | Core practice

Listening and speaking

Listen to the exchanges (a – d) and mark the statements (part i) true ⊤, false ⎡F⎤ or unclear ⎡U⎤. Then, working with a partner, practise the exchanges indicated in part ii.

a i The customer orders more than he wants. ☐
  ii Practise calling a supplier and confirming an order.

b i The customer is being overcharged. ☐
  ii Practise querying an invoice.

c i The extra items should be at the full price because this is a new order. ☐
  ii Practise changing and / or increasing an order.

d i The supplier is not to blame for the delay. ☐
  ii Practise calling a customer to say a delivery is going to be late.

2 | Language check

Refer to the Language Notes on page 92 as you complete the examples below using the choices provided – only one is correct. Then prepare a version of each example that you might use.

1 The goods .... loaded when the buyer called .... the order.
  a are / canceling
  b were being / to cancel
  c were / to be cancelled

2 The client's .... seem .... forgotten in this case.
  a instructions / to have been
  b needs / being
  c wants / to have

3 Customers are being .... unrealistic delivery dates – nobody likes .... let down.
  a give / to be
  b gave / to have been
  c given / being

4 The reason we are not going to be able to deliver your order on time is .... there was a hold up with the paperwork at your ....
  a because / side
  b so / part
  c that / end

5 We order on-line .... we can .... deliveries and cut costs.
  a in order to / make
  b so that / track
  c so as to / follow

6 The unit is 55cm by 30cm by 2.3m – it has .... of about 0.35 ....
  a an area / square metres
  b a volume / cubic metres
  c a capacity / metres

7 It .... 7 metres by 4 metres – the .... is 28 square metres.
  a measures / area
  b has / size
  c weighs / dimension

8 We'd like to take you .... your offer, if it's still ....
  a out for / on
  b up on / open
  c down for / good

9 They wanted to .... an order but they couldn't meet our price – their .... are very tight.
  a place / margins
  b take / profits
  c make / costs

10 .... discounts are not available to retail customers, but this range is .... special offer.
  a Bulk / for
  b Wholesale / in
  c Trade / on

3 Listening

In a sales office

Listen to some sales administrators in a light engineering company and answer the questions.

a i What is the relationship between the two speakers?

ii What are the implications of this order for production schedules?

iii How else could you say, 'but there isn't much cushion'?

b i What is the problem with the order?

ii How does the seller hope to sort out the problem?

iii How else could you say, 'Let's keep our fingers crossed'?

4 Writing

A home page

1 Read the information adapted from the Conversis website home page. In pairs, discuss the service. Would you use it? How would you use it?

2 Prepare a message you might send to Conversis via its website asking for details of its services and charges. Use your own business circumstances as a basis for the message. See page 136 for some Useful Language.

Comunicaçion
En cualquier idioma

Conversis

| US ENGLISH | FRANCAIS | ESPANOL | DEUTSCH | ITALIANO |

TRANSLATIONS FOR SUCCESS, IN ANY LANGUAGE

To do business throughout the world you need to speak the right language. Everywhere. But communicating effectively requires much more than accurate translations. It also requires ensuring that your products and marketing messages will meet with sales success in any global market.

That's why you need to know more about Conversis. As a full-service translation and localisation company, we offer the entire suite of services, including:

- high-quality translations of marketing and product information
- website and branding globalisation
- international desktop publishing
- quality assurance and testing services.

Conversis has all the multinational programmes you require to distribute your products or services on time and within budget – delivering high-quality translations that see a consistent return on your investment.

In any language, Conversis is the translation company you have been looking for.

Contact with a possible supplier

Partner A: You are interested in purchasing a Customer Information System. You have received a mail shot from Guidex Systems – see page 136. You access the information below on the company's website, then call the company. You get through to **Partner B** in Customer Information.

Partner B: You work for Guidex. You process first enquiries, identify needs, and pass prospects on to specialist advisers and sales teams. See page 136 for more information.

Possible areas for discussion

- Specific needs
- Guideline prices
- Installation dates and times
- Training and Service support

GUIDEX*systems*

Systems and products

Our work – over forty years in all – has given us immense experience in all aspects of transport system management. We are the industry leaders in the rail sector. Read more.

Customer management

Understanding and responding to customers is a vital part of our success. Intelligent queuing and meeting agenda systems will transform the way your business runs.

Customer displays

Leading edge designs driven by an integrated information platform ensure the clearest and most user-friendly monitor displays available.

FROM first TO last

From conception to completion, we offer full project life-cycle management to meet all our customers' requirements.

From a simple face-on monitor display to a fully integrated transport infrastructure management system, we will work closely with *you* to guarantee *you* achieve *your* desired outcomes.

We will work closely with you to guarantee you achieve your desired outcomes.

LANGUAGE REFERENCE

Language Notes

For further notes on these points, see the accompanying Business Grammar Guide (BGG).

More on passives: Continuous, Infinitive and *-ing* forms (BGG 4)

- Continuous

e.g. Your order **is being prepared**.
Where **are** the goods **being stored**?
The order **was being loaded** when the customer cancelled it.
Buyers **were being given** unrealistic delivery dates.
Deliveries **weren't being checked**.

- Infinitives

e.g. The boxes used **to be made** by hand.
We didn't expect the order **to be cancelled**.
This job is not due **to be delivered** till the 19th.
We ought **to have been informed**.
The client's instructions seem **to have been ignored**.

- *-ing* forms

e.g. Some suppliers insist on **being paid** in advance.
Our customers can't stand **being kept** waiting.
They rely on **being given** the facts.
We all dislike **being overcharged**.
Nobody enjoys **being criticised**.

Giving reasons / explanations (BGG 18.1)

e.g. We order on-line **because** the prices are lower / **because of** the low prices.
We order on-line **in order to** / **so as to** cut costs.
We order on-line **so that** we get a good price.
As / **Since** it's cheaper, we order on-line.
It's cheaper **so** we order on-line.
Our reason for ordering on-line **is that** the prices are lower.
That's **the reason**. That's **why**.

Some measurements (BGG 24.2, 24.3)

e.g. The dimensions are 20 feet by 8 feet by 5 feet.
The unit measures 17 metres by 5 metres.
The (surface) area is 85 square metres.
It has a volume of $2\frac{3}{4}$ cubic metres.
The gross weight is 20 tons. / It weighs 20 tons.
It is 2 metres long / wide / high / deep.
The length / width / height / depth is 2 metres.

sq cm = square centimetre
cu m = cubic metre
1 foot = 0.305 metres (2 feet = 0.610 metres)

Vocabulary

- Terms used in retail / wholesale sales

retail, retailer, a retail chain,
wholesale, wholesaler,
an account / a trade customer,
a quantity / trade discount,
a bulk order,
a margin of 10%, a mark-up of 25%,
credit terms, credit limit,
to be in stock / to be out of stock,
to be on special offer,
to be reduced to clear,
to buy something on sale or return

- Verbs and verb phrases

e.g. I'm calling to **place an order**.
We'd like to **take** you **up on** your offer, if it's still open.
We had to **put** our prices **up** / **down**.
We are not going to **meet the deadline**.
Could you **batch** part of the order **through** tomorrow?
We try never to **let** a customer **down**.

Useful Phrases

The unit weighs 2.5 kilos.
It has a volume of 1.5 cubic metres.
The screen measures 17 centimetres by 5.
The surface area is 85 square centimetres.
We offer a quantity discount and generous credit terms.

I can let you have them for $62.
They are on special offer.
Can you supply them on sale or return?

I'm calling to place an order.
We'd like to take you up on your offer.
You quoted us $9 per hundred.
I'll check if we have them in stock.

Our quote was subject to the cost of raw materials.
We had to put our prices up.
That wasn't made clear.
We ought to have been informed.
Our margins are very tight.

I'm afraid we're not going to be able to deliver on time.
But time is critical at this end.
Our instructions seem to have been ignored.
We are being given unrealistic delivery dates.
We rely on being given the facts.
We could batch through part of the order on Wednesday.

Sometimes customers order on-line (in order) to cut costs.
That's the reason. That's why.

UNIT 21 Customer care

1 Core practice

Listening and speaking

Listen to the exchanges (a – d) and mark the statements (part i) true ☐T☐,
false ☐F☐ or unclear ☐U☐. Then, working with a partner, practise the
exchanges indicated in part ii of the questions.

a i The company's efforts in the area of customer care are mainly
window dressing.

  ii Practise talking about the care culture in your organisation.

b i The problem with the machine has been going on for over two
hours.

  ii Practise calling a supplier and getting the service support you need.

c i The boss is actively promoting good customer relations.

  ii Practise trying to persuade your boss to support a customer care
idea that will cost some money.

d i The customer is not telling the whole story.

  ii Practise dealing with a retail customer who wants his / her money
back although the problem is not covered by the guarantee.

> **Preparation**
>
> Think about the customers of your
> organisation – internal or external. How
> are they satisfied? How are problems
> dealth with? Come prepared to talk about
> the customer care they receive. Refer to
> the Useful Phrases on page 96. If possible,
> bring to the class emails or letters relating
> to a customer care issue you have been
> involved in.

2 Language check

Refer to the Language Notes on page 96 as you complete the examples below using the choices provided – only one
is correct. Then prepare a version of each example that you might use.

1 The call-out time .... to
be one hour. We're very
unhappy .... the way
we're being treated.
  a is / for
  b is not / with
  c is supposed / about

2 I am calling to complain ....
the .... we received from
your service engineer.
  a for / care
  b about / service
  c for / support

3 The best companies ....
their customers first; we try
never to let a customer
....
  a put / down
  b make / off
  c have / go

4 Could you .... it with me?
I'll .... into the problem
and .... back to you.

  a look / get / leave
  b get / leave / look
  c leave / look / get

5 The guarantee does not cover
damage .... misuse.
  a due for
  b leading to
  c caused by

6 Damage that is ....
customer neglect is not ....
the terms of the guarantee.
  a the result of / covered under
  b because / under
  c caused by / fixed by

7 Are these statements aggressive
or polite?
  i I'm fed up with being treated
like this.
  ii I completely understand and
I apologise.
  a polite / aggressive
  b aggressive / polite
  c aggressive / aggressive

8 .... the warranty, if
.... has caused this
problem the company will
replace the goods free of
charge.
  a By / misuse
  b Under / a manufacturing
fault
  c In / mistreatment

9 They agreed to .... back
immediately. It's almost
.... they knew it was
faulty when they sold it.
  a give us our money / as if
  b exchange it / as
  c take it / if

10 It .... if the machine is
overheating. What kind of
.... contract do you have?
  a sounds as / service
  b seems as / protection
  c looks / warranty

3 | Listening

The customer is right

1 Listen to the two speakers and tick the points they refer to. Do they speak as customers or as suppliers?
2 In pairs, discuss a time when you complained. What was the cause? Which factors in the table were involved?

Factors affecting customer relations

	Speakers: 1	2
Standard of service	☐	☐
Value for money	☐	☐
Interest in customer's needs	☐	☐
Credit control procedures	☐	☐
Frequency of sales calls	☐	☐
Hospitality / entertainment	☐	☐

From The Manager's Handbook

4 | Writing

Letter of complaint

1 Your boss asks you to rewrite the letter below. He / She says it is too long and too wordy – it also needs a heading. Work in pairs.
2 Write a letter relating to a case when you complained.

Dear …

I am writing to complain about the poor service we have received on our order dated 20 July – I attach a copy.

1 You may recall that when we placed the order, I explained that this was for a new overseas customer. I requested delivery not later than 7 September. You assured me that the goods, modified according to our specifications, would be delivered by 4 September.

2 On 15 August, our distribution manager tried to call your Customer Services department to get confirmation of the delivery. Having called a number of times and failed to make contact, he asked for the manager, Teresa Fardio. He was told she was too busy to come to the phone. He finally sent an email, and received a reply signed by a T. Larrick, stating that the job was on schedule.

3 When the goods were finally received this morning:
   • the order was two boxes short
   • the colour was cream, not white
   • the monogrammed logo was 'DV Hotels', not 'PV Hotels'.

I have to say that I am very upset by the way the order has been handled. This is an important opportunity for us, and it is now in jeopardy as a result of your negligence. The customer has not cancelled yet, but I have had to promise very fast delivery.

I would very much regret ending a business relationship that goes back a long time, but I will be obliged to make other arrangements if I do not receive a satisfactory reply and acceptable delivery dates before the end of the day.

Yours sincerely

Fair trading

1 Read the leaflet and discuss the questions in pairs.
  a How might a document like this be distributed?
  b What is its purpose?
  c How is it intended to improve customer relations? Discuss in pairs.
2 Work in pairs. Practise returning some shoes to a Cobra shop.

  Partner A returns the shoes.
  Partner B is the sales assistant.
  Refer to the document
  below, where
  necessary.

Possible reasons for return of shoes
- They have worn badly.
- A defect has been noticed.
- They are an unwanted gift.
- They are the wrong colour.
- They don't fit.

Possible outcomes
- Refusal to replace them
- A refund
- A credit note
- Replacement shoes
- An apology

cobra
SPORTS SHOE EXPERTS

FAIR TRADING POLICY

We WILL exchange or refund if:

The goods you bought are agreed by our store manager to be faulty, not of merchantable quality or not fit for the purpose for which they were designed as long as you have the till receipt.

OR

The goods are returned, in the original packaging, with the appropriate till receipt and in an unused condition suitable for resale.

We WILL NOT exchange or refund if:

The goods returned show signs of damage which are not obviously the result of a manufacturing fault; this applies to both accidental and malicious damage.

The goods have been worn in an obviously unsuitable or inappropriate way – for example:
- ladies shoes worn by men
- shoes worn for long periods with the laces unfastened.

The goods have been mistreated – for example:
- washed in a machine in a hot or cold wash when not specifically stated as suitable by the manufacturer

- machine dried or dried by excessive heat (radiator, airing cupboard).

The goods have obviously been used for purposes other than those for which they were designed – for example:
- aerobics shoe being used for skateboarding
- running shoes being used for football kickabouts
- aerobic shoes for indoor use, used in wet conditions outdoors.

(Please ensure that you take advice on the design function of a pair of shoes before purchase.)

If you do not agree with our store manager on whether or not your goods are exchangeable or refundable, he or she may offer to send them (at our expense) to their manufacturer, for their expert opinion. If this does not satisfy you, the matter can be taken further via the Office of Fair Trading.

We hope you find this helpful, and believe that by maintaining a consistent but, more importantly, fair approach to returned products, we will be ensuring the best value for all our customers.

This policy is actively endorsed by our suppliers.

LANGUAGE REFERENCE

Language Notes

For further notes on these points, see the accompanying Business Grammar Guide (BGG).

Impressions: examples with *seem* / *look* / *sound* and *as if* / *as though* (BGG 20.2)

e.g. They **seem** to be the wrong size.
The guarantee **doesn't seem** to have been stamped.
It **looks as if** / **as though** it was cleaned with solvents.
It **doesn't sound as if** they're going to change it.
It **doesn't look like** a new pair to me.
It's **almost as if** they don't believe you.

Cause and effect: some examples (BGG 18.1)

e.g. The damage **was caused by** misuse.
This is **the result of** using the wrong fuel.
They've shrunk **because** they were washed in a machine.
In our view, the wear and tear **is due to** heavy use.
The cold weather **resulted in** a number of cancellations.
A manufacturing fault **led to** the machine overheating.

Complaining: some examples

e.g. I'm calling **to complain about** the fact that …
We're very **unhappy about** the way …
According to the brochure, **it's** (**not**) **supposed to** …
When we bought it, we **were assured** that …
The trouble is … / **It's too** …
It's just **not good enough**.

Referring to warranties / guarantees: some examples

e.g. It's still **under guarantee** / **warranty**.
Can I get this fixed **under the guarantee** / **warranty**?
Under the terms of the guarantee / **warranty** …
The guarantee / warranty **covers** parts and labour.
The guarantee / warranty **does not cover** defects caused by neglect.
According to the contract, call-out time is one hour.

Vocabulary

- Words and phrases
  customer focus, customer facing,
  call-out time, downtime,
  fault, defect, defective part,
  neglect, misuse, wear and tear,
  refund, replacement, credit note

- Verbs and verb phrases
e.g. The best companies **put** their customers **first**.
We try never **to let** a customer **down**.
It was faulty / damaged so I **took it back**.
We're not **happy with it** – we'd **like our money back**.
We're really **fed up with** being treated like this.
Could you **put** your complaint **in writing**.
If you leave it with me, I'll **look into** the problem and get back to you.

Useful Phrases

I want to make a complaint. Who should I speak to?
Can I take the details?
Are you sure it's plugged in properly?

According to the instructions it's supposed to be silent.
Is this covered by the guarantee?
Leave it with me – I'll get our technical support to call you.

It sounds as if the machine is overheating.
Do you have a service contract?
Call-out time is supposed to be two hours.
This isn't the result of normal wear and tear.
We're very unhappy about the way we're being treated.

I was thinking of sending the buyer at SLX tickets for the Cup Final.
There might be some questions.
It would be better if you took him yourself.

I bought these shoes three days ago – here's the receipt.
They are brand new and the soles are coming away.
It looks as if they've been washed in a machine.
In our view, the wear and tear is due to heavy use, not to a manufacturing fault.
The guarantee doesn't cover defects caused by misuse.

Do you want to exchange them for a new pair, or would you prefer a refund?
Sorry for any inconvenience. Please accept our apologies.
Get back to us if you have any more problems.

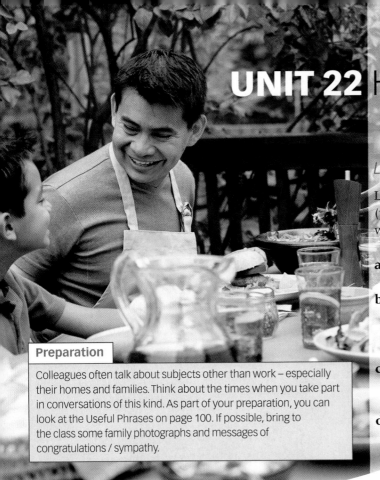

UNIT 22 Home and family

1 Core practice

Listening and speaking

Listen to the exchanges (a – d) and mark the statements (part i) true ☐T☐, false ☐F☐ or unclear ☐U☐. Then, working with a partner, practise the exchanges indicated in part ii.

a i The apartment block is on a hill.
ii Practise talking about your home. ☐

b i From the time he gets up, the speaker has an hour to get ready and have breakfast before he leaves. ☐
ii Practise talking about your morning routines. ☐

c i This is the speaker's second marriage. ☐
ii Practise showing photos and talking about your family.

d i They employ a cleaner. ☐
ii Practise talking about your domestic arrangements – how are they organised?

Preparation

Colleagues often talk about subjects other than work – especially their homes and families. Think about the times when you take part in conversations of this kind. As part of your preparation, you can look at the Useful Phrases on page 100. If possible, bring to the class some family photographs and messages of congratulations / sympathy.

2 Language check

Refer to the Language Notes on page 100 as you complete the examples below using the choices provided – only one is correct. Then prepare a version of each example that you might use.

1 .... three children look very .... to their mother.
   a All / similar
   b All of / the same
   c All of the / like

2 The .... property we had in Jakarta was very .... from the place where we live here.
   a leasehold / unlike
   b rented / opposite
   c freehold / different

3 Although they are twins, they are very different from ....
   a every other
   b each other
   c each one

4 We are getting .... next week. .... of my relations has sent a wedding present.

   a divorced / All
   b engaged / Every
   c married / Each

5 She is staying with a friend of ....
   a her mother
   b her mother's
   c her mothers'

6 We're looking .... my .... cat; they're away on holiday.
   a after / boss's children's
   b for / boss's children's
   c at / boss' children's

7 When my mother .... , I suddenly had two new .... sisters and a .... father.
   a remarried / half / step
   b got married / step / half
   c got divorced / ex- / no

8 They fell in love, got .... , and five months later got .... A year after that my mother got .... and I was born.
   a married / separated / broke up
   b married / split up / divorced
   c engaged / married / pregnant

9 She's .... the children .... her own at the same time as doing a full-time job.
   a growing up / by
   b bringing up / on
   c looking after / with

10 We are moving .... a top-floor apartment .... the river, with parking .... the basement.
   a into / overlooking / in
   b in / with a view / on
   c to / next / down

3 Listening

Family background

1 Listen, and match the speakers with the photographs (A – C).
2 In pairs, talk about your background. Refer to family photos where possible.

A

B

C

4 Writing

A request for time off

Write a letter or email requesting time off – see the Useful Phrases on page 137.

Before writing
- Check if there are company guidelines covering the situation. Adjust your request to fit the requirements, if possible.
- Decide what you want and the grounds for your request. Is it:
  - part of your holiday entitlement?
  - time off in lieu of overtime pay?
  - time off on compassionate grounds?
  - unpaid leave?
- Think about the business situation.
  - Is it a busy time?
  - How will your work be covered?

In the letter or email
- Provide a clear heading.
- Indicate your request and explain why it is important (if this is not obvious).
- Indicate the basis of your request – holiday entitlement, unpaid leave, etc.
- Show that you understand the business situation and put forward solutions to possible problems.
- If necessary, refer to the in-house guidelines.
- Be brief.

Couples in business

1 Read the article. Working in pairs, go through the notes on the article. Do they cover the main points? Add / delete as necessary.
2 Think about your own partner or a close friend. Could you go into business together? Would you like your partner to be your boss? Prepare your thoughts, then compare notes with the group.

MARRIED TO THE JOB

When graphic designer Debbie Mole was looking for a business partner she had a clear idea of what she did not want. After working in previous design partnerships she was very wary of getting involved with someone who wouldn't pull their weight.

But this time she found the answer close to home. Two years ago she set up a business with her husband Alan, also a designer. Now their company, Design Conspiracy, is thriving – and the marriage is still going strong.

But results vary. When they were running The Body Shop, Gordon and Anita Roddick apparently thrived on the pressures of running an international business. In the world of publishing, Anthony and Rosie Cheetham are established names. But business woman Jennifer d'Abo, who bought and sold the Ryman Stationery chain, ended up divorced from her husband, and says business and marriage don't mix. And George Davies, who worked with his wife Liz at Next, lost both – even now he prefers not to talk about it.

The importance of knowing each other's strengths and weaknesses was stressed by one of the most famous

Anita and Gordon Roddick: a partnership in business and marriage

couples in business, Anita and Gordon Roddick. 'I'm good out front, dealing with the public and the customers, and Gordon is a fantastic behind-the-scenes organiser,' says Anita in her book, *Body and Soul*. 'His strengths are my weakness, and vice versa; that is why we're a good partnership. I think we are able to work together successfully because we don't interfere with each other and we have confidence in each other's abilities.'

This does not mean there were never any rows. 'Anita and I have lived together for many years,' says Gordon. 'We've had hundreds of blazing rows.

That's how we operate – anything else would be fairly uninteresting.' He adds that in design matters, she has the final say, but on the business or financial side, she defers to him.

'One of the benefits of working with your emotional partner should be that you can talk freely and make constructive criticism without the other person taking it literally,' says Zelda West-Meads of the marriage guidance agency Relate. 'But you must have a good relationship to start with.'

Notes on the article

- Debbie Mole was wary because previous partner was lazy.
- Results vary. Works for G & A Roddick & A & R Cheetham, not for George D (Next).
- The Roddicks believe rows not a problem.
- Zelda West-Meads (Relate) – need good relationship to start with.

Adapted from an article by Sarah Hegarty

LANGUAGE REFERENCE

Language Notes

For further notes on these points, see the accompanying Business Grammar Guide (BGG).

Similarities and differences (BGG 15)

• *same as, similar to, different from, etc.*

e.g. My husband's taste in music is very **similar to** mine.

We spent **the same** amount on our holiday this year **as** we did last year.

When I'm at home I'm very **different from** the way I am at work.

My wife is **the opposite** of my mother – she is very calm.

• Verb forms

e.g. My daughter **resembles** her mother.

The children **don't look like** their parents at all.

This top **matches** your skirt.

Our methods may **differ**, but we have **the same** aims.

each, every, all (BGG 10.3)

• *each*

e.g. **Each** child is responsible for certain jobs.

Each of my brothers has married a business woman.

My brothers have **each** married a business woman.

I take the kids to school **each** / **every** morning.

In a small flat, you tend to get in **each other's** way.

• *every*

e.g. **Every** marriage is a compromise of some sort.

Every other person I meet seems to be getting engaged.

Not **everyone** wants to get married and have children.

We had to check **every single** item on the bill.

We have the washing machine serviced **every** two years.

• *all*

e.g. **All** (**of**) my relatives live in Ireland.

I keep in touch with **all of** them / them all.

We keep in touch **all the time**. Don't all couples?

We **all** make mistakes.

I was away **all** (last) week.

Possessive 's (BGG 11.2, 11.3)

e.g. My **children's** future

Her **parents'** house

John and Mary's family

My great **grandmother's** best friend

A friend of my **sister's**

A cousin of **John's**

She was wearing her **mother's** hat / a hat of her **mother's**.

Vocabulary

• Relationships

single, engaged, married, divorced, mother / father-in-law, grandfather / grandmother, first / second cousin, boyfriend / girlfriend, step mother / father / children, half brother / sister, ex-wife / husband, partner

• Homes

a ground-floor flat, a top-floor apartment, a rented flat, a terraced house, a bungalow, a freehold / leasehold property, on two floors, with parking in the basement, overlooking the river, with a view of the sea, a three-year lease, a 20-year mortgage

• Verb phrases

e.g. Where I **grew up**, the streets were relatively safe.

I **drop** the children **off** at the child minder.

She's **bringing up** the children on her own.

My mother gave up her career to **look after** her children.

Useful Phrases

In this picture you can see the house where we live.

This was taken at my father's 70th birthday party.

That's my son – he doesn't look like me at all; he resembles his mother.

This is where we lived when I was working in Korea.

That's my mother-in-law in the front there.

We have a freehold property overlooking the river.

We live in a terraced house with a small garden.

It's a quiet neighbourhood / a residential area.

We're surrounded by trees. We have a view of the sea.

There's a local shop just round the corner.

Our place is rented; we have a three-year lease.

We're on two floors.

Upstairs, there are two bedrooms and a bathroom.

We're about 15 minutes from the centre of town.

The apartment is fully serviced.

Since we broke up, I've been on my own.

I have a flatmate who contributes to the rent.

We have a cleaner who comes twice a week.

We share the housework.

The alarm usually goes off just before 6 o'clock.

I get up at about 6.15.

It takes me about 20 minutes to shower and dress.

The children are old enough to get themselves ready.

I drop them off at school on the way to the station.

My commute is about 45 minutes.

UNIT 23 Work / life balance

1 Core practice

Listening and speaking

Listen to the exchanges (a – d) and mark the statements (part i) true ☐T☐, false ☐F☐ or unclear ☐U☐. Then, working with a partner, practise the exchanges indicated in part ii.

a i The speaker puts his family first. ☐
  ii Practise talking about your work / life balance.
b i The speaker is a junior manager. ☐
  ii Practise talking about what you like to do in the evenings.
c i The speakers are old friends. ☐
  ii Practise making a social arrangement.
d i The speaker's children are between six and 14. ☐
  ii Practise talking about how you spend your weekends.

> ### Preparation
>
> In this unit you will review and practise the language used by business people to talk about family, leisure activities, interests outside work. Come prepared to talk about how you achieve balance in your life. You can prepare by looking at the Useful Phrases on page 104. If possible, bring to the class printed materials relating to a hobby or interest.

2 Language check

Refer to the Language Notes on page 104 as you complete the examples below using the choices provided – only one is correct. Then prepare a version of each example that you might use.

1 Reading is a lot more relaxing than .... TV.
  a watch
  b watching
  c to watch
2 I do weight training – there are .... more places where you can do it than there were when I started.
  a much
  b many
  c a bit
3 The apartment we had in Mexico City was twice .... the one we have here.
  a as big as
  b as big than
  c bigger than
4 I'm quite tired. I'd .... rather go home and watch TV than attend my Spanish evening class.

  a far
  b very far
  c a lot
5 I .... what you're saying but I don't .... you.
  a understand / agree with
  b understand / accept
  c accept / agree
6 I'm .... agreement with Theo – I think he has a very good ....
  a at / reason
  b on / argument
  c in / point
7 I'm a member of the Parent's Committee at my son's school – we don't meet on .... but it's still a big commitment.
  a regular way
  b regular days
  c a regular basis

8 .... , you must be John's brother – you look just like him.
  a Ooops
  b Phew
  c Ah
9 The place where you are staying is quite near us – you must .... round for a meal sometime .... your husband.
  a walk / and
  b come / and bring
  c go / and take
10 I used to collect coins but I gave .... because it takes .... a lot of time.
  a them away / off
  b up / away
  c it up / up

Exercising the brain

Read the article, then discuss it in pairs.

Partner A: Your role in the discussion is to support the case put forward in the article below. Use the information presented and your own experience. There are some Useful Phrases on page 137.

Partner B: Your role is to argue against the case. Your information is on pages 137.

Pumping iron can pump up your brain power

GERAD EVANS in Los Angeles

EXERCISING really can make you smarter, claims a new study. Keeping fit helps the brain stay healthy and sharp in old age. It may even prevent Alzheimer's disease and other mental disorders associated with aging. The American study is the first to show that intelligence factors in the brain – the compounds responsible for the brain's health – can be controlled by exercise.

Those who pump iron live longer and score higher on mental agility tests. Dr Carl Cotman, of the University of California, said: 'Here's another argument for getting active and staying active.'

Dr Cotman conducted his research on rats. Those that exercised had much higher levels of BDNF – brain-derived neurotrophic factor – the most widely distributed growth factor in the brain and one reported to decline with the onset of Alzheimer's.

The study showed a minimum level of exercise was enough to raise the levels of growth factor. The rats were permitted to choose how much exercise they wanted to do.

Some were 'couch rats', who rarely climbed on the treadmill, and others were 'runaholics' who would jog up to five miles a night. Prime examples of humans who have turned muscle power to their advantage are Arnold Schwarzenegger and Jean-Claude Van Damme. Despite their humble backgrounds, both fitness fanatics negotiated their way to the top of the Hollywood pile.

'The brain really is a muscle. When you exercise it the mind grows and is capable of handling more projects and complex problems,' he added.

Adapted from *Los Angeles News Service*

4 Writing

Reading habits

1 Study the statistics relating to book buying. Then work in pairs. Discuss your reading habits in relation to these statistics.
2 Write a summary of the information contained in the statistics. You'll find some Useful Language on page 138.

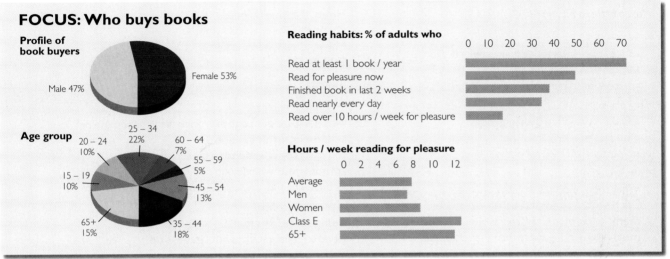

From *Books and the Consumer*

5 Feature

An interview

1 Listen to the speaker and complete the questionnaire on her behalf. What is the speaker's score?
2 In pairs, complete the questionnaire. Compare results. Does the analysis seem correct?

Do you balance work and leisure successfully?

		TRUE	FALSE
1	I often go through an entire weekend without spending any time on work brought home from the office.	☐	☐
2	Events at work sometimes force me to miss occasions at home that my family have particularly asked me to get back for.	☐	☐
3	I never dream about work problems.	☐	☐
4	I have at least three significant leisure interests that have nothing to do with my work.	☐	☐
5	When I am ill, I tend to take work to bed with me.	☐	☐
6	I find it easier to talk to work colleagues than to my partner or friends.	☐	☐
7	It is very unusual for me to ring home and say I'm going to be back later than planned.	☐	☐
8	I have had to cancel at least one holiday due to pressure of work.	☐	☐
9	When I'm trying to read a book or magazine, I find my mind keeps wandering back to work problems.	☐	☐
10	I find it a relief to meet new people who have nothing whatever to do with my line of business.	☐	☐

Score 2 points for every 'True' answer to statements 1, 3, 4, 7 and 10.

Score 0 for every 'False' response.

For statements 2, 5, 6, 8 and 9, score 2 points for each 'False' reply, and 0 for every 'True'.

A score of **16 or more** suggests that you have managed to achieve a healthy balance between your professional and private life. It's not that you are not fully committed to your job, just that you recognise the price of professional success does not have to be failure in other areas of life.

A score of **12 – 14** suggests that when office and domestic or leisure interests come into conflict, work comes first. Improving your performance in the office would reduce the number of occasions when you feel forced to disappoint your family and friends.

A score of **10 or less** points to workaholism. For you, life outside the office hardly counts.

From *How Do You Manage?*

LANGUAGE REFERENCE

Language Notes

For further notes on these points, see the accompanying Business Grammar Guide (BGG).

Comparisons with modifiers: *much / many, far, a lot, a little, a bit, no* (BGG 13.3, 15)

Activity A is …
… **much** more interesting than activity B.
… **far** less tiring than this one.
… **a lot** easier to play than the other one.

Mary plays …
… **a little** more often than John does.
… **a bit** less regularly than I do.
… **no** better than the rest of the team.

My new club has …
… **a few** more facilities than the old one.
… **a little** more atmosphere than yours does.
… **many** fewer members than its rival.
… **much** less parking space than the other one.

Adverbs, alternative forms (BGG 14.7)

e.g. I take exercise regularly.
I take exercises **on a regular basis**.

He plays **very competitively**.
He plays **in a very competitive way**.

Drive **carefully**.
Drive **with care**.

Preferences: some examples (BGG 20.4, 20.8)

e.g. 1 **I (much / far) prefer** going out to entertaining at home.
We'd (much / far) prefer to go out than to stay in.
Would you prefer not to eat till later?

e.g. 2 **I'd (much / far) rather** go to a movie than watch TV.
Would you rather we went by taxi?
I'd rather not use the tube at night.

e.g. 3 Why did they choose movie A **rather than** movie B?
They chose this **in preference to** that.

Agreeing / disagreeing (BGG 21.2)

• Agreeing with people
e.g. I'm **in agreement with** John.
I **can't / don't agree with** the government.
I **disagree with** what you are saying.

• Agreeing with facts / ideas
e.g. I **accept** your point.
I'm **in agreement with** what you said earlier.
I very much **agree / disagree with** your position.

Non-verbal communication: some examples

e.g. **Ah**, there you are.
Hey, is that your new car?
Oh, I'm sorry I thought the seat was free.
Oops – I've made a mistake!
Hmm, that smells good.
Ouch, this water is boiling hot!
Phew, it' very warm in here!
Ssh! Be quiet!

Vocabulary

• Verb phrases: meeting
e.g. Why don't we **get together** for a drink or something?
Let's **meet up** after work.
You must **come around** to dinner sometime.
I'm **going out with** Bruno on Friday.
At the weekend, we have some friends round for a meal.

• Verb phrases: activities
e.g. **Going round** a museum is not my idea of fun.
I used to collect stamps but I **gave it up**.
Hobbies can **take up** a lot of time.
I **go running** because it helps me **keep fit**.
I'm very **keen on** golf – it helps me unwind.

Useful Phrases

How's your work / life balance?
OK. I'm very keen on golf.
It's fun and I find it helps me unwind.
I take exercise on a regular basis.
We play in a very competitive way.
I go running because it keeps me fit.

At the weekend we have a few friends round for a meal.
For me it's a time to relax and spend time with the family.
We might all go for a walk, if the weather is good.
As a parent, I find it difficult to balance work and domestic commitments.

I much prefer going out to entertaining at home.
It's far more fun and a lot less hassle.
What I like best is meeting up with some friends.
During the week I have to entertain clients.

Saturday is a day for family and shopping.
During the week, my wife has to handle the domestic demands.
Does she accept that?
She agrees with it completely.
She isn't in agreement with it at all.

Do you take work home.
I do from time to time, but I try not to.
I'll work late during the week rather than work over the weekend.

Hey, why don't we don't we get together for a meal or something?
Wow, that would be nice – shall we meet up for lunch on Sunday?
Hmm, OK. Shall we fix a time?

UNIT 24 Getting away

1 Core practice

Listening and speaking

Listen to the exchanges (a – d) and mark the statements (part i) true ☐T☐, false ☐F☐ or unclear ☐U☐. Then, working with a partner, practise the exchanges indicated in part ii.

a i The break is in addition to the speaker's annual holiday.
  ii Practise organising a mini-break. ☐

b i In the area referred to, the off-season is between July and October.
  ii Practise getting advice and information about a place you plan to visit. ☐

c i The Imperial Palace is between Fulong and Gretik. ☐
  ii Practise asking for travel instructions to a tourist attraction.

d i The speaker is on a business trip. ☐
  ii Practise making arrangements to cut a trip short.

Preparation

Modern work patterns and global working can mean ongoing pressure and the need for breaks. Come ready to talk about a recent holiday. You can prepare by looking at the Useful Phrases on page 108. If possible, bring to the class a holiday postcard you received from a colleague, plus some photographs you took while on holiday.

2 Language check

Refer to the Language Notes on page 108 as you complete the examples below using the choices provided – only one is correct. Then prepare a version of each example that you might use.

1 The .... is very good value .... the fact that it is slightly more expensive.
  a airport tax / despite
  b mini-break / however
  c special package / in spite of

2 I put a label on my bag, and when I checked .... the clerk tagged it. .... the airline managed to lose it.
  a in / Even so
  b out / Even though
  c through / All the same

3 You .... a visa or any inoculations, but in my opinion .... to get an anti-tetanus jab.
  a need / it would be best
  b don't need / it would be a good idea
  c don't require / I suggest

4 We're staying in a small hotel right .... the beach. It's very popular .... my friends.
  a beyond / for
  b beneath / with
  c beside / among

5 I want to get .... for a few days, so I'm heading .... the coast, stopping on the way.
  a off / by
  b away / towards
  c out / for

6 – I'd like an early call in the morning.
  – Certainly; .... ?
  a when for
  b who from
  c where to

7 We can take the bus or the train – .... comes first.
  a which
  b whichever
  c whenever

8 I have to .... out in the morning. Could you prepare my .... , please?
  a leave / invoice
  b go / account
  c check / bill

9 I'm afraid this ticket isn't valid on .... flights; if you want to travel tomorrow, you'll have to .... to business class.
  a package / re-book
  b scheduled / upgrade
  c charter / improve

10 *(A booking clerk)* The flight is .... at the moment. Shall I put you on .... ?
  a booked / the list
  b overbooked / waiting list
  c fully booked / stand-by

3 | Listening

Holiday destinations

Listen to the three speakers talking about holidays and short breaks. Where do they like to go? Then complete the table to the right.

When on holiday	Speakers:	1	2	3
I like to relax and forget work.		☐	☐	☐
I like to be somewhere hot.		☐	☐	☐
I like to visit the sea.		☐	☐	☐
I like sightseeing / experiencing a different culture.		☐	☐	☐
I like to try the local food.		☐	☐	☐
I spend time with my children / family.		☐	☐	☐
I enjoy taking exercise.		☐	☐	☐
I like reading.		☐	☐	☐
I take work with me.		☐	☐	☐

4 | Writing

Greetings to colleagues

Imagine you are on holiday. Send email greetings to your colleagues in the office. Think of your last holiday and write a message you might have sent them. Refer to some of the points listed below. See the Useful Language on page 138.

- When you arrived
- How you are feeling
- Your journey
- The area
- Your hotel
- Local details (food, weather, people)
- Your plans
- Your contact details

1 Work in pairs.
  Partner A: Read the extract below.
  Partner B: Read the extract on page 138.
  Make notes.

2 **Partner A:** Tell **Partner B** that you are going to New York for a mini break. Also mention the suggestions for first-time visitors you have seen in the guide below.
  Partner B: Use the information given on page 138, plus your own experience (if you have been to New York), to advise **Partner A**.

THE APPLE OF TEMPTATIONS IS IRRESISTIBLE FOR FIRST-TIMERS

IF IT IS YOUR FIRST TIME in the city, I recommend you start with a taster.

Stroll Central Park early morning when legions of joggers join the dog-walkers. Starting from Central Park South, skirt the Pond and the open-air Wollman Rink and its ice-skaters. Pick up a calendar of park events from the Visitor Center at the rear of the Victorian Gothic Dairy. There's plenty more to see in the park: 58 miles of bridleways and footpaths and 30 bridges, the ornamental Bethesda Fountain and Terrace, Strawberry Fields (a memorial to John Lennon who was shot outside the nearby Dakota Building) and Belvedere Castle. Take the elevator to the 102nd floor of the Empire State Building, where you'll be able to see for 80 miles if it's a clear day. Entrance is at 350 5th Avenue, between 33rd and 34th Streets.

Hop aboard the Staten Island ferry for its one-hour, round-trip from Battery Park at State Street. Stroll down Madison Avenue and Fifth Avenue from around 49th up to around 75th – smart people, smart shops. Walk through Greenwich (known simply as the Village) and SoHo, and finally sample what you fancy from the many museums, shops, restaurants, bars and theaters available in the Big Apple.

From Ewan MacNaughton Consultants

LANGUAGE REFERENCE

Language Notes

For further notes on these points, see the accompanying Business Grammar Guide (BGG).

Contrast clauses: *although*, *in spite of*, etc. (BGG 18.2)

e.g. 1 Prices are generally low, **but** petrol is quite expensive.

Although prices are generally low, petrol is quite expensive.

Even though prices are generally low, petrol is quite expensive.

While prices are generally low, petrol is quite expensive.

Prices are generally low; petrol is quite expensive, **though**.

e.g. 2 The flight was fully booked, **but** we managed to get a seat.

We managed to get a seat **in spite of** the fact that the flight was fully booked.

We managed to get a seat **despite** the fact that the flight was fully booked.

We managed to get a seat **regardless of** the fact that the flight was fully booked.

e.g. 3 We had fully confirmed first-class tickets …

… **but** we couldn't get on the plane.

… **Even so**, we couldn't get on the plane.

… **However**, we couldn't get on the plane.

… **All the same**, we couldn't get on the plane.

Holiday travel tips: giving advice (BGG 21.1)

e.g. **I would advise you** (not) to drink the local wine / water.

My advice is to leave your valuables in the hotel safe.

I suggest you get an anti-tetanus jab.

It's best (not) to change money at a bank.

It's (not) **a good idea to** book in advance.

Always / Never carry your ID / large notes.

Look / Watch out for unlicensed taxis.

Short form *wh-* questions (BGG 17.2)

e.g.
I'd like a ticket.	→ **Where to?**
I want to get away.	→ **How long for?**
I have to get back.	→ **When by?**
There was a phone call.	→ **Who for?**
I need a doctor.	→ **What for?**
There is a good restaurant.	→ **Where?**
Down by the port.	**Whereabouts?**

whatever, *wherever*, *whoever*, etc. (BGG 20.6)

e.g. It'll be crowded **wherever** we go, at this time of year.

When we're away the children go to bed **whenever** they want.

Whatever you do, don't drink the water.

We can go by taxi or take the courtesy bus – **whichever** is more convenient.

Come out – **whoever** you are!

Vocabulary

• Words and phrases

e.g. **people:** travel agent, local rep, first class / standby passengers

holidays: package holiday, mini-break, high / off season

travel details: scheduled / charter flight, aisle / window seat

prices/money: inclusive prices, hidden extras, refund

booking: fully booked, overbooked, waiting list, on standby

accommodation: full / half board, self-catering, bed-and-breakfast

formalities: visa, accident insurance, inoculation certificate

• Verbs and verb phrases

e.g. I'm hoping **to get away** next week for a few days.

When I go on holiday it takes me a day or two **to unwind**.

We're **heading / making for** the south of France this year.

Could you **write down** the directions?

I need **to get back to** my office.

I'll be **checking in / out** in the morning.

Useful Phrases

The climate is good, although it can be chilly at night.
The countryside round the city is unspoilt.
The people are warm but fairly reserved.
Do I need a visa?
No, but I advise you to have an anti-tetanus jab.

I'd like to book a mini-break.
Where to? What do you have in mind?
Flights to the Caribbean are fully booked.
Could you let me know if you get a cancellation?
The package includes accommodation at a three-star hotel.
Departing at 14.20 on the 17th and returning on …

The documents are all in this wallet.
Can I see your passport and driving licence?
Could you sign here and here, please?
Which road do I take for Kalinski?
Follow the signs for the coast, and then take Route 27.

What's the best way of getting to the Summer Palace?
It's beyond Fulong, towards Gretik.
It's difficult by public transport; there's no direct service.
It'll take you a long time whichever way you go because it's a very bad road.

I'd like an early check out, please.
I'm afraid you can't use this ticket on a scheduled flight.
If you want to travel tomorrow, you'll have to upgrade to business class.
How much would it cost to upgrade?
I've booked you on to the 12 o'clock flight.

UNIT 25 Politics and business

1 Core practice

Listening and speaking

Listen to the exchanges (a – d) and mark the statements (part i) true $\boxed{T}$, false $\boxed{F}$ or unclear $\boxed{U}$. Then, working with a partner, practise the exchanges indicated in part ii.

a i The new ten-mile zone has been rejected. ☐
   ii Practise discussing your country's relations with one of its neighbours.

b i The new restrictions are designed to encourage rail transport. ☐
   ii Practise discussing a government policy you believe is having a bad impact on business.

c i The speaker supports the current government. ☐
   ii Practise discussing the strength of the government's position.

d i The socialists are in power. ☐
   ii Practise discussing the prospects of the main parties in a forthcoming election.

Preparation

Think about when and where you talk about politics? Do you discuss political or economic questions with your colleagues? Do you have to discuss the impact of such questions on your work? As part of your preparation you can look at the Useful Phrases on page 112. If possible, bring to the class newspaper articles on issues that are relevant to your work.

2 Language check

Refer to the Language Notes on page 112 as you complete the examples below using the choices provided – only one is correct. Then prepare a version of each example that you might use.

1 The minister .... receiving the money.
   a advised
   b denied
   c refused

2 The embassy .... us not to go out alone.
   a suggested
   b said
   c warned

3 It is difficult .... what the outcome ....
   a to predict / will be
   b anticipating / was
   c believe / is going to be

4 I .... Sophie Bouvet .... to be selected. She is easily the best candidate.
   a don't think / is going
   b think / is unlikely
   c reckon / is bound

5 The centre .... won a majority in the .... so we anticipate that they will form the next ....
   a party / election / government
   b government / referendum / opposition
   c politicians / voting / joint venture

6 The .... is rising. People are far better .... than they were ten years ago.
   a cost of living / up
   b standard of living / off
   c rate of inflation / on

7 Public .... borrowing is too high and this is having an impact on the .... of inflation.
   a area / cost
   b sector / rate
   c party / speed

8 We could .... a vote now, or .... , we could leave it till the next meeting.
   a make / nevertheless
   b take / alternatively
   c give / on the other hand

9 I .... with most of what you said. .... , there is one point which I don't agree with at all.
   a agree / However
   b accept / On the other hand
   c don't agree / Whereas

10 If the government .... a referendum on .... smoking in public – I intend to vote .... the ban.
   a holds / banning / for
   b makes / finishing / on
   c take / leaving / against

3 | Listening

Politically correct

Listen to the interview with Kathleen Kelly Reardon, author of *It's All Politics: Winning in a World Where Hard Work and Talent Aren't Enough*. Then answer the questions. According to the author:

a What skills do you need to win in office politics? Do you agree?
b What should you do if you say the wrong thing in a meeting with your boss? Do you agree?
c What are the three biggest political mistakes you can make in an office. Do you agree?

4 | Writing

Country profile

Read the text and label the points: economic E, geographical G, historical H, political P or social S. Write an 'international briefing' on your country or area.

INTERNATIONAL BRIEFING
Venezuela

a Venezuela, in northern South America, was named after Venice by 15th-century European explorers who found native houses on stilts round Lake Maracaibo. H

b It is a country of striking natural beauty, with snow-capped Andean peaks in the west, Amazonian jungles in the south, and beaches in the north. ☐

c Venezuela is one of the most highly urbanised countries in Latin America. Most Venezuelan's live in cities on the Caribbean coast. ☐

d The country is one of the oldest democracies in South America (elections since 1958). ☐

e A founding member of the Organization of Petroleum Exporting Countries (OPEC), Venezuela has the largest proven oil reserves in the Western Hemisphere – and the second largest natural gas reserves (after the USA). It also has huge quantities of coal, iron ore, bauxite and gold. ☐

f If you meet a business traveller in Venezuela, there's a good chance they work in the petroleum industry. It is by far the nation's leading export, accounting for well over two-thirds of all export revenue. ☐

g Because of the fluctuating oil market, the country has been involved in an ambitious programme to develop its tourism industry. ☐

h There have been attempts at radical reform by the political leadership designed to reduce unemployment and raise living standards. ☐

i Venezuela has sought to strengthen its regional position through stronger economic and diplomatic ties with other South American and Caribbean countries, and also with China, a major customer for the country's oil. These efforts are seen, in part, as a move to counter US influence. ☐

Quick facts

- Population: 26.6 million
- Capital: Caracas
- Area: 881,050sq km (340,561sq miles)
- Life expectancy: 70 years (men), 76 years (wor
- Monetary unit: 1 bolivar = 100 centimos
- Main exports: petroleum, bauxite and aluminiu steel, chemicals, agricultural products
- GNI per capita: US$4,030
- Internet domain: .ve
- International dialling code: +58

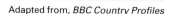

Adapted from, *BBC Country Profiles*

Rail privatisation

Read the article and then discuss the issues.
Partner A: You are in favour of privatisation. See the notes on page 138.
Partner B: You are against. See the notes on page 138.

In line with a global trend

Governments around the world are privatising their railways in an attempt to reduce losses and create more efficient passenger and freight networks. None has plans as far reaching as those of Britain – which broke up its railway into more than 80 separate companies – but many are determined to split up larger public sector monopolies.

Countries as diverse as New Zealand, Argentina, Sweden and the Czech Republic have privatised or are thinking of privatising their railways. Others are splitting railway companies into smaller units with an aim of introducing greater competition.

The division of train operations from ownership of the track – one of the most criticised aspects of British Rail's privatisation – is not unique to Europe. But most have opted for a railway with train and track ownership in the same hands.

The debate on rail privatisation is brought into sharp focus by accidents and the resulting concerns over safety. Who is responsible? Is it the fault of the government? The regulators? The operating companies?

From *The Financial Times*

LANGUAGE REFERENCE

Language Notes

For further notes on these points, see the accompanying Business Grammar Guide (BGG).

Verbs of reporting (BGG 5)

- + (that) + clause

e.g. She **said** (that) she supported the Christian Democrats.

I **explained** (that) I'm not interested in politics.

It's **reported** that the Prime Minister has resigned.

- + object + (that) + clause

e.g. The police **warned** us (that) the demonstration might be dangerous.

He **told** me (that) he was going to resign.

A spokesperson **informed** us (that) the vote would take place tomorrow.

- + infinitive

e.g. The government has **refused** to compromise.

The authorities **promised** not to interfere.

He **claims** to be speaking on behalf of the unions.

- + object + infinitive

e.g. They **advised** us to call the police.

We **warned** him not to get involved.

He **persuaded** a lot of people to vote for him.

- + -ing

e.g. She **admitted** photocopying the report.

The senator **denied** receiving the money.

A colleague **suggested** calling you.

- + object

e.g. She **presented** the arguments very clearly.

The government **outlined** its plans.

The President **announced** his resignation.

Contrasts and alternatives (BGG 18.2, 18.3)

e.g. I am a Democrat. **However**, this time I voted Republican.

I am a Democrat, **whereas** my sister is Republican.

We disagree politically; **otherwise** we get on well.

I usually vote Democrat. This time I voted Green **instead**.

I might vote Democrat. **Alternatively**, I might stay at home.

I believe we have a democratic responsibility to vote. **Nevertheless / At the same time**, I accept that many people disagree.

Vocabulary

- Political terms

e.g. local / state / federal government, a democracy, a one-party state, a republic, the government / the opposition, a pressure group, a left-wing / right-wing party, the socialist party, an election, a referendum, a vote, a majority / a minority (government), a politician, a minister, a member of parliament

- Economic terms

e.g. balance of payments, imports, exports, exchange rate, government borrowing / expenditure, private / public sector, privatisation, the rate of inflation / interest, boom, slump, the cost / standard of living, monopoly, competition, joint venture, merger, takeover

- Verbs and verb phrases

e.g. They plan to **hold a referendum** on the issue.

Are you planning to **vote for** or **against** the policy?

We should **take a vote** to find out the level of support for the policy.

Most people **are better / worse off** since we joined the EU.

What **impact are** the new taxes **having on** the economy?

The Social Democrats **have been in power** for years.

The left **is ahead** in the opinion polls.

Useful Phrases

The government is a coalition between parties of the left and centre.
It has been in power for five years.

It is difficult to predict who will win the next election.
It's almost impossible to forecast the result.
The social democrats are ahead in the opinion polls.

Nevertheless, the right have a good chance.
There has been a strong swing to the right.
However, the left are still ahead.
We don't think the electorate will elect a right-wing government.

Relations with our neighbours are good.
They announced a new trade agreement on the news.
A spokesperson informed us that they would take a vote tomorrow.
There are pressure groups who are against the agreement.
They say the government should ban imports from the area.

What's your position on rail privatisation?
I'm for it – I'm in favour.
I'm very much against it.

The evidence against privatisation is very clear.
In most cases, prices have risen.
Experience shows that service deteriorates.

I don't agree at all.
Statistics show that passenger numbers go up.
Investment increases faster than it does under state control.
The fact is that privatisation increases efficiency.

In my view, the government should hold a referendum.

UNIT 26 Taxation

1 Core practice

Listening and speaking

Preparation

Review conversations you have about tax – personal and corporate. What do you need to say? Prepare by looking at the Useful Phrases on page 116. If possible, bring to the class correspondence relating to tax. Come prepared to talk about the tax system in your country.

Listen to the exchanges (a – d) and mark the statements (part i) true ⊤, false ⨍ or unclear Ⓤ. Then, working with a partner, practise the exchanges indicated in part ii.

a i The first speaker is not a tax expert. ☐
  ii Practise talking about sales tax in your area. Do you have one? Can visitors reclaim it?
b i The government has recently cut corporation tax. ☐
  ii Practise talking about tax rates in your area.
c i Generally, the taxes mentioned are designed to encourage saving. ☐
  ii Practise talking about schemes which allow you to avoid tax.
d i Basically, the speakers agree with each other. ☐
  ii Practise talking about a case of tax evasion.

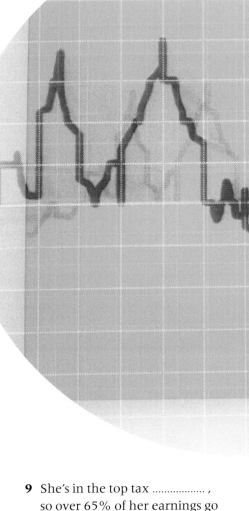

2 Language check

Refer to the Language Notes on page 116 as you complete the examples below using the choices provided – only one is correct. Then prepare a version of each example that you might use.

1 The tax .... needs to be completed by the end of the month.
  a liability
  b relief
  c return

2 Is business entertaining a tax .... expense?
  a exempt
  b deductible
  c relief

3 Don't .... me, but I think there are some serious .... in the accounts.
  a quote / discrepancies
  b take / errors
  c say / mistakes

4 .... the tax inspector is coming this afternoon.
  a I'm not an expert but
  b As far as I know
  c Off the top of my head

5 The Finance Director .... me if I .... about the tax situation in Chad.
  a told / would know
  b asked / knew
  c requested / know

6 The auditors said that they .... in touch with us .... week.
  a were / next
  b will be / the following
  c would be / the following

7 They warned me I .... to pay a late filing ....
  a would have / penalty
  b had / rate
  c was having / charge

8 I was .... that the money had been transferred ....
  a informed / few days before
  b instructed / in a few days time
  c advised / a few days ago

9 She's in the top tax .... , so over 65% of her earnings go .... tax.
  a category / after
  b bracket / in
  c level / to

10 We have managed to get the money .... to pay off our tax ....
  a together / arrears
  b behind / bill
  c in / sum

3 Listening

Tax liabilities

Read the short case studies from an accountancy firm's brochure about how they can help people to reduce their tax liability. Then listen and match the speakers to the cases.

Case studies — *Some typical projects tackled by our tax consultancy team include case studies 1 – 5, below.*

CASE 1

A retail pharmacist was facing a tax bill for £150,000 (€222,000) following an Inland Revenue investigation. Our team prepared a report that led to the bill being reduced to £5,250 (€7,770).

CASE 2

A printing business received a VAT assessment for £45,000 (€66,670). We advised the client to appeal, and after discussion with Customs and Excise the entire VAT bill was waived.

CASE 3

A timber wholesaler asked our advice on tax structuring. We set up a self-administered pension scheme and an innovative bonus scheme for directors, and thus reduced a potential tax liability of £120,000 (€177,800) to just £5,000 (€7,400). Our recommendations had the added benefits of providing attractive incentives for key directors and creating better pension provisions.

CASE 4

One of the principal shareholders in a wholesaling business wanted to retire and agreed to sell his shares to another shareholder. Acting for the purchaser, we restructured the transaction to leave the seller with the same net proceeds while saving our client over £40,000 (€59,250). We also created significantly better financing arrangements for him to complete the transaction.

CASE 5

A family farming business faced a potential inheritance tax bill of over £230,000 (€340,620). Our team devised a strategy to achieve a smooth transfer of ownership to the next generation while reducing the tax liability to virtually nil.

From Solomon Hare Chartered Accountants

4 Writing

Tax queries

1 Read queries a and b, along with the advice given. Using the knowledge you already have, change the advice to fit the laws in your area, as far as you can.

2 Discuss queries c – f and write responses, again based on your existing knowledge.

3 Compare your opinions with answers taken from Findlaw.com – see pages 138 – 139.

a **I hired a babysitter to care for my children in my home. Do I need to withhold taxes on her wages?**
If you pay a household employee wages of $1,100 (€930) or more in a calendar year, you must withhold social security and healthcare taxes from all wages you pay to that employee.

b **If my part-time employees receive less than $20 (€17) a month in tips, are they required to report them?**
Employees who receive less then $20 (€17) per month in tips are not required to report the tips to their employer, but they must include them in gross income on their tax return.

c **Do I have to pay tax on my bonus or award?**

d **Do I have to pay tax on gifts, bequests or inheritances?**

e **Do I have to pay tax on my hobby income?**

f **Do I have to pay tax on meals and lodging provided by my employer?**

From Findlaw.com

Read the article and answer the questions.

a What's tax avoidance?

b What is tax evasion

c In what way are death and taxes the same?

d In what ways are they different?

Taxing times

They say death and taxes are the two things you can't dodge. But while we can't avoid the Grim Reaper, taxes are another matter …

GEORGE PITCHER

THIS TIME OF YEAR – THE END OF the tax year – always reminds me of an annoying popular saying. Benjamin Franklin is supposed to have said: 'Nothing is certain but death and taxes.' It is annoying because it's one of those sayings that doesn't mean anything.

The certainty of taxes and their comparison with death is just one of those things that people say when they can't be bothered to think. It's devoid of meaning. The essential difference between death and taxes is the same as that between avoidance and evasion.

You can avoid death – by choosing not to paddle a kayak over Niagara Falls, for example – but you cannot evade it. Not being able to evade it is the whole point of death – it's what makes it so certain.

On the other hand, you most certainly can both avoid and evade taxes. You might say that's the whole point of them. It's precisely what makes taxes uncertain, as any accountant will tell you.

Tax avoidance is what you pay your accountant's fee for. Evasion, being illegal, brings fines and imprisonment, if detected. But the whole business of perfectly legal avoidance is what makes it so uncertain. I have a friend who recently received a tax demand for £1.16 – rather less, I imagine,

than the despatch of the demand cost. He writes travel guides and claims his 'researches' against his tax bill.

At a corporate level, taxes are no more certain. Companies will tell you that they invest millions in worthy community causes, while boasting to their shareholders that they save billions by being domiciled for tax purposes in a tax haven. (Where is the social responsibility in that?)

Perhaps what Benjamin Franklin really meant was that concern about taxes is always in the air, just as we are always aware of our own mortality. If this is the case, I think that the way forward is clearly to put taxes and mortality on an equal footing.

I don't mean that we should give tax inspectors powers of execution. They seem too bureaucratic for that. Rather, I mean that every effort should be made to keep alive those who evade their taxes, so that they are paying taxes well into their old age to make up for their shortfall.

The prospect of having to fill in tax returns while receiving their pensions should have the evaders begging for release from this world.

George Pitcher is a founding partner of the strategic communications consultancy Luther Pendragon.

Adapted from *BA magazine*

LANGUAGE REFERENCE

Language Notes

For further notes on these points, see the accompanying Business Grammar Guide (BGG).

Reported speech (BGG 5)

- Some examples

e.g. Our accountant **says** the tax inspector is tough but fair.

The auditors **asked** us if the accounts were clear.

The government **announced** it would cut the rate to 15%.

The tax office **informed** us they had received our letter.

They **claimed** the refund had been sent.

He **urged** me not to tell anyone else about it.

Did you **mention** your pay rise?

- Time frames

e.g. tomorrow ➡ the next day / the following day

yesterday ➡ the day before / the previous day

next week / year ➡ the following week / year

last week / year ➡ the previous week / year

two days ago ➡ two days before, two days earlier

in two days' time ➡ two days after (that), two days later

Terms used to qualify statements

e.g. As far as I know …

I'm not an expert, but …

It's not really my area, but …

Don't quote me, but …

You need to check, but I think …

Off the top of my head, I'd say …

Speaking form memory, I believe …

Taxation: vocabulary

- Some tax terms

liability for tax	tax deductible
before / after tax	tax exempt
taxable income	tax relief
tax allowances	tax rebate
tax revenue	tax refund
tax rate / rate of tax	tax assessment
tax free	tax holiday
tax bill	tax arrears
direct / indirect tax	late filing penalty

discrepancy, mistake, error,

income tax, cooperation tax, sales tax,

inheritance tax, capital gains tax

- Some tax verbs

to **pay** $1,000 **in** tax

to **pay** tax **on** your income

to **pay** tax **at** 40%

to **pay** 40% **in** the pound / dollar

to **fill in** a tax return

to **be in** a low / high tax bracket

- Verbs and verb phrases

e.g. Half my salary **goes on** / **in** tax.

Tax rates have **gone up** / **down**.

I hope that rates will **come down**.

We are trying **to get** the money **together**.

You can **set** the money you pay into a pension scheme **against** tax.

Useful Phrases

How much did we pay in tax last year?

Companies are taxed at a rate of 25%.

Three years ago the government announced it would cut the rate to 15% the following year.

As far as I know, it didn't happen.

Our tax bill was $500,000.

I pay tax at 40% on an income of £50,000 per year.

The tax authorities informed us that we had to pay a late filing penalty.

We were late filing our tax return.

Our accountant promised she'd file the return the next day.

The tax office claim it arrived late.

As far as I know, you can reclaim the tax.

You have to fill in a special form.

You take the form to the refunds office at the airport.

The tax rate / burden is very high.

How much does a middle manager pay in tax?

About 30% of my salary goes in tax.

We're not taxed on the first $5,000 we earn.

You can set against tax the money you pay into a pension scheme.

A capital gain on the sale of a private house is tax free.

It's very tax efficient.

Is there much tax evasion in your country?

I'm not an expert, but my accountant claims most companies are above board.

UNIT 27 Legal matters

1 Core practice

Listening and speaking

Listen to the exchanges (a – d) and mark the statements (part i) true ☐T☐, false ☐F☐ or unclear ☐U☐. Then, working with a partner, practise the exchanges indicated in part ii.

a i The compensation they received did not cover the legal costs. ☐
  ii Practise talking about a civil case – one you were involved in or one you've read about.

b i The company is extremely hard on late payers. ☐
  ii Talk about techniques you use to get customers to settle.

c i They now have no chance of being paid. ☐
  ii Practise talking about a company that has gone bankrupt.

d i They are correcting the hard copy before making the corrections on screen. ☐
  ii Practise correcting a document and improving the layout.

> **Preparation**
>
> How much do you get involved in legal issues at work? Are there particular laws which regulate how you or your team perform? Think about the points you need to communicate and the statements you need to understand. You can prepare by looking at the Useful Phrases on page 120. If possible, bring to the class a document you consider to be poorly laid out, so you can point out how to improve it.

2 Language check

Refer to the Language Notes on page 120 as you complete the examples below using the choices provided – only one is correct. Then prepare a version of each example that you might use.

1 Once it has been signed, the agreement will be .... on both ....
  a concerning / sides
  b acting / prosecution and defence
  c binding / parties

2 We have decided to start legal .... against them.
  a prosecution
  b proceedings
  c damages

3 He was .... guilty of fraud but as he .... no previous convictions, they .... him off with a warning.
  a found / had / let
  b let / found / had
  c had / let / found

4 With .... to the fax you sent us yesterday, could you please forward a list of the .... questions?
  a connection / the prosecution's
  b regarding / judge's
  c reference / regulator's

5 I'd like to speak to you. It's .... with the final demand .... you sent us.
  a in connection / notice
  b with regard / warning
  c concerning / agreement

6 You need to study the .... at .... of the page.
  a bracket / the margin
  b small print / the bottom
  c paragraph / top left-hand corner

7 The key text is clearly shown .... bold. I think we need to .... a full stop after each bullet point.
  a from / put in
  b of / take out
  c in / add

8 The court .... the defendant guilty and .... a substantial fine.
  a found / imposed
  b convicted / enforced
  c ordered / awarded

9 I .... to sue unless they had a good case.
  a warned them that
  b advised them not
  c advised them

10 The tribunal .... the company to pay compensation and ordered it to comply .... the regulations in future.
  a cautioned / for
  b instructed / with
  c warned / to

3 | Listening

Medical malpractice

Listen to Doug Wojcieszak of the *Boston Globe* talking about medical liability. Then tick the summary that is most accurate.

a ☐ Harvard Medical School advises doctors to drop their defensive posture in cases of malpractice because it is unfair and wastes time.

b ☐ Lexington VA hospital in Kentucky introduced the policy of saying sorry when their defensive posture was criticised for being expensive and unprofessional.

c ☐ Experience in America shows that when doctors apologise and offer fair compensation, malpractice cases are settled quickly and reasonably.

4 | Reading

Legal advice

1 Read the briefing document and answer the questions below.
  a How can you show a seller of unsolicited goods that you do not want the products?
  b When you write, what should you say?
  c Why should you give proof of posting?
  d In what circumstances should you pay for unsolicited goods?
2 Find simpler words you might use in place of: *deemed, thereby, unsolicited, prohibitively.*

Unsolicited goods and services

What action should you take if you find your business billed for products you didn't order?

Don't ignore it. If you do it might be deemed as accepting the goods and thereby give a 'reasonable cause' for the sender to believe there is a right to payment.

Don't use the goods. Keep them safe and, if opened, replace them in their original packaging if possible.

Write to the sender. Advise that you do not intend to pay because the goods are unsolicited. State that the goods are being kept safe and secure, and request collection by a given date. Keep copies of all correspondence and get proof of posting.

Inform your local authorities. The sender may already be known to them and they may be able to give useful information. They may investigate if they consider an offence may have been committed.

If threatened with legal action get advice from your local authorities or your solicitor. Don't be intimidated by such threats, which are often a bluff. If the sum concerned is less than £1,000 (US$1,780) and the sender does go to court, the matter will be dealt with in the Small Claims Court where you don't need a solicitor and costs are strictly limited.

If you have used the goods, you must pay for them. To avoid further deliveries write to the sender. State clearly that no more goods should be sent. Keep a copy and get proof of posting.

With regard to goods sent from abroad, it is virtually impossible for the local authorities to exercise any control. Recovery of any payments already made may require legal proceedings in the sender's country which could be prohibitively expensive.

Adapted from the Chamber of Commerce

5 | Feature

Customers' rights

1 Identify the section of the text referred to (a – e) in the box.

2 Relate the text to your own experience.
- Have you ever returned goods to a shop?
- What was the reason?
- What was the response?
- Compare the laws that apply in your country with these guidelines.

> **a** The point at the beginning of the second paragraph.
> **b** If you look at the first phrase in bold …
> **c** It's the second to last point mentioned.
> **d** It's the third bullet point down.
> **e** The word just before the bracket near the end.

Goods bought from a retailer must be fit for the purpose for which they were designed (or purposes for which products of that kind are commonly bought). They must also be fit for any purposes made known by the buyer to the seller.

If the goods are found to be faulty (that is, not fit for the purposes for which they were designed), the buyer can return the goods and get a refund, exchange or credit note (whichever the buyer wants).

However, the longer the buyer keeps the goods, the stronger the evidence will be that the goods have been accepted, and thus more likely that the buyer will only be offered a part refund for faults found. The seller may also offer to exchange the goods or repair them as an alternative to a refund. Receipts make it clear as to when and where the goods were bought, and such proof would be required for a valid claim.

There are situations where the buyer **will not be able to seek** any redress for **faulty goods**, and where the seller **has no legal obligation** to the buyer. Instances where dissatisfaction with goods will not constitute 'faulty' under the Sale of Goods Act include the following.

→ Where the buyer simply changes his or her mind.

→ Where the buyer chooses the wrong colour / type of article.

→ If the goods are found to be cheaper elsewhere.

→ If the goods are sold at a cheaper price because they are 'seconds', 'imperfects', 'shop soiled', 'fire damaged' or 'flood-salvage stock' there will be no redress to the buyer.

→ If the buyer examines the goods prior to buying (and is satisfied).

→ If the fault was pointed out to the buyer and at a later date the buyer is no longer happy with the fault.

→ If the goods 'hurt' the buyer in the shop but the buyer insists on having them.

Language Notes

For further notes on these points, see the accompanying Business Grammar Guide (BGG).

More on reported speech (BGG 5.4 , 5.5)

- Advice / warnings

e.g. Our lawyer **advised** us not to sign the agreement.

She **warned** her client that the room might be bugged.

- Commands

e.g. We were **instructed** not to discuss the case.

The court **ordered** the company to pay.

- Questions

e.g. They **wanted to know** our fax number.

He would **like to know** if this is your car.

Making reference (*concerning, with regard to*, etc.)

- Mid-position

e.g. The legal department wants to talk to you

… **about** the court case.

… **concerning** / **regarding** our legal position.

… **in connection with** the regulator's questions.

… **with regard** to the new laws.

- Front position

e.g. **With reference** to the court case …

With regard to the new legislation …

Regarding the regulator's questions …

Concerning the new sex discrimination laws …

Terms related to text layout

e.g. heading / sub-heading

It needs to be

… **in** bold / italics.

… **in** capitals / **in** lower case / underlined.

… centred / right aligned / left aligned.

- Position on the page / in the text

e.g. **At** the top / bottom of the page.

In the margin.

In the small print.

In the first bullet point / sentence / paragraph.

In the top left-hand / right-hand corner.

- Verb phrases

e.g. I suggest we **take out** the italics / **delete** that paragraph.

We need to **put in** a comma / to **add** a full stop.

Did you **run** it **through** the spellcheck?

Did you **spellcheck** it?

Vocabulary

- Legal

new **laws** / **legislation**

to **obey** / **enforce** / **break** the law

to **comply with** the regulations

to be **in breach of** contract / the regulations

a (fair) **trial**, a (court) **case**

to **appeal against** a decision

- Criminal cases

the **judge**, the **jury**, the **verdict**

to be **arrested** for / **charged** with (assault)

to **prosecute**, to be prosecuted

the court found the defendant **guilty** / **not guilty** (innocent)

to be **convicted** (of fraud)

to be **fined**, the court **imposed** a fine

to **let** someone **off** with a caution

- Civil cases

a **binding** contract / agreement

to **go** to court, to **start** legal proceedings, to **take** legal action

to **sue for** damages / infringing our patent / breach of contract

to **bring a case** for (unfair dismissal)

to **contest** a claim, to **settle** out of court

the court / tribunal **awarded** us compensation / damages

- Bankruptcy

to **go into** receivership

to go **bankrupt** / to go **bust**

to **file for** bankruptcy

Useful Phrases

Our lawyers have warned us it wouldn't be worth going to court.

We hope to settle out of court.

We are prepared to consider arbitration.

We would like to avoid a lengthy court case.

We took legal advice.

We were advised that we had a strong case.

We decided to sue for breach of contract.

We took them to court.

They contested the claim.

How did it turn out?

The court awarded us compensation.

The judge ordered them to pay our costs.

The company went bankrupt last week.

The receivers have been called in.

Their finance director was convicted of fraud.

Why weren't we notified?

I thought it was required by law.

By law I'm entitled to three weeks' annual holiday.

That doesn't mean I get it.

This layout is a mess.

The logo needs to go in the top, left-hand corner.

We need to add another bullet point.

It shouldn't be in bold – it should be in italics.

Shall we take out the third point?

That should be a comma, not a semi-colon.

Did you run it through the spellcheck?

UNIT 28 Planning

1 Core practice

Listening and speaking

Listen to the speakers (a – d) and mark the statements (part i) true ☐T☐, false ☐F☐ or unclear ☐U☐. Then, working with a partner, practise the exchanges indicated in part ii.

a i The pilot scheme started on time. ☐
  ii Practise looking back and reviewing a project that is complete.
b i The speaker is part of the project management team. ☐
  ii Practise taking about a current project and your role in it.
c i The scheme was badly planned. ☐
  ii Practise talking about a piece of work that went wrong.
d i The speaker is behind with her tax. ☐
  ii Practise talking about outstanding paperwork and planning immediate commitments.

Preparation

This unit is about planning, especially as it relates to projects and work commitments. How do you organise your work? Prepare to talk about the way you plan. Before the class, look at the Useful Phrases on page 124. If possible, bring to the class examples of action plans or 'to do' lists you have used.

2 Language check

Refer to the Language Notes on page 124 as you complete the examples below using the choices provided – only one is correct. Then prepare a version of each example that you might use.

1 The first .... is to call a meeting of the interested parties, to make an .... and then ....
  a phase / action / priorities
  b stage / prioritise / action plan
  c step / action plan / prioritise
2 .... with, I read through all the correspondence relating to the scheme.
  a First
  b In the first place
  c To start
3 .... building the prototype, we were planning the field-study.
  a On completion of
  b At the same time as
  c After
4 There were a few .... in the early stages, but everything worked out OK ....

a setbacks / in the end
b set-ups / finally
c set-downs / lastly
5 If we modify the prototype at this stage, the completion date will have to be put back. .... I think we should do it.
  a For another thing
  b All the same
  c Besides
6 If any member of the consortium needs more information, ... should contact .... team leader.
  a he / his
  b she / her
  c they / their
7 The company .... said that in her view the increased costings weren't a major set-back.
  a spokesperson
  b spokesman
  c spokeswoman

8 – It really isn't possible to .... freak circumstances like these.
  – You weren't expecting them, were you?
  – .... (Agree)
  a plan / Yes, we weren't
  b plan for / No, we weren't
  c anticipate / Yes, we were
9 There are a number of key factors to .... into account when assessing a project like this.
  a put
  b draw
  c take
10 We didn't .... this in our contingency plan, so the end-date will have to be put ....
  a make allowances for / back
  b make for / right
  c allow for / forward

3 Listening

A project

Read the list below. Then listen to the project manager responsible for planning and running a scheme to build an automated waste-sorting system. Tick the categories he mentions.

Planning is an essential part of managing a project and is a means of:

a deciding who does what, when, how and why ☐

b determining the resources required ☐

c allocating these resources on a time-phased basis ☐

d allocating and defining responsibility ☐

e integrating the work of all the organisations involved ☐

f liaising with all those involved in the projects ☐

g controlling progress ☐

h estimating time to completion ☐

i handling unexpected events and changes. ☐

From Harrison and Gower, *Advanced project management*

Automated waste sorting system

4 Case study

A start-up

1 Read the case study. Then discuss in groups how the two women can make this project a success. What are the steps involved?

2 Write up your advice as a short report.

Sally-Anne Duke

Sally-Anne Duke and Carola Sutton both have thriving careers, but want to give them up to start a part-time business. They are both married, and expect to have children, but want an interest that will take them outside the home and family as well as provide an independent income. Although they haven't given up their jobs yet, they have decided to start a service for people who need to buy antique furniture for pleasure or investment, but who lack the knowledge or time to undertake the considerable work involved.

The idea is only a hunch. They both love antiques and they are both interested in them. But they have to prove to themselves before committing money to the scheme that a market exists. They have no professional experience of the antiques world, or of market research. Their only assets at this stage are, therefore, that they like their goal, and that it fits their perception of where they would like to be in a few years' time.

Carola Sutton

Adapted from *Getting Things Done*

1 Complete the article, using words from the box.
2 In pairs or as a group, conduct a simple project assessment.
 • How feasible is the project?
 • What are the main obstacles?
 • What will the benefits be?
 • Do you think it'll go ahead?

► conditions
► counterparts
► feasibility
► members
► project
► research
► techniques
► vision
► consortium
► drawing
► fulfil
► obstacle
► realised
► study
► venture

A tunnel linking Russia to America

A **a** .... of Russians and Americans is **b** .... up plans to build a tunnel under the Bering Strait – the icy 60-mile (96km) stretch of sea between Alaska and Russia – in a bold **c** .... to link two continents and boost global commerce.

It might sound far-fetched, but engineers in both countries are confident the **d** .... can be **e** .... Undeterred by the fact that thousands of miles of track would have to be laid just to link the tunnel to existing rail networks, they are lobbying governments and private enterprise with their **f** .... of a new trade route across the top of the world.

The Interhemispheric Bering Strait Tunnel and Railroad Group has united Americans, Canadians and Russians in a common vision: 'The tunnel project will finally **g** .... Columbus's dream,' said George Koumal, a Czech-born engineer leading the American branch. 'It will be possible to reach India in the east by going west.'

A big **h** .... is money. Koumal, who estimated the costs at $37 billion admits it has been hard enough to raise funds for the **i** .... study, which is being funded by consortium **j** ....

The Russian prime minister has ordered the cabinet to conduct its own **k** .... before releasing **l** .... money. Tunnel supporters are forging ahead all the same, with talk of revolutionising world commerce: carried by rail through the Bering Strait, foods from China would reach America in half the time it takes by sea, they maintain.

The idea of burrowing under the Bering Strait is not new; in 1905 an American consortium raised $5 million to build the 'Trans Alaska Siberian Railroad'. But the First World War, the Russian civil war and then the Cold War put paid to the plans.

Russian engineers, who have invited their American **m** .... to a Moscow 'tunnel conference' are confident the digging could be done in four years, using the same **n** .... employed by Britain and France in the Channel tunnel.

They say drilling **o** .... are more favourable under the Bering Strait than under the Channel, and the position of two islands in the middle of the Strait means no stretch of tunnel would be longer than the one now linking Britain and France.

Times

LANGUAGE REFERENCE

Language Notes

For further notes on these points, see the accompanying Business Grammar Guide (BGG).

Indicating sequence

e.g. To start with, …
In the second stage, …
In the final phase, …
Prior to that … Before that …
On completion of the feasibility study, we will …
At the same time as costing the plan, we were …
Subsequently, we had to revise the timetable.

Some terms for structuring ideas / arguments

e.g. first, in the first place, first of all
then, finally, lastly / last
in addition to that, as well as that
anyway, besides
all the same, on the other hand
such as, for instance
apart from, except for
and so on, etc.
in other words, that is to say
in most cases, on the whole

Gender-free reference (BGG 12.3)

• Some examples
e.g. If any member of the team has a complaint, **they** should …
If a participant has a query, **he** or **she** should speak to …
No employer wants to lose **their** best staff.
Everyone has **their** price.

• Some terms
chair person / chair (for chairman)
spokesperson (for spokesman)
business person / people (for businessman / men)
author (for authoress)
waiter (for waitress)
flight attendant (for stewardess)
police officer (for policeman / woman)

Tag questions (BGG 17.1)

• Affirmative point of view
e.g. You understand the situation.
You understand the situation, **don't you?**
You do, **don't you?**
Agreement: Yes, I do.
Disagreement: No, I don't.

• Negative point of view
e.g. You don't understand.
You don't understand, **do you?**
You don't, **do you?**
Agreement: No, I don't.
Disagreement: Yes, I do.

Vocabulary

• Words and phrases
e.g. schedule, timetable, deadline,
phase, stage, milestone,
partner, participant, stakeholder,
start date, end date,
feasibility study, contingency plan,
field study, site test, live test,
setback, hold-up,
on target, on schedule, on track

• Verbs and verb phrases
e.g. We need **to break** the job **down into** specific tasks.
The are several factors **to take into account**.
Have you **made allowances for** the weather?
We may have to **put back / forward** the start date.
The system **goes live** next week.
We plan **to roll out** the programme in January.

Useful Phrases

The scheme was planned in three phases.
My role was to liaise with the other participants.
It was mainly a trouble-shooting role, wasn't it?
Yes, it was; I had to keep the work on track.

There were a number of unforeseen hold-ups.
We didn't allow enough time for research.
We missed a key milestone.
We had to reschedule the live testing.
The end date had to be put back a month.

A key member of the project team has had to drop out.
They have some family problems.
So we are a little behind schedule.
This could seriously affect the timetable.
We didn't anticipate this in our contingency plan.

These papers relate to a court case we're involved in.
There's no action required at the moment.
This is junk mail which I want to look through.
It's low priority, so I keep putting it off.
The deadline for this is the 24th.
I need to chase them – I'd better do that today.

In the first place, I need to make an action plan.
Then I need to prioritise.
There are a number of factors that have to be taken into account.
It's sometimes difficult to keep to the plan.
My main obstacle is lack of time.
At the moment I am on schedule.

UNIT 29 Work in progress

Preparation

Delivering the job (or service) on time and in budget depends on reviewing and controlling the work in progress. Come ready to talk about how you monitor work in progress. You can prepare for the lesson by looking at the Useful Phrases on page 128. If possible, bring examples of graphs and tables that relate to your work.

1 Core practice

Listening and speaking

Listen to the exchanges (a – d) and mark the statements (part i) true ☐T, false ☐F or unclear ☐U. Then, working with a partner, practise the exchanges indicated in part ii.

a i OK Cosmetics does not communicate well enough with it's customers. ☐
 ii Practise giving your manager an update on a project involving an external company.
b i The delay is the subcontractor's fault. ☐
 ii Practise talking about a specific hold-up and making a contingency plan.
c i The project will be completed in two days. ☐
 ii Practise discussing changes in a project plan required by an inspector, and agreeing a new end-date.
d i The speaker expects electronic products to outsell other products. ☐
 ii Practise presenting information from graphs and tables.

2 Language check

Refer to the Language Notes on page 128 as you complete the examples below using the choices provided – only one is correct. Then prepare a version of each example that you might use.

1 We are in the .... of refurbishing your head office.
 a progress
 b process
 c point
2 We expect to finish .... good time.
 a in
 b on
 c with
3 That's a good question and it .... my next point.
 a brings
 b brings me
 c brings me to
4 I'll begin by giving you a brief .... of the subject.
 a overlook
 b overview
 c oversee

5 The .... line here shows units completed per day.
 a broken
 b solid
 c dotted
6 At this point on the curve there is a .... in output.
 a significant fall
 b gradual decline
 c slight rise
7 As you can see, production levels are being ....
 a raised moderately
 b cut back a little
 c maintained at the same level
8 We are currently processing over 300 applications per day. That represents a ....
 a 100% reduction
 b 100% improvement
 c 50% rise

9 – What's .... you up?
 – We're .... for a delivery of fasteners.
 a holding / waiting
 b waiting / working
 c keeping / holding
10 .... is the work coming along? .... have you got to with it?
 a When / Who
 b Why / Where
 c How / Where

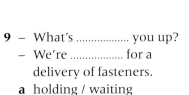

3 | Listening

Progress reports

Listen to the speakers and make notes. Then prepare a short progress report using a template like the one below.

PROGRESS REPORT		
Report by	Project description	Progress / Comments

4 | Writing

Progress chasing

Work in pairs.

Partner A: You are the administration manager of a company which is having its offices in Dublin, Ireland, refurbished. Call **Partner B**, the project manager who is overseeing the job, and check what is happening. You need information on the points listed in the checklist below.

Partner B: Your information is on page 139.

After the call, work together to draft a project update for **Partner A**'s management committee.

CHECKLIST

- Installation of new telephone and IT circuits.
- Refurbishment of cloakrooms and washrooms.
- Kitchen facilities upgrade – including flooring and wall tiling.
- Installation of new office furniture.
- Construction of a new fire escape.

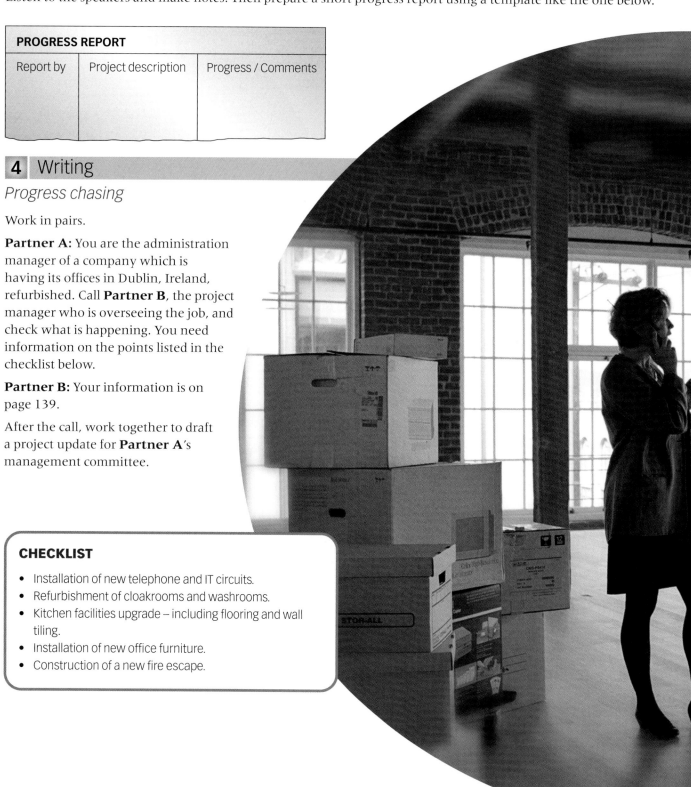

People Tree: a company review

Conduct an informal review of People Tree, a leading brand in fair trade fashion.

Step 1

Read the statement from the company's home page and its mission statement below. Then answer these questions.

- What is your experience of socially responsible trade?
- How far are you willing to go to support socially responsible companies?
- In your view, are they sustainable in the open market?

Step 2

In pairs and groups, read the newspaper article about People Tree on page 139. On the basis of the information given:

- review the company's performance against its mission statement
- review the company's progress. Where has it come from? Where is it now? Where is it going?

Present your conclusions to the group.

PEOPLE TREE — Fair Trade – Ecology – Fashion

People Tree is a pioneer in Fair Trade and Ecology Fashion. We work in close partnership with 70 producer groups in 20 countries across Asia, Africa and Latin America, helping some of the world's most marginalized communities to improve their lives through Fair Trade.

We help groups develop their skills and produce designs, and give them a fair price, regular orders and advance payment as needed. We also supply village welfare projects and schools for our producers' children.

MISSION STATEMENT

1 Trading Partners / Producers
To support producer partners' efforts toward economic independence and improvement of their social position.

2 Environment
Take care to protect the environment in production, packaging and transportation of products and throughout the business.

3 Customers
To supply to customers healthy, safe and attractive products with good service, together with information about the background of the products, producers and lifestyle alternatives. To give customers an opportunity to participate in a trading partnership that supports people and the environment. To ensure that the customer is always satisfied.

4 Us
To allow people to use their ability and creativity as fully as possible in an environment that is nurturing and supportive.

5 Wider
To set an example to the wider general public, to business and to government, of Fair Trade as a form of business which is based on mutual respect between producer, trader and consumer. To develop a business that proves that Fair Trade is successful.

© People Tree

LANGUAGE REFERENCE

Language Notes

For further notes on these points, see the accompanying Business Grammar Guide (BGG).

Reporting on the state of play

• Plans

e.g. Everything is going according to plan.
     We are in the process of revising our estimate.
     We are having to revise our plans.
     We are due to / about to sign the contract.
     We won't / can't begin till next week.
     Is the meeting still in progress?

• Time

e.g. It should be completed in good time.
     The work is behind / on / ahead of schedule.
     We expect / are expecting to finish on time.
     We won't have finished by then.
     It should have been completed by now.
     We are supposed to go live on the 27th.

Some terms used in presentations

e.g. The aim of this presentation is to …
     I'll begin by saying a few words about … , then …
     I'll say more about that in a moment.
     That brings me to my next point.
     In my view, the first / next step is to …
     Does everyone follow that?
     So, to summarise the key points …
     Well, that was a brief overview of the subject.
     Are there any questions?

Referring to graphs / tables

e.g. The solid / broken line represents …
     As you can see from the dotted line …
     Time is on the horizontal axis.
     At this point on the curve, there is a dramatic rise in …
     This table gives a breakdown of …
     The pie chart shows sales by country.
     If you look at the red segment / green bar …
     The number of store-openings rises dramatically here.
     Complaints peak in June.

Describing trends

e.g. Current orders are worth …
     That's a 12% increase on last year.
     That's a drop of 25% over three years.
     That represents a rise of 10% in three months.

     In spite of the recession …
     … demand has remained steady.
     … demand has gone up significantly.
     … demand has not changed dramatically.

     At the moment we're spending …
     So the budget has been cut back slightly.
     So the budget is being raised gradually.
     So the budget is being maintained at the same level.

Vocabulary

• Words and phrases

e.g. an update, a progress check, an overview, progress monitoring, progress chasing, a contingency plan, an alternative, a plan B, bar chart, pie chart, graph, table, dotted line, broken line, solid line

• Verbs and verb phrases

e.g. Where **are you up to** now?
     How is the work **coming along**?
     Where have you **got to with** this project?
     Progress is **being held up by** the weather.
     Our supplier **let us down** with a delivery.
     How long has this been **going on**?
     Could you **chase them up**?

Useful Phrases

What's the position with regard to this project?
I need an update on the state of play.
The project has fallen behind schedule.
Do we have a contingency plan?

We are in the process of revising our estimate.
It should be completed in good time.
The work is ahead of schedule.
We expect to finish on time.
We are supposed to go live on the 27th.

Progress is being held up by the weather.
Our supplier let us down with the delivery.
How long has this been going on?
Could you chase them up?

I'll begin by saying a few words about the delays.
I'll say more about them in a moment.
In my view, the next step is to establish the facts.

This table shows the current position.
The dotted line indicates costs.
Current orders are worth $10 million.
That's a 12% increase on last year.
At the moment we're spending too much.
So the budget has been cut back slightly.

Does everyone follow that?
Before I summarise the key points, are there any questions?

UNIT 30 Feedback and review

1 Core practice

Listening and speaking

Listen to the exchanges (a – d) and mark the statements (part i) true ☐T☐, false ☐F☐ or unclear ☐U☐. Then, working with a partner, practise the exchanges indicated in part ii.

a **i** The speaker suggests an area for improvement. ☐
   ii Practise reviewing an event you have been involved in.
b **i** The speaker didn't take the test because she hadn't done enough work. ☐
   ii Practise taking part in an individual performance review, talking about successes and disappointments.
c **i** The speaker is mainly positive about the course. ☐
   ii Practise discussing the strengths and weaknesses of a course like this one, for example.
d **i** The speaker has a clear action plan. ☐
   ii Practise talking about next steps.

> **Preparation**
>
> A significant number of the interactions that take place at work are some form of review or feedback – checking what has happened, identifying ways to improve. Think about the reviews you get involved in. As usual, you can prepare by looking at the Useful Phrases on page 132. If possible, come prepared to talk about a review process you have been involved in.

2 Language check

Refer to the Language Notes on page 132 as you complete the examples below using the choices provided – only one is correct. Then prepare a version of each example that you might use.

1 In my .... his performance was .... second-rate.
   a thought / absolutely
   b view / rather
   c impression / a bit
2 I have absolutely .... that her performance will improve now the .... are clear.
   a sure / achievements
   b the impression / points
   c no doubt / objectives
3 Everyone says that the presentation was .... outstanding.
   a really
   b highly
   c slightly
4 – The admin wasn't too .... , in fact it was very .... I was quite pleased.
   a good / bad
   b bad / good
   c good / good

5 .... the whole, the feedback .... that we are on the right lines.
   a At / maintains
   b In / suggests
   c On / indicates
6 Looking .... , it is fairly .... that we didn't prepare carefully enough.
   a down / obvious
   b back / clear
   c in / true
7 .... the lack of time available for preparation, I .... the conference achieved a lot.
   a Bearing in mind / think
   b From the point of view of / guess
   c Speaking about / have no doubt

8 Speaking .... someone who doesn't like studying, I thought the course was .... good.
   a for / really
   b to / a bit
   c as / pretty
9 Having read through the feedback .... , I can .... up my reaction in two words – 'well done'.
   a forms / sum
   b questionnaires / summarise
   c sheets / speak
10 1 don't think we should .... any conclusions till we see the results of the ....
   a come / research
   b draw / survey
   c make / rating

3 | Application

Self-assessment

Read the advice on self-assessment. Then, working in pairs, take it in turns to assess the progress you have made in your English studies, and your current standard.

Begin the review process by asking yourself these questions.

- What were your aims and objectives when you started the course?
- What strengths did you show?
- What were your weaknesses?
- How did you apply your strengths?
- How did you overcome your weaknesses?
- How satisfied were you with the progress you made?
- How much recommended reading and homework did you do for the course?
- What are your new goals?
- What are your next steps?

4 | Questionnaire

Work styles

Assess your work style by completing this questionnaire. Compare your results with other members of the group. Do you agree with the analysis?

Twenty questions to test if you are a workaholic

Michael Douglas declared that 'lunch is for wimps' in the classic film *Wall Street*. His ruthless character Gordon Gekko demonstrated one extreme of workaholism – focused attention, endless activity, and a strong desire to be in control. At its worst, it can lead to extreme stress. Find out if you are a workaholic by completing this simple test.

1. Do you work before breakfast?
   Always (2) Sometimes (1) Never (0)
2. Are you usually the last to leave the office?
   Always (2) Sometimes (1) Never (0)
3. Do you work through your lunch break?
   Always (2) Sometimes (1) Never (0)
4. Do you contact colleagues outside working hours to discuss work-related problems?
   Always (2) When needed (1) Never (0)
5. Do you take work home at weekends?
   Always (2) Usually (1) Never (0)
6. Do you take your full holiday entitlement?
   Always (2) Usually (1) Never (0)
7. Have you ever cancelled a holiday because of work?
   Yes (2) No (0)

8. Do you ever contact the office while you are on holiday?
   Yes (2) No (0)
9. Do you take work with you on holiday?
   Yes (2) No (0)
10. Do you lie awake at night thinking of work problems?
    Often (2) Sometimes (1) Never (0)
11. Do you ever get up during the night and begin working?
    Often (2) Sometimes (1) Never (0)
12. Have you ever refused to attend training programmes because of pressure of work?
    Usually (2) Occasionally (1) Never (0)
13. Have members of your family ever complained about the hours you work?
    Often (2) Occasionally (1) Never (0)
14. Have you ever been advised by a doctor to take things easy?
    Occasionally (2) Once (1) Never (0)
15. Have you ever cancelled a family outing or celebration because of work pressure?
    Often (2) Occasionally (1) Never (0)
16. Do you read material unrelated to work in your spare time?
    Never (2) Sometimes (1) All the time (0)

17. Do you work at home in the evenings?
    Often (2) Sometimes (1) Never (0)
18. Do you find it difficult to do nothing?
    Yes (2) Sometimes (1) No (0)
19. Do you dread retirement?
    A lot (2) A little (1) No (0)
20. Do you look forward to the start of the working week?
    Often (2) Occasionally (1) Never (0)

Assessing your scores

0 – 10 Your work holds very little interest for you. Perhaps you need a change?

11 – 20 You are motoring along in a low gear. Are you making the most of your career?

21 – 27 You have a reasonable balance between work and leisure and a healthy lifestyle.

28 – 34 You are a hard worker, perhaps internally driven or simply in a highly pressurised job.

35 – 40 You are a workaholic – maybe you should reassess your priorities.

Performance review

Listen to the excerpts (1 – 3) from a job appraisal interview in a food wholesale company, and answer questions 1, 3 and 4 below. On the basis of the information in the form, write an answer to question 2.

Name: Theo Coman

Title: Sales Rep

Department: Health Foods

Reports to: Jana Cossich

Title: Sales Manager

Review Period: First 4 months of employment (April – July)

Performance should be assessed in relation to the key responsibilities / tasks of the job and any specific objectives previously agreed with the job-holder and his/her manager / supervisor.

Performance rating against key responsibilities/tasks of the job:

Exceeded requirements: A
Achieved requirements: B
Partially achieved requirements: C
Did not achieve requirements: D

Use the comments column to help qualify or justify the rating given.

Key responsibilities / Tasks	Rating	Comments / Actions for the future
To visit wholesalers and retailers in his area to promote Febex products and secure orders, and to gain market information on competing products.		**(Question 1 – recorded excerpt 1)**
To attend trade fairs, conferences and exhibitions to promote the Febex name and product lines.	A	*This is an aspect of the job Theo does particularly well. He needs to ensure that he keeps up to date with his paperwork.*
To assist in the development of telemarketing by supplying leads and suggestions based on information gained in the field.	B	*Theo's leads are excellent, but he needs to pass them on more quickly.*
To liaise with the Sales Manager to ensure that the customer database and mailing lists are kept up to date.	C	*He needs to keep more in touch and to confirm key information in writing.*
What skills, knowledge or personal attributes has the job-holder shown in carrying out his / her job?	Theo has extensive knowledge of competing products on the market; enthusiasm and energy in carrying out hectic visiting schedules; an excellent telephone manner; the ability to absorb product information quickly.	
Are there areas (skills, knowledge or behaviour) which require improvement or development?	**(Question 2)**	
What key actions are necessary to ensure improvement or further development? (This may include training, extra guidance, exposure to additional tasks, etc.)	Work with the Sales Manager on planning itineraries. Theo to work on his keyboard skills. The company to allow Theo to take a laptop home so he can write follow-up information while it is still fresh in his mind.	
General: use this section to make any additional comments. (This may include areas of future interest; skills or knowledge which are not currently being utilised; career aspirations; etc.)	**(Question 3 – recorded excerpt 2)**	

Job-holder's comments: **(Question 4 – recorded excerpt 3)**

Signed .... Date ....

Signature of Appraiser:

Jana Cossich

Date: 11th August

LANGUAGE REFERENCE

Language Notes

For further notes on these points, see the accompanying Business Grammar Guide (BGG).

More on giving opinions (BGG 21.3)

- Strong opinions

e.g. I'm absolutely sure / positive / convinced / certain (that) … I have absolutely no doubt (that)…
I strongly / firmly believe / maintain (that) …
I definitely / certainly think / believe / consider (that) …
I really (do) think / feel / believe / consider (that) …

- Neutral opinions

e.g. I think / feel / consider / believe / reckon (that) …
My view / opinion is (that) …
In my view / opinion …
As far as I'm concerned …
As I see it …
To my mind …
From my point of view …

- Moderate / polite opinions

e.g. I'm inclined to think (that) …
I tend to think (that) …
I'd say / guess (that) …
I have/get the impression (that) …
Don't you think (that) … ?
I would have thought (that) …

Some terms used in evaluating (BGG 14.4)

- Strongly positive

highly original, really outstanding, truly exceptional, absolutely first class, extremely high quality

- Weakly positive

quite good, fairly interesting, moderately good value, rather nice, pretty well-made, not too bad, more or less OK

- Weakly negative

not very good, rather boring, fairly dirty, pretty bad, quite disappointing, a bit second rate, slightly messy

- Strongly negative

absolutely awful, very bad indeed, not right at all, extremely bad, completely disorganised, terribly inefficient

Summarising / drawing conclusions

e.g. So to sum up / to summarise, I'd say …
My overall view / feeling / assessment is …
Overall / Generally / On the whole, we feel / consider / believe …
The evidence / feedback suggests / indicates …

The assessment forms show / indicate / prove …
Looking back, it's (pretty) obvious / clear …

Indicating in what context you are speaking

e.g. From a training point of view, it's clear …
In business terms, we feel …
Bearing in mind the time involved …
Speaking as someone who …
As the person responsible …
Considering the cost / time implications …

Vocabulary

- Words and phrases

self-assessment, peer review, performance evaluation, development needs, progress monitoring, measurement criteria, overall aim, personal target, corporate objective, to rate, to score, to evaluate, achievements, successes, quick wins, disappointment, weaknesses, areas for improvement

- Verbs and verb phrases

e.g. The feedback suggests we **are on the right lines / on target**.
I'm disappointed we **didn't meet our targets**.
I **took the test** but I didn't **pass it** / didn't **get through it**.
My next step is to **put** what I learned **into practice**.
The evaluation **came to the conclusion** she **made good progress**.
Let me **sum up** by saying you did a good job.

Useful Phrases

How would you evaluate the course?
What's your overall assessment?
On a scale of one 1 to 10, how would you rate your performance?

I'd give it 8 out of 10.
In my view it was really excellent.
Parts were OK, but overall I thought it was below standard.
Frankly, it was absolutely awful.

Bearing in mind the circumstances, I reckon you did really well.
Speaking as someone who finds studying quite difficult, I found the instruction first class.
We didn't do too badly, considering the circumstances.

I'm inclined to think the products were rather second rate.
As far as I'm concerned, it was on the right lines.
I have absolutely no doubt her performance can improve.

On the whole, I felt the content was extremely well-planned.
Generally, the feedback suggests the material is more or less OK.
My overall conclusion is that we made good progress.

But I'm disappointed I didn't meet my targets.
To sum up, I'd say you did a good job.
What are your next steps?

Support materials

UNIT 5 Culture and values

4 Listening

Email message

> **Useful Phrases**
>
> I am writing in connection with … with regard to …
> As you may know, I am due to …
> Before …, I have to / need to … I would be grateful if / for …
> Present as a list if possible, please.
> Could you let me have / know … ?
> I would also appreciate / welcome … advice on matters such as …
> Finally, can / could you recommend … ?

5 Questionnaire

Score your answers as indicated, then interpret your total by consulting the text in the box.

Scoring:

1: a 0; b 1; c 3. **2:** a 0; b 3; c 0. **3:** a 0; b 1; c 3; d 0. **4:** Score 2 for each tick, plus possible bonus. **5:** a 0; b 3; c 2; d 1. **6:** a 0; b 4; c 2. **7:** Score 2 for each tick, plus possible bonus. **8:** a 0; b 2; c 0; d 3. **9:** a 1; b 2. **10:** Deduct 2 for each tick.

> **Interpretation**
> **38 and over:** Above average – people probably like working for you, and work well.
> **28 and over:** Average – your courtesy needs to be more consistent, doesn't it?
> **Under 28:** Below average – you tend to lack respect for other people. How can you expect respect when you don't give it?

UNIT 6 Environmental issues

4 Writing

Information for Partner B: Partner A is responsible for preparing a response to the environmental complaint. He / She has asked you to work on the draft because you have the necessary knowledge (for the sake of the exercise, improvise if necessary). Use the notes below to help you advise **Partner A**.

Replying to a message of complaint.

- Acknowledge that you have received the complaint and thank the sender for informing you.
- You may be able to deal with the complaint or you may need time to look into it. Either way, tell the sender what you intend to do. Indicate time frames.
- If the complaint is justified, explain how the mistake occurred and how you intend to solve the problem.
- Invite the sender to contact you direct if he / she has further concerns.
- In closing, indicate where possible that the mistake or error is an exception that is very unlikely to happen again. And apologise to the sender for any inconvenience or discomfort.

UNIT 7 Recruitment and training

5 Application

Use this completed planner as a model for your own.

	Focus area	Where now	Objective
1	Time management	Work sometimes late Desk area is cluttered	To be well planned and punctual in all areas
2	Networking	No focus on this Few people know who I am	To feel comfortable meeting people To know people in all the key function areas
3	Report writing	Takes too long Too long Not readable	To write reports that get read To reduce writing time by 50% To know people in all the key function areas

	Actions	Timing
1	Go on a course Find a coach	Start: ASAP Ongoing
2	To talk to one stranger per day To call someone useful once a week To meet up with some useful once a month	Start: next week Ongoing
3	To take a report-writing course To study for 30 minutes per day To ask for feedback	Start: now / asap End: six months (October)

UNIT 8 Staff relations

5 Questionnaire

Here is the scoring for your completed questionnaire.

> - Score 2 points for each 'True' answer to questions 2, 3, 5, 7 and 10. Score 0 for each 'False'.
> - For questions 1, 4, 6, 8 and 9, score 2 points for each 'False', and 0 for each 'True' answer.
>
> The higher your score, the more satisfied you are.
>
> - A score of 14 or more suggests that you find your job worthwhile – personally and financially.
> - A score of 6 or less indicates that you are getting less pleasure from your work than most people do – and less than is healthy for you.

UNIT 9 Retirement and redundancy

4 Writing

1 Sue Nickson's reply – she works in Britain.

Even though your employer has paid enhanced redundancy payments in the past, it does not automatically mean you are entitled to the same.

It will depend on what your contract of employment and company redundancy policy states, what your boss has said to you directly, and what has been done in the past.

If you are not explicitly entitled to the amount that former workers have received, you may still have a right to more if your employer has led you to believe that you would receive such a payment.

In 2002, a case in the Court of Appeal held that if an enhanced payment was implied in an employee's contract of employment, then they were entitled to the greater amount.

In that case, the decision was reached because enhanced redundancy terms had been drawn to the attention of the workers and therefore all the employees had a reasonable expectation that they would be paid more.

From *Financial Mail on Sunday*

2 Here is some useful language that you could use in a letter of regret that a colleague is leaving.

> **Useful Language**
>
> Il was (very) sorry / shocked to hear …
> sad news …
> We will all miss …
> friendly personality …
>
> professionalism / dedication
> … great pleasure working with …
> a really good holiday
> Keep in touch …

5 Case studies

Information for **Partner B**: Read the article about Nick Filleul and prepare to recount the information to **Partner A**.

How they told me I'd lost my job

After losing his job in February, Nick set up his own business in May. He is now an independent distributor of water and air filters.

Nick Filleul, 29, was a project manager for a company relocation firm until the business was hit by the recession. On the day he was told he must go, he recalls: 'I immediately tried to argue. A few months before I had approached the company to ask that, if they were going to make me redundant, could they give me as much notice as possible. I felt an element of trust had been broken.

Being made redundant still came as a surprise. The two company directors, both good friends of mine, called a meeting one lunch time after having been to see the bank. They told me the company was going to have to let me go that week.

I'd had suspicions about the company fortunes for four or five months and knew that I would be asked to leave at some point. I was also told the company couldn't afford to pay my final month's salary, although they eventually gave me one of the company PCs instead. I was pretty unhappy, but I did expect it.

After the meeting, I went back into the office to tie up all the loose ends. It was all very frantic and I didn't have much time to think of anything else. I'm still fairly good friends with the directors and we see each other socially. The positive side of it is that I've had the opportunity to set up on my own.

UNIT 10 Conferences and exhibitions

4 Application

Information for **Group B**: You are representatives from various companies who are going to visit the stand run by **Group A**. Research indicates that people at trade exhibitions visit stands for the reasons listed below. Each member of **Group B** should adopt one (or more) of the roles listed. Think through the language needed, then begin the exercise.

> **Main reasons people at exhibitions visit stands**
>
> - The display or demonstration has caught their attention.
> - They have heard about the company and would like to know more.
> - They know about the products and have a specific enquiry.
> - They are users and need advice.
> - They are users and have a complaint.
> - They are users and want to know about upgrades.
> - They are users and want to chat / express appreciation.
> - They are looking for a job.

UNIT 11 Networking

4 Writing

A letter of invitation

> **Useful Phrases**
>
> … we are organising …
> … we hope that you will …
> … private facilities have been booked …
> … refreshments will be available …
> … the [tennis] promises to be good …
> … we would be grateful if you would confirm …
> … please present the enclosed card at the main gate …
> … [play] starts at …
> … we look forward …

UNIT 12 Security abroad

5 Feature

Covering message

> **Useful Phrases**
>
> … I attach a copy …
> … mentioned over the phone …
> … a matter of common sense …
> … stories about tourists having problems …
> … worth being careful …
> … one point that is worth stressing / that isn't listed is the fact
>   that …
> … caused some embarrassment …
> … have a good trip …

UNIT 13 Salaries, incentives and rewards

4 Writing

> **Useful Phrases**
>
> - Message supporting
>   … I am writing to support …
>   … John Fu served the organisation well …
>   … assets grew …
>   … costs fell …
>   … high performance should be rewarded …
>   … the exit package is in line with similar rewards …
>   … effective leaders need to be encouraged …
>   … the policy was rejected by 10% of the members …
>   … 90% voted in favour …
> - Message criticising
>   … I am writing to make clear my opposition …
>   … Mr Fu was fairly rewarded …
>   … his pension entitlements are estimated to be …
>   … there is absolutely no need to give him …
>   … he is also to receive £18,000 per year …
>   … non-executive directors are supposed to be independent …
>   … Mr Fu does not qualify …
>   … in my view and the view of many shareholders …
>   … we demand …

5 Application

Information for **Partner B**: Take part in a simple pay review with your manager, **Partner A**, using the detail's below.

> **Factors to think about before the meeting**
>
> - Identify the items in your package you would like to
>   improve – see the list on page 63.
> - Prepare arguments to support your case:
>   - value added (your performance or productivity figures)
>   - extra responsibilities taken on
>   - contributions to the bottom line
>   - parity with similar workers in the company or industry
>   - increased profit (company price rises, increases
>   in turnover)
>   - cost of living increases (inflation).
> - Think in particular how your proposed increases will
>   benefit the company.

> **Useful Phrases for Partner B**
>
> When would be a good time to review my salary?
> When I accepted the extra responsibilities, you said I would receive
>   an increase in salary.
> I feel the company should recognise contributions of this kind.
> Who does the award have to be signed off by?
> It would be easy to feel undervalued in a situation like this.
> This can't be their final offer.
> What would you do if you were in my position / my shoes?
> Do you think they could be persuaded to reconsider?

UNIT 14 Personal and company finances

4 Writing

> **Useful Phrases**
>
> … I very much appreciate the opportunity I have had …
> … I feel I have contributed significantly …
> … for example, in the last six months, I have …
> … as you know, I'm still working for the salary we agreed …
> … when I joined, we agreed to renegotiate …
> … in the light of my overall performance …
> … I think it would now be fair to review my salary …
> … to bring my salary into line with payments to people with
>   similar responsibilities …
> … for the record this would involve an increase in the region
>   of 6% …
> … I would like to thank you for the development opportunities …
> … I am very much looking forward to the challenges ahead …
> … please let me know if you need more information …

UNIT 15 Managing credit

5 Feature

Information for **Partner B**: **Partner A** has read an article on ID theft and has called you for advice. Use your own experience and the information below to respond.

Check it, shred it and beat the crooks

CHECK your credit file regularly. Reports are available from around £2. Visit a credit reporting agency like experian.co.uk
SIGN up to a mail filtering service like the Mail Preference Service at mpsonline.org.uk, to cut junk mail.
BUY a shredder to destroy card slips and junk mail.
REGISTER with an anti-fraud register like the Cifas Protective Registration Service at cifas.org.uk
NEVER disclose your pin. Give card and address details over the phone only to companies you know and trust.
REPORT the loss or theft of personal documents straight away.
READ bank and credit card statements thoroughly.
TELL all financial companies you deal with immediately if

From Financial Mail

UNIT 16 Time management

5 Feature

Information for **Partner B: Partner A**, a potential customer, would like some details about TMI. Use the information below, supplied by TMI, to respond. If you are asked questions not covered here, improvise.

- TMI stands for Time Management International. TMI is a worldwide training consultancy, with local centres in 36 countries.
- TMI offers a variety of courses / programmes, including a two-day time management course – this is goal focused and based on a printed time organiser called a Time Manager. During the two days, participants learn how to realise their goals using Time Manager as a planning tool.
- Course / programmes are normally held in a business centre or hotel. They are non-residential.
- The basic costs of the two-day time management course is US$1,920, inclusive of materials, lunch and refreshments. Numbers are between 20 and 54.
- On the first day the focus is on 'what you do' – a review of goals and priorities. On Day 2, the focus moves to 'when and how you do it' – ways of implementing your goals. On each day, there are three sessions in the morning and three in the afternoon, with breaks for refreshments.
- The telephone hotline is a free back-up service – anyone who has completed a TMI course may call for help and advice.
- The free update evenings provide customers with a chance to review progress and discuss problems. They last two hours.
- The optional tune-up day provides customers with a chance to review progress and to extend the use of the system in their key areas. Price US$1,010.

UNIT 18 Working practices

5 Questionnaire

Here is the scoring for the questionnaire.

1 Score 2 for each tick. **2:** a 3; b 0; c 1. **3:** a 3; b 1; c 1; d 0.
4: a 2; b 2; c 2; d 0. **5:** a 3; b 2; c 0; d 0. **6:** a 0; b 2; c 3; d 0.
7: a 3; b 1; c 0. **8:** a 2; b 3. **9:** a 0; b 1; c 3. **10:** a 1; b 3; c 0; d 2

---

30 – 40: Your company is well above average.

20 – 30: Can your company really afford to make clients feel so unimportant even some of the time?

Under 20: Are you fighting your clients or trying to please them? Remember, those who are unimportant today could be important tomorrow.

UNIT 20 Offers and orders

4 Writing

A message asking for details of service and charges.

Useful Language

We are [an Egyptian trading company].
We are interested in …
We would like details of …
Our problem is …
We need help with …
Specifically we need …
Could you let me have details of your charges?
We would like details of any discounts available.
Do you offer quantity discounts?
Do you have any introductory offers?
We are concerned about confidentiality.
How do you process sensitive / confidential documents?
Would you be able to supply a copy of your client list?
We would like references / testimonials from satisfied clients.

5 Application

Information for **Partner A**: Below is the mail shot from Guidex Systems.

Dear Sir / Madam

Please find enclosed details of the Customer Information Systems available exclusively from **GUIDEX SYSTEMS**.

GUIDEX SYSTEMS has been established for 42 years and has acquired an enviable reputation with our major customers. These include railway companies, airport authorities and metro systems.

As part of our work with these major customers we have acquired a range of expertise in the design of information display systems. We specialise in the operator interface design and display quality.

We can offer quality systems for large and small applications at a very reasonable price.

I trust that you will find a system application to meet your requirements. Please note that our systems are readily extendable and can be configured to meet your exact requirements.

Please contact me for further technical information and prices for these products and other information display systems that **GUIDEX SYSTEMS** supplies and installs.

Yours faithfully

Information for **Partner B**: You work in a call centre processing first enquiries from people interested in Postfield Systems. In the exercise, use the information in the display panel to help you. If you are asked questions not covered there, improvise.

INFORMATION DISPLAY

Benefits

- Display available at all strategic points
- Instantly updatable
- Venue changes highlighted by flashing display
- Special messages display facility
- Up to 96 separate courses can be displayed on four monitors at one location
- For more courses these can be scrolled
- Standard systems available ex-stock
- Special facilities may be added as required
- Cost-effective
- Flexible
- Adaptable
- Site proven

Prices depend on proposed usage – the size of the building, the number and location of monitors, the quantity of information to be displayed, etc. The following costing is a guide.

Supply and installation for an office block on ten floors.

Software	7,900
Hardware	18,200[1]
Monitors: €1,100 each	5,500
Cabling	440
Installation: €980 per monitor	4,900
Training: €970 per person per day	1,940[2]
Total	**€38,880**

[1] Hardware includes computer parts.
[2] Length of course depends on complexity of software.

From Postfield Information Systems

UNIT 22 Home and family

4 Writing

Useful Phrases

… I'm writing to ask for time off.
… to attend (my daughter's wedding) …
… I realise this is a busy time …
… rearrange the work …
… willing to cover for me …
… everything is up to date …
… my holiday entitlement …
… unpaid leave …

UNIT 23 Work / life balance

3 Reading

Information for **Partner B**: Your role is to question the key ideas in the article. Is it true that people who take exercise are cleverer than others? Use the information presented below and your own experience. See also the Useful Phrases below.

Is it true that exercise improves intelligence?

The article on page 102 reports on an American study which shows that taking exercise improves your mental ability and helps the brain to stay healthy in old age. Dr Carl Cotman of the University of California claims that the brain is a muscle that benefits from exercise.

Dr Cotman supports his claims with the examples of Arnold Schwarzenegger and Jean-Claude Van Damme – both fitness fanatics who started from humble backgrounds. But it seems possible that there are other reasons for the success of these men. Both are obviously extremely ambitious and dedicated to improving themselves.

And it is not clear that intelligent people in the past have been interested in physical fitness. Did Einstein take exercise? What about Newton, Marconi, Mozart, Dante? In fact, many brilliant people died young. Steven Hawking, one of the most talented mathematicians and philosophers of our own time, is crippled by a wasting disease and cannot move.

Common sense tells us that it is easier to perform successfully if you are fit and healthy. Everything becomes more difficult if you are unwell, including clear thinking. Dr Cotman's research goes beyond this simple idea and suggests that taking exercise increases mental ability. Perhaps the truth is that brilliant people in the past like Einstein would have achieved more if they had spent more time jogging.

Useful Phrases

Opening	What do you think of … ?
	What's your view of / on … ?
Giving an opinion	I feel / think that …
	It seems to me …
Asking an opinion	What's your view on / of this?
	What do you think is going to happen?
Clarifying	How do you mean?
	Are you saying that … ?
Persuading	Don't you think … ?
	Don't you agree that … ?
Accepting a point	That's a good point.
	I think you are right, up to a point.
Not accepting	I don't (really) agree.
	I'm not sure about that.
Persisting	What I'm trying to say is …
	What's more …
Asking for clarification	What do you mean by … ?
	I'm not sure what you're saying.
Offering clarification	Let me put it this way.
	What it means is …
Querying exhalations	Is that really so?
	I find that difficult to believe / accept that …
Summarising	So what I'm saying is …
	So basically … to sum up …

4 Writing

Useful language to help you write the summary.

> ### Useful Language
>
> The four charts give a picture of …
> The profile indicates that …
> A pie chart breaks the total down into age groups.
> There is a bar chart showing … / which shows …
> A second bar chart gives …
> Here the largest / smallest group is …
> It is interesting / striking that …
> The biggest group is between 25 and 34.
> This group represents 22% of the total.
> 53% of book buyers are female.
> 18% are between 35 and 44.
> 70% read at least one book year.
> The average is 8 hours per week.

UNIT 24 Getting away

4 Writing

Here is some useful language that you can include in your email to office colleagues.

> ### Useful Language
>
> Greetings from …
> We arrived two days ago; we had a good flight / journey …
> The food / weather / people here is / are …
> The place where we are staying is not far from … . There is a castle nearby / two kilometres away, which … . This area is famous for … . Tomorrow we are going to … .
> Hope you are surviving without me / us! If you need to make contact, the number is … .
> See you next week.

5 Feature

Information for **Partner B**: Read the text below and pass on the information when **Partner A** calls.

THE WALK

If I were doing just one walk, I'd head for Greenwich Village and then slip down into SoHo. Bleecker Street still has psychedelic posters and awnings from the first time round. Here you'll find Zapp Records, Afghan Friend Importers, psychic counselling and cafes with names like Mother Hubbard's. Try the pastries and espressos at Cafés Bargia or Le Figaro. Bedford and Carmine are typically gracious Village streets with handsome 19th-century red-brick buildings with black zig-zag fire escapes.

Turn south down West Broadway and head into the gallery area of SoHo. Browse in the antiques, fashion and art houses here and on Spring, Prince and Green Streets before buying yourself a treat at the exquisite Dean and DeLuca deli at 560 Broadway.

From The Weekend Telegraph

UNIT 25 Politics and business

5 Case study

Notes on rail privatisation for **Partner A** – you are 'for'.

> - Privatisation is the best possible thing for the railways. In almost all cases passenger numbers go up and investment increases faster than it does under state control. The fact is that privatisation increases efficiency.
> - Generally there is more competition. Governments tend to split up the industry when it is privatised and competition between firms gives much better results for consumers.
> - Governments tend to invest too little in railways, so problems build up. The operating companies have to correct years of neglect.
> - The market is a more effective way of allocating resources. If there is a demand for services then the market will provide them in the most efficient way.
> - Statistics show that rail is the safest way to travel – privatised or not.
> - That's why more people are using the railways and why the reliability figures are so much better than before.

Notes on rail privatisation for **Partner B** – you are 'against'.

> - The railways should not be privatised. Experience shows that service deteriorates and safety is compromised.
> - Railways are a monopoly and privatising a monopoly leaves the company in a position to exploit consumers. Creating a private monopoly just makes the situation worse.
> - Look at the profits train operating companies make. Shareholders make money, while the railway system suffers.
> - For privatisation to work, the railways must be properly regulated, but usually the regulators have no teeth.
> - In many areas, including the UK, the safety record alone tells us that railways should never be privatised.
> - The evidence against privatisation is very clear to users. In most cases, prices have risen and services and reliability have deteriorated.

UNIT 26 Taxation

4 Writing

Compare your written responses with these professional opinions, which are based on the position in the USA.

c Do I have to pay tax on my bonus or award?
Generally, a bonus or award paid to you for outstanding work is taxable income that you must report on your tax return.

d Do I have to pay tax on gifts, bequests or inheritances?
Generally, property you receive as a gift, bequest or inheritance is not included in your taxable income on your tax return for income tax purposes. However, the property may be subject to gift tax, estate tax or inheritance tax.

e Do I have to pay tax on my hobby income?
You must include hobby income on your tax return. Tax deductions for expenses related to hobby income are limited to the amount of hobby income you report on your tax

return. If you collect stamps, coins or other items as a hobby for recreation and pleasure, and you sell any of the hobby collection items, your gain is taxable as a capital gain on your tax return. However, if you sell items from your hobby collection at a loss, you cannot deduct a net loss on your tax return.

f   Do I have to pay tax on meals and lodging provided by an employer?

Generally, no. Do not include in your taxable income on your tax return the value of meals and lodging provided to you and your family by your employer at no charge if the following conditions are met.

The meals must be:
* furnished on the business premises of your employer
* furnished for the convenience of your employer.

The lodging must be:
* furnished on the business premises of your employer
* furnished for the convenience of your employer.

Adapted from WorldWideWeb Tax™

UNIT 29   Work in progress

4   Writing

Partner B's information: You are the project manager responsible for refurbishing.
Partner A's offices: You have had a number of problems, mainly caused by your sub-contractors, and the work will not be finished for a couple of months at least. You are apologetic, but things are outside your control. See the information below.

Installation of new telephone and IT circuits
No problems – the work is on schedule and will finish on time.

Refurbishment of cloakrooms and washrooms
Behind schedule. New washbasins have not been delivered. Expected next week. Estimated completion – ten days from then.

Kitchen facilities upgraded – including flooring and wall tiling
At least three weeks behind schedule. Again, a problem with the supply of materials. Supervisor has had flu.

Installation of new office furniture
No problems expected. It's all in a warehouse awaiting delivery to the site.

Construction of a new fire escape
Progressing well. Expect to finish by the end of the week – ahead of schedule.

---

5   Case study

Use the information below to complete the tasks in Step 2 of the Case Study on page 127.

Fashion with a conscience

In 2001 Ms Minney launched her company in the UK. 'We sell our products through mail order and it was harder than I expected to get the business off the ground in the UK. In Japan, we already had a market presence through the Fair Trade Company. We weren't as well known here,' she says.

After hiring two full-time members of staff, Ms Minney bought commercial mail order lists, but quickly realised that this was not the way to go.

'We couldn't get across what was special about the product,' she says, 'We were determined to highlight the differences between us and other mail order clothing firms. It was a difficult nut to crack. We then decided to work in partnership with like-minded shops such as Aveda, which worked well.'

Their early catalogues – printed on 100% recycled paper, of course – were well received.

The company grew 50% in 12 months and Selfridges showcased its first People Tree collection – a significant milestone for the fair trade fashion industry.

The company's products are now available by mail order and in fair trade shops throughout the UK, Italy and Japan, which is also home to its only flagship store. Ms Minney is looking for partners to open the first shop in Britain.

What sets People Tree apart from its main market competition is that it pays its producers a fair price, provides technical assistance with product design and quality control, and commits to ordering regularly.

Ms Minney says: 'Fair trade helps people to revive their livelihoods and develop their communities. We work with 20 textile artisan groups in 20 developing countries to help them to meet environmental standards and develop market potential.'

People Tree now has five full-time designers on the team, which consists of 40 employees in Tokyo and eight in London.

The company pays 50% of the operating costs of two primary schools in Nepal and Bangladesh, and is in the early stages of supporting a third school in Tirupur, the T-shirt capital of India, where child labour is rife.

Ms Minney says that the 10,000 people around the world working for People Tree receive up to 70% more in wages than they would earn otherwise. Ms Minney now hopes to educate consumers and show them what they are capable of achieving through the choices they make when they shop.

Adapted from The Times

Audioscripts

UNIT 1 Business travel

1 Core practice

a – Come and see for yourself what we're doing here. I think you'd find it interesting.
  – Yes, I'd like to. But my diary is pretty full till July.
  – There aren't many people here then – it's holiday time. Why don't you fly down in June? I can show you round and introduce you to some of our people. What about the week of the 12th?
  – Er, no, I'm afraid I'm busy that week.
  – Well how about the 19th? That's the following week.
  – That's Tuesday, isn't it?
  – Yes, or Wednesday would be OK, if that suits you better.
  – Er, can we make it Tuesday?
  – Sure. Just let me know what time you are arriving and I'll pick you up from the airport.

b – Remember to bring your skiing gear; we're only 30 minutes from the mountains.
  – I didn't realise you were near mountains.
  – Yes, we're in an agricultural area between the mountains and the sea. It's good for farming – the countryside round here is quite flat and we get plenty of rain.
  – So is it going to be cold?
  – In the mountains, it's about minus five at this time of the year.

c – We've had to change your hotel arrangements.
  – That's OK, but I'm afraid something has come up, and I'm not going to be able to make the 17th.
  – But it's all set up.
  – I know, I'm really sorry but there's not a lot I can do. I'd like to put the trip off till the 28th. Do you think that would be possible?
  – I'm sure it's possible, but they won't like it.
  – Well, let's reschedule for the 28th provisionally.
  – And if that doesn't work for them, we'll have to set up a telephone conference.

d – How do I get to you?
  – The easiest way is by public transport – take the express bus. They leave from outside the arrival hall in Terminal 1, about every 12 minutes. It's a direct service to Central Square. Where are you staying?
  – It's a place called the Shereema Lodge.
  – The stop is right outside.
  – OK. And where are your offices in relation to that?
  – Pen Avenue South is about two blocks from Central Square. I'll send you a link to our map for visitors.

3 Listening

Speaker 1

You know, there are often delays with long journeys, and when you arrive in India everything closes very early, so therefore you know it's always a bit of a worry if you arrive after eight o'clock in the evening for instance. And then one thing that er you know, anybody going to India should remember – is that … people appear very, very helpful. In fact they are all very, very keen to … you know, offer you accommodation and so on, but one has to, you know, kind of discriminate about that, because … you know, people just could take you anywhere, so one has to be very careful. But … you know, hotels are definitely wonderful in India and … you know it is very cheap for us, so it is lovely to actually … indulge and … go to a, you know, kind of little palace really.

Speaker 2

Last year I went to Phoenix in Arizona … er … to the Phoenican Resort Hotel er to attend a convention. And the convention was of people in the fund management business in America and their wives. And the Phoenician Resort Hotel is quite far from the airport but you don't need to hire a car because the convention people provide a lift for you from the airport er to the hotel. Dress is very informal in that sort of place. Umm, shorts and a shirt or jeans and T-shirt are there. But in the evening and … when there are formal dinners, then of course a suit and tie is a good idea.

UNIT 2 Representing your company

1 Core practice

a We're a medium-size manufacturing company – we're part of the Melox group, which has its head office in Toulouse. We're based here in South Wales – our main plant is in Swansea, where we produce a range of state-of-the-art domestic cookers. The organisation consists of three divisions: production, marketing and strategic services (which includes finance). Since the tie-up with Melox, export sales have more than doubled. At present we operate a two-shift system, but we are planning to introduce a third shift from the beginning of next month.

b This is what we're working on at the moment. It's an automated sorting and packing machine, linked to our computer database. We're having one or two teething problems, but when the system is up and running, it'll make it possible for us to turn orders round in four hours.

c – Look, come and meet our building manager, Mel d'Abo, he's responsible for project planning. He's the best person to answer your query. He's just over here. Mel, this is Donna Ng; she's with the management group from Shanghai.
  – Hello, welcome to Sydney.
  – Thank you. Pleased to meet you.
  – Donna has a question for you.

d – Have we lost anyone?
  – No, I think we're all here.
  – OK, please follow me. We go down these stairs and through the swing doors.
  – Is there any chance of seeing the new high-speed processor you mentioned?
  – No, I'm afraid not – it's still being trialled by our R&D people. And the R&D area is closed to visitors.
  – Oh, that's a pity.
  – I can show you an older model which we're in the process of modifying. It's just along here on the left. This is it. Mind your clothes, the paint might be wet.

3 Listening

Extract 1

– Well, good morning. I'd like to welcome you to Van Breda Footware, and to thank you for coming. Did anyone get lost?
– No, I think we're all here.
– OK, we have an interesting programme for you today. First of all we'll go up to our boardroom. I've organised some coffee

for us, and during the course of coffee I'll introduce you to some of the guys who run the place. Our Managing Director is joining us. The first presentation starts at 10.00. Then we can have a look round the plant and show you what we're working on.

Extract 2
– First of all then, while we're waiting for coffee, can I introduce you to Jan Ruse, who is our MD.
– Hello and welcome. It's good to see you all here. I'll be joining you for the round-up session, so if you have any questions specifically for me, you can catch me then – OK? I hope you enjoy your tour.
– Thanks, Jan. Jan is responsible to our head office in Brazil for the running of this site and the whole of our European operation.

Extract 3
– Aah, there's a slight change of plan – there's a fire inspection in the plant this morning, so we're going to look round the showroom first. Are we all here?
– Yes, I think so.
– Right … as you can see, this is where our samples are on display. As you know, we make a whole range of leather shoes and we specialise in all-weather footwear. You can see some samples on those racks over there.

Extract 4
This is the new XL20. Can everyone see? It heat-welds the uppers to the soles. It's a state-of-the-art machine, which more or less runs itself. The only trouble is, it's very sensitive. We're having a few teething problems with it, because it keeps stopping. Can you see these gauges down here? Mind your heads. If the reading goes into the red, the whole machine shuts down.

Extract 5
– Excuse me, the boardroom is along here, through the swing doors.
– Oh …
– Mind the step! In fact we're a little early; we're not meeting Jan for another 10 minutes. Anybody need the toilet? It's on the left here. OK, where were we? Oh yes – you had a question …
– Yes, I was wondering how many people you employ.
– Do you mean on this site or in the whole company?

UNIT 3 Following up

1 Core practice

a This is a message for Jan Somensky from Ron Lomax. I'm just following up on our meeting. Have you been able to get hold of those samples yet? As far as I know, we haven't received anything at this end. Umm … do you know how soon we can expect them? Anyway, I'd be grateful if you could call me and let me know the state of play. Thanks.

b – I managed to get hold of the figures you wanted.
   – Oh, thanks for getting back to me.
   – That's OK, but I'm calling because we're having problems with the samples. But I understand you don't need them now.
   – Er, look, I'm in a meeting right now – can I call you back in about 10 minutes?
   – Yes, of course. Could you call my landline? My mobile keeps switching to silent – there's something wrong with it.

c – I'm calling to find out if I left some papers behind. They were in a green folder marked 'Liaison'.
   – Er, I didn't see anything. Do you know where you left it?

– I'm pretty sure I put it down in the reception area.
– I'll call them and check whether anyone has handed it in.
– I'm sorry to bother you with this.
– That's OK. People are always leaving things behind. I'll contact you as soon as we find it.

d – I'm just calling to thank you for organising such an interesting visit for us.
   – I'm glad you could come.
   – Thanks a lot for showing us round. It was very interesting.
   – I hope you found it useful.
   – Oh, we did. And next time you must visit us.
   – We'd like to, very much.
   – Just let me know when you want to come, and I'll organise it. We're looking forward to taking our relationship with your company to the next stage.

5 Case study

DY = Donna Yang
PB = Peter Baska

DY: How are you progressing with the Ray Felli business? Did he meet the deadline?
PB: The information relating to his bank account? You remember he was asked to account for the movement of company funds into and out of his personal account.
DY: Yes, by the 21st of February.
PB: Well, we didn't get the information on the date requested, but after a few reminders we did finally get it. Our position now is that we're satisfied with the information we've received, and we're going ahead more or less as recommended in my report. They're setting up the new procedures which will standardise most of the regular money transactions. From the beginning of next month regular cheques will be paid at a regular time each month. The new petty cash system for irregular cash payments is already up and running. Er … we've reviewed the situation of the part-time accountant and we've decided to retain his services, but to bring in someone from one of the international accounting firms to do a month-end review.
DY: You decided not to find someone else.
PB: No. The matter of any missing money has also been reviewed and our view again is that this is not misconduct, but mismanagement. Plus the decision not to pay any further funds into Ray Felli's personal account has helped the situation a lot.

UNIT 4 Dealing with change

1 Core practice

a – I started work on the new catalogue in February. The work went well and I finished the job in about five and a half weeks. Then, at the beginning of May, I had to revise it all because the marketing director wanted to include a range of products we'd just bought in. But he said the Board didn't want the production timetable delayed in any way. At first I didn't think it would be possible, but once I'd entered all the new data, I found that the job wasn't as difficult as I'd expected. The team helped a lot.
   – Did you meet the deadline?
   – Yes, but just prior to the delivery they tried to change the spec again.

b – There have been some changes in the last few months. As you know, a new managing director has just been appointed. He became MD three weeks ago.
   – Was he an internal appointment?

    – In a way. He was from within the group, although I'd
      never met him. He'd been running our Spanish
      subsidiary.
    – Who did he take over from?
    – Beatrice Guyon, the previous MD; she's been promoted
      to the main board. She's now group financial controller.

c Our factory in Scotland has just been closed down.
We used to make our industrial filters there, but recently
production has been switched to China. Nowadays,
margins are so tight that we can't afford to manufacture
locally. In the last year, we've been forced to cut prices
twice. These days, the European end of the operation
concentrates on planning and marketing – that's all. Head
Office has even cut back on R&D.

d – What difference will the reorganisation make?
    – We used to process orders locally, but now the back and
      middle office functions are moving to Milan, orders are
      going to be processed centrally.
    – So, the transactions you used to handle here are
      moving?
    – Yes, to the global customer care team.
    – How will it affect the service for people like me?
    – There should be no difference in the day-to-day
      running of your account. But if you have any problems
      you can always call me.

3 Listening

Mark Jarvis works in aircraft manufacturing
I woke this morning and turned on my PDA to check my
overnight emails, which I then replied to in the taxi to Heathrow
Terminal 1. Next, I checked in and settled into the departure
lounge, where, with a hot latté, I connected to the Internet and
downloaded my corporate mail with attachments. How different
from when I started work at British Aerospace 22 years ago. I had
a desk with a telephone and a filing tray. What did I do every
day? Imagine coming to the office and sitting down at your desk
with only a phone and not even direct dial – to place an outside
call, you had to ask the operator to connect you. If I needed a
letter typed, I had to write it and give it to the typing pool. They
would type it with carbon copies that I would proofread and
correct. There was one photocopier for 3,000 people that you
needed authorisation to use! If you travelled overseas, for
example to Nepal, you would be gone for two weeks and nobody
could phone you – and you couldn't phone them.
(Adapted from *Business Life Magazine*; the words of Mark Jarvis are
spoken by an actor.)

UNIT 5 Culture and values

1 Core practice

a We use to be a middle-of-the road company; the workforce
    was skilled but fairly unmotivated – it was the kind of place
    where if your face didn't fit you couldn't get on. The
    management were living in the past. Then, 18 months ago,
    we were taken over, and we got a new managing director –
    an American. And the change was dramatic. She
    introduced new technology – we all had to learn new skills.

b – We used to produce high quality products that sold at
      premium prices, at the top end of the market. Many of
      the processes were still done by hand. I wanted to
      mechanise some of the operations, but the bosses
      weren't interested. They were only concerned about
      one thing – the exclusivity of their products. And they
      weren't concerned about modern ideas of staff relations.
    – How were the workers motivated?

    – Erm, they used to pay well. They weren't bad
      employers; the management style was just very
      old fashioned.
    – What about staff turnover?
    – It was quite low. Some people couldn't stand the
      atmosphere and walked out, but unemployment in the
      area was over 17%.
    – How long were you there?
    – Only six months; I didn't fit in.

c The people I work for are very willing to try out new ideas.
It's a young company – we're involved in a lot of cutting-
edge technology and we're working in an expanding
market. It's one of the so-called 'sunshine industries'.
So my work is changing all the time. Change is the norm.
It's like a constant learning and retraining process. The
atmosphere is extremely businesslike, but it isn't at all
formal. We work together in teams – whoever has the
right mix of skills becomes responsible for the job.
The management attach a lot of importance to motivation
– they expect you to think for yourself.

d I'd never worked with Japanese managers before – this is a
joint venture with a Japanese company. Previously I'd
been working with manual systems, and here all the
equipment is state of the art – we use all the most up-to-
date methods. About 80% of the operation is automated.
It took me a little time to get used to it. But everyone here
is very supportive. The company is very well run. Everyone
in the company from the top to the bottom knows the
importance of quality and customer service – the
management won't put up with low-quality work.

4 Listening

– People in the factory have been very kind to me. I've really
  enjoyed my stay here so far.
– You have not found it difficult to get on with people, and to do
  your job here?
– Not at all. No. Everyone's been very friendly and helpful. I've
  been really welcomed into the group, so to speak. And when I
  have tried to learn Dutch they are all very helpful. I've been
  having lessons here, and I attended some intensive training
  courses before I came.
– So you have learnt quite a lot.
– I really don't know if it's quite a lot, but I try to manage. There
  are some people who refuse to speak anything but Dutch, and
  I have to be able to say something and to understand
  something in the factory.
– How are you getting on in your job here? What is your job
  exactly?
– Well, this is the first factory for Hub Textiles in Holland, and
  that's why everything is new, not only for me but for the
  whole organisation. I suppose that my main role is to be the
  contact person between the new company here and our head
  office in Manchester. I need to find out a lot more about this
  market, the area, how customers behave here, and how the
  factory needs to operate in the market. To report this
  information back to the UK is possibly my most important job.

UNIT 6 Environmental issues

1 Core practice

a – As far as I'm concerned the key issue is population
      control.
    – What about global warming?
    – I agree that exhaust emissions and so on are a big
      problem. But I think the central issue, the cause, is
      overpopulation. The earth's resources are being used up

at an alarming rate. In my view, we have to ensure that we deal with the cause, not the effects.

  – I agree on the whole …
b – We tend to take energy supplies for granted. But the truth is that oil and natural gas supplies will only last a few decades.
  – I take your point, but I don't really go along with the idea that the world has an energy problem. We have enough coal to last hundreds of years – and there are many alternative sources of energy.
  – Look, I don't think we can rely on green technologies to supply all our energy needs.
  – OK, but what about nuclear power? We have enough uranium to last thousands of years.
  – And what about the environment costs?
c – Where do you stand on green issues?
  – As a company we believe it makes sound business sense to have environmentally friendly policies. New environmental regulations are coming in every year.
  – Specifically, how does the situation affect your company?
  – Well, we are moving over to an environmental procurement policy. This means that when we are awarding contracts to suppliers, we ask questions about their environmental practices. Environmental performance is now a competitive issue.
d – We manufacture soft drinks which we sell in aluminium cans, and the new government legislation requires us to recycle 50% of the cans used. Basically, they're running out of landfill sites where they can bury rubbish.
  – How does the legislation affect you?
  – From our point of view it's bad news. We're having to spend a lot more on collection. I suppose something has to be done about pollution, but my personal view is that the volume of environmental legislation is too high at the moment.

5 Case study

– Can you explain to me, what is an environmental audit?
– These days, environmental auditing is defined quite well in various textbooks and even now in European Law. An audit really is an opportunity to take stock of your environmental performance against a set of benchmarks or standards which are now universally accepted. But within … for example, the European Union Eco-management and Audit Regulation, the audit is only one part of an overall, comprehensive approach to minimising and managing your effects on the environment.
– Now could you tell me something about your packaging policy?
– The Body Shop has a quite radical approach to packaging which follows … best practice, we believe, and also the most forward thinking approaches that … come from a non-profit sector. And we have a very very strong commitment to minimising waste in the first instance, so anyone who walks into one of our stores will see that the … packaging we use is absolutely minimal. We are dead against having … secondary packaging just to make the products look good; we are absolutely against that. Er, but we go further, so once we have minimised, we are committed to … reusing packaging, so again we have a fairly unique system for refilling our packaging where customers can bring their bottles back to the stores and have them refilled … with a discount on the purchase price … for the item that they are buying.

UNIT 7 Recruitment and training

1 Core practice

a – We normally use small ads in the local paper when we want to recruit operators, clerical staff, etc.
  – What about managerial staff?
  – Sometimes we advertise in the national press, but more often we post vacancies on the net – there are one or two specialised job-search sites we use. And for top positions we sometimes use head hunters.
b – Is that the recruitment manager?
  – Yes, it is.
  – Hello, my name's Jeb Milhey. I'm calling about your advert for a Business Support Manager. The reference number is 27216. I sent you a couple of emails, but I don't think you got them.
  – I'm sorry – let me check. Jeb Milhey – when did you send them?
  – I sent the last one this morning.
  – No, I didn't get it. If you give me your address, I'll send you the details and the application form – or you can get them from our website.
c I left school when I was 18 and started life as a trainee clerk in the bank. I actually just walked into the bank one day and asked if they had any vacancies. To my amazement, they took me on. I was sent on day-release courses and took various banking exams. By the time I was 30, I was manager of a local branch. Not long after that I was transferred to Head Office.
d – I'm very keen to go on an export documentation course. Do you know of any? There have been so many changes recently that I'm very much out of date. Is the training department running anything at the moment? I've looked on the training portal and can't see anything.
  – There's nothing at the moment, but we're thinking of doing something. We've had a lot of similar requests.

3 Listening

Speaker 1
I work in market research, in qualitative research. I've been doing it for about 12 years. The training I've had has been almost entirely on the job because I've worked in small companies which don't have strict training regimes. It's basically been to do with developing interviewing skills, developing the ability to listen to people as well as to talk to get the most out of people. Other training … has been to do with expressing myself verbally and in writing … and again that's been largely on the job with the help of people who have got more experience than I have.

Speaker 2
I'm an accountant and my job title is Assistant Business Support Manager, which basically involves producing month-end reports for both of the business managers and the US parent of the company. I have a degree in biochemistry – that was my initial degree – and after that I sat the Certified Institute of Management Accountancy exams while I was working. I've now been qualified for four years and I've been in my present job for four and a half years. Most of my training has been on-the-job training. I've done a few courses, but they were related to sitting and passing the accountancy exams.

UNIT 8 Staff relations

1 Core practice

a Things aren't so good at the moment. There was a pay freeze last year, then an overtime ban. As you can imagine, the atmosphere in the plant deteriorated badly. It is very unfortunate because we used to have an excellent working relationship here. We were famous for it. If you ask me, the place has gone downhill.

b – How is it at Tenco these days?
   – Things are going well. We had a new production manager who started at the beginning of the year and he's really turned things round. There's no more of that 'them' and 'us' nonsense. It's mainly because of him that the Workers' Council is now making a real contribution. He makes sure they really understand the business plan, and buy into the business objectives.

c – Can I have a word?
   – Sure? What's the problem?
   – I need a couple of days off next week. I hope that's OK.
   – We're pretty busy at the moment.
   – Yes, I know, but I think Nina can handle it.
   – Which days are we talking about?
   – Wednesday and Thursday.
   – Is this holiday or what?
   – No, I'm owed five days – time off in lieu of overtime.
   – Yes, OK … that's fine by me – but make sure everything is covered!

d – What we're looking for is an across-the-board increase of 5% on current pay levels. We'd also like to see a review of the company health-care plan. The current plan does not really cover our present needs.
   – Yes, I agree with your point about the health plan, but obviously we will need to look at all your proposals in detail.

3 Listening

Speaker 1 (a 23 year-old TV researcher)
The best thing I ever did was to ask my boss for weekly update meetings. I'd been fumbling in the dark for so long that I finally decided to confront him and ask for these sessions when I could check that everything was OK and that there wasn't anything else he needed. After all, I'm not a mind reader. It took courage to ask him, but I believed that I had to do it. In the end he was really pleased that I'd taken the initiative.

Speaker 2 (a 21 year-old personal assistant)
My boss was a cool and withdrawn person, and I found it difficult to break the ice. She never praised me and I never asked her how she thought I was doing. I thought that she wasn't very happy with my performance. When a chance for promotion came up, I didn't apply for the job and someone else was brought in. I later found out that my boss was surprised that I hadn't gone for the job as she thought that I was ready for it. You can imagine how frustrated I felt.
(Note: the words of the TV Researcher and the Personal Assistant are spoken by actors.)

UNIT 9 Retirement and redundancy

1 Core practice

a – How did you manage during the summer? Did you have to stop any of the machines?
   – We did, unfortunately, yes. We laid off one of the machine crews and a couple of people in the warehouse. But things are picking up now and everyone is back at work. The summer was a difficult time for us all.

b Can I have everyone's attention, please? I would like, on behalf of everyone here, to wish Paul a very happy retirement. As you know, Paul has been with the company for the best part of 25 years, and I know that I speak for all of us here when I say that we will all miss him enormously. Paul, I know that you have many plans for the future, not least …

c – In this company we let people retire early at 55 – that's men and women. The policy's been very popular. There is no pressure to go, but many people have seized the chance of taking early retirement.
   – I'm not surprised. I would if I could. In my firm we have to stay until 65. If we leave before then, we lose some of our pension entitlement.
   – I opted out of our scheme. I have a private plan, which I run myself.

d – I was terribly sorry to hear what happened. How long had you been with the firm?
   – Just over two years. No one expected them to close us down. We were expecting this plant to expand if anything.
   – It must have come as a terrible shock. But I'm sure you'll find another job soon.
   – I hope so, but I'm not so optimistic. At my age it's not so easy.
   – Well, good luck – keep in touch.

3 Listening

Speaker 1
The idea of being able to take time out to start thinking and planning and doing new things is very attractive, but I think … that is a luxury in a sense because first of all I think the economic thing has to be sorted out. I would have to be very clear in my own head that … umm … I wouldn't have an impoverished retirement. I think that's probably quite important so we've got a plan for all of that. Part-time working possibilities are obviously … attractive and I guess I think about that quite a lot – although I think it has to be said that my … the thing I really like about my job is that I work with some very good and interesting people.

Speaker 2
Uhh … it's quite funny actually because I got made redundant from a large firm, having just turned 50. And that was, I suppose, at one level quite fortunate, because it meant that, number one, I was eligible for a pension. So I was in the peculiar position of having a pension every month until I die, as of that age, which seems far too early to actually be pensioned off. And also, of course, in leaving a large company I had the opportunity of a lump sum, in lieu of redundancy, which means therefore there is enough money to create an investment base if one actually wanted to start a small business, which is exactly what's happened.

UNIT 10 Conferences and exhibitions

1 Core practice

a – We have a stand at the Focus 49 exhibition. Why don't you come over and visit us?
   – Where is the exhibition?
   – In the Dubcek Centre. It would be good to meet up. Could you spare the time?
   – I don't think I can make it today. How long is it going on?

-   It ends on Friday. Why don't you come tomorrow? We could have lunch. I'd like to show you our new product range.
-   OK …
-   That's great. We're on stand 27 in the ground floor display area. I'll leave a pass for you with the information desk at the main entrance.

b – When is your first lecture?
-   Tomorrow at 10.00.
-   Have you got everything you need?
-   Oh, I haven't had time to look at the room yet.
-   OK, but let me know if you need anything. My pager number is on the back of your pass.
-   OK, thanks.
-   The organisers would like to take you out … show you some of the sights and give you dinner. Would that be possible?
-   Of course – that's very kind of them.

c – Can I help you?
-   I'm not sure. We're thinking of upgrading our waste separators so we're looking to see what's available. We saw your display – it's very impressive.
-   Thank you. It's our latest model – the Solvex B. Can I ask what you are using at the moment?
-   We have two Nemco B24s and two old Bemat Maxi machines. We produce a range of disinfectant and antibacterial products.
-   Look – would you like to come and sit down? It's a bit quieter and we can talk without being disturbed?

d – I'm sorry to keep you waiting. We've been very busy this morning. How can I help you?
-   I have one of your products – an SA 9,000 – and I'd like to find out what upgrades are available.
-   If you come this way, they are on display at the back of the stand.
-   Will I be able to try them out? Do you have them here?
-   We have some – some you can check on the display screens. There's 15% discount if you order during the exhibition.

3 Listening

- Hello, Intermark. You are speaking to Carla Choudry. How may I help you?
- I'm calling about your one-day Internet Marketing Conference. Are there any vacancies left?
- Let me check – there's been a lot of interest in this. How many tickets do you want?
- Two.
- Yes, that's fine.
- And is it going to be at the address given in your mailout?
- Yes – the Floris Hotel.
- Could you tell me what level the programme is at? Will it cover the basics?
- Whether you are a seasoned pro or a new entrepreneur, the programme will have something for you.
- So it'll cover how to get started?
- Oh yes – the first session is called 'Why start a website?'.
- OK … What's the difference between 'Search engine techniques' and 'Search strategies'?
- I'm not the expert, but I guess search engine techniques are the technical details – how search engines work. The session on search strategies is more strategic.
- OK … Will you be covering on-line selling techniques?
- Let me check … Yes, that will be covered in the lecture entitled 'Getting ready to sell on the Internet'.
- OK – and what about website construction?
- Look, why don't I send you a link to the full programme? It has notes and everything.

- OK, thanks – and can I book on-line?
- Sure.

UNIT 11 Networking

1 Core practice

a – I wanted to say 'hello' because Silke Ollek suggested I contact you.
-   Oh – how do you know Silke?
-   We work together.
-   Oh. I see …
-   I was wondering if I could come and see you sometime.
-   Sure! What's it about?
-   Well we have a problem, and Silke says you are a great problem solver.
-   I don't know about that – but why don't you call my office and fix an appointment?
-   I'd be glad to. Do you have a card or something?
-   Sure … here you are.
-   Thanks … and these are my details.
-   Thanks … Well, I think I'd better circulate. It was nice meeting you.

b – So what do you do?
-   I'm a nuclear service engineer? What do you do?
-   I'm the safety and compliance manager at the plant in Rossas.
-   So you're in the business.
-   That's right. Maybe we should get together … and explore common ground.
-   Why not?
-   Here's my card.

c – I'm planning to contact Juanita Curtiz in Mexico City. Do you have any advice?
-   Well, she's really into sailing …
-   I don't know anything about sailing.
-   You can ask questions, show an interest.
-   OK. And any points I should watch out for?
-   Well, yes … she's pretty right wing and has strong views, so it's probably best not to talk about politics or religion.
-   That's useful. Thanks. Can I mention your name?

d – It's Gerry Atailer.
-   Sorry …
-   Gerry Atailer – we met at the conference in Manheim.
-   You mean in June?
-   That's right. Do you remember? We talked about our new anti-corrosion techniques and you said you might be interested. You asked me to call you.
-   Oh yes, I remember. You were supposed to send me some details.

3 Listening

- What are the benefits of these corporate entertainment packages in real terms? Can firms use hospitality to help secure contracts?
- Corporate entertainment is the most direct form of target marketing there is. It's tangible and provides companies with the opportunity not only to invite potential clients to discuss new business, but also to network with existing customers and spend time running through current and future contracts. A successful company nurtures its clients in order to maintain and develop relationships and achieve good communication. Corporate entertainment provides the opportunity for such relationships to develop.
- But does 'wining and dining' really make that much difference? Are companies that don't spend money in this way, that can't afford this kind of package, losing out?
- Wining and dining provides the opportunity for relaxed discussion, and it's often during such occasions that clients

provide their host with additional – and useful – business information. The matter of cost isn't always significant. A wine bar lunch can be just as effective, if planned properly to meet a specific objective.
- So how much choice is there in this market? What's the Rolls-Royce of the hospitality market?
- The Rolls-Royce package in the UK (and one of the most sought-after invitations) is probably finals day at Wimbledon All England Lawn Tennis Championships, which can cost as much as £4,000 per head for the men's final.
- Oh gosh!

UNIT 12 Security abroad

1 Core practice

a – I'm sorry, we do not accept credit cards.
- Oh, I don't have any cash. Is there a bank nearby where I can change some money?
- Yes, there's a bank at the end of the street, but I think they will have closed by the time you get there – it's lunch time. We'll be closing soon.
- So what do you suggest?
- We could accept euros, but there would be a supplement.

b – I've been waiting half an hour for my baggage. There's still no sign of it.
- Which flight were you on, sir?
- The Athens flight.
- Yes, I'm sorry we have some staff shortages at the moment. We expect the bags will be coming through soon.

c – Hotel security.
- Oh, come in. I have to report a theft. My wallet was stolen while I was in the shower.
- When was this?
- About half an hour ago.
- You weren't using the mini safe …?
- No it has a faulty lock; it isn't working. Are the police coming? My insurance company will need a police report number.
- Yes, they'll be here in about half an hour.
- Oh – I'll have left by then. I have a meeting.
- When will you be returning to the hotel?

d – Your car has been towed away.
- But it doesn't say 'No Parking'.
- It was incorrectly parked.
- Oh. Do you know where it was taken?
- You need to phone this number.
- Oh, right. How much will I have to pay to get it back?
- Usually the fine is 400 US dollars.
- I don't believe it! That's ridiculous.

3 Listening

During the course of my employment with Lonely Planet I have visited some rather interesting places and many beautiful places in Mexico, which is why Torreon was a surprise. Torreon is a city that built itself around a lead smelter. Like most other mining operations, it is in the middle of the desert – the smelting operations belching out clouds of zinc and lead dusts. And it is, of course, hot.

I arrived in this charming location with a migraine headache … and in a foul mood, because I had my credit card declined when I went to purchase the plane ticket in Monterrey. It turned out to be a fraud! Then, when I got to the hotel, the clerk claimed he had no reservation for me. Nor did he have a room. We finally sorted it out, and I shuffled off to my room. To my relief my

colleagues from Mexico City arrived and I was marginally better as we sat down to eat.

I have never seen steak served in so many new and interesting ways. But unfortunately dinner was cut short by the return of my migraine. In the end, my stay in Torreon was a success. Mexican hospitality worked its magic, but it was a tough trip.

Paul Talley's words are spoken by an actor.

UNIT 13 Salaries, incentives and rewards

1 Core practice

a – We all get a bonus at New Year. It's based on the company's results – it approximately equals one and a half week's salary.
- Do you have child-care facilities?
- One in three of the workforce are women, and most of them have children, so the company has to provide a crèche on-site. It's very good, but we have to pay for it.

b – Do you receive any perks?
- The main thing we get is a discount on company products – we get 7% off. Also the canteen is subsidised – it's very good value. I'm sure the top managers get all sorts of executive perks like free cars, free health insurance and so on, but I don't qualify for those yet.
- Do you have sports facilities?
- Not of our own, but we have the use of the facilities at a local club.

c – My basic salary is in the region of €5,000 a month, and then on top of that I get 5% commission on sales. What I get depends on my figures. In a good month I might clear €8,000. In addition I get an incentive bonus of 3% on sales above my monthly target. After deductions, it's not a fortune but I get by. According to my contract I am expected to work a 35-hour week – in fact, it's usually more than that.
- Do you get paid overtime?
- No, because I'm not on an hourly contract. But when I'm away overnight, I get an allowance for unsocial hours.

d – I'm really enjoying my new supervisor role. And I think the team is doing well – we've been meeting our targets …
- Yes, you are doing a good job.
- Thanks – so when would be a good time to review my salary? When I accepted the extra responsibilities, you said we'd review my package after the trial period.
- Yes I know, but I'm afraid this is not a good time.
- Oh, I see … So what would you advise? I'm very happy to do the work, but I feel the company should recognise my contribution.
- I agree – but right now a pay demand is very unlikely to succeed.
- So, what would you suggest?
- Look … put your request in writing, and I'll see what I can do.

3 Listening

Speaker 1

I get paid on a monthly basis in arrears – normally a week before the end of each month. It's quite a large salary, and so I don't get paid for overtime, etc. But that … well, my salary is … includes what I would consider a payment for that overtime. I'm also benefiting from a non-contributory company pension. They also fully finance my car, everything bar petrol from home to work. Paid holidays, I get 20 days but in keeping with my job, time is slightly more flexible and you can accrue days off because of the amount of extra hours you do during the weekends, etc. We do have sports facilities; we don't have sports facilities on-site, but we are provided with discounts for certain sports centres in the area – although I don't actually choose to take up that option. The major perk I get in my job is a company car, which, as I say, is fully financed by the company.

Speaker 2
I'm a consulting engineer … mainly involved in the domestic house market. Er … generally speaking, we're rewarded for our work in the form of fees which are sometimes based on an hourly rate. Alternatively, we can agree a fixed fee with the client prior to the work being carried out and then we are paid that, either in one full payment at the … when the work is completed, or sometimes, if the work goes on for a very long time, we can be paid in a number of stages.

UNIT 14 Personal and company finances

1 Core practice

a We performed reasonably well – sales rose by 7% and we met our sales targets in all our key markets. We also achieved our quality targets in most areas. But unfortunately our financial results were a bit disappointing. We're in a very competitive field, and our margins were hit by price cuts. In addition, earlier in the year we had to pay higher-than-expected interest charges, which had an effect on the bottom line. And then in the last quarter we had to write off a bad debt when a customer went into liquidation.

b As a rough guide, I'd say last year our day-to-day living expenses came to around $3,000 a month altogether. I suppose about half of that went on the basics – I'm not sure where the rest went! I think we must have been spending more than usual on entertaining. I know from my credit card statements that our expenditure on vacations amounted to $7,000 in all. We should really cut back on that, but we're a large family and it's not easy. And, of course, all that's on top of the usual fixed outgoings like mortgage, pension, local tax and so on. I can't really break the figures down for you – my wife keeps the accounts.

c Our main asset is our house, which hasn't increased in value much during the past year but at least the value hasn't fallen. At the moment the signs are that the housing market is improving gradually, thank goodness. In June we had rather a setback when my husband was made redundant but he did receive a lump sum payment, which we put into government bonds. Er … what else? Well, we traded in our car for an up-to-date model.

d – We try to keep our overheads down to 25% of sales. That's been difficult in the last year because our core management costs are up by 4%, mainly because we've been in a period of reorganisation. We're moving into franchising, and we've been setting up a new franchise division, which has involved us in a number of one-off reorganisation costs. But these developments haven't yet led to an increase in turnover.
   – Can you tell me what your fixed costs came to overall?
   – I'm afraid I don't have the exact figure in my head. I should have brought a copy of our accounts with me.

3 Listening

Caffè Nero today revealed that not only has it avoided the downward trend in consumer spending, it has also exceeded analysts' forecasts as its sales for the financial year to the end of May rose 7.5% on a same-store basis. A spokesperson for the 230 coffee houses went further, saying that in June, July and August – when other retailers really began to feel the effect of slower consumer spending – its sales were up by 34%. Nero plans to open a further 25 cafés by the end of its current financial year next May. It opened 52 last year.

Chairman and chief executive Gerry Ford said: 'Caffè Nero is going to have another strong year. Much like last year, all the main ingredients remain in place for us to excel – a thriving retail coffee market, a favourable retail property environment with extensive availability of sites at reasonable prices, a coffee brand highly rated by UK consumers, and self-generated funds sufficient to finance the group's growth.' He added that the group now generates as much cash as it spends on expansion and has €5.9 million in the bank.

UNIT 15 Managing credit

1 Core practice

a – I'm calling about our invoice number AK-40 7/AZ for €450.
   – How can I help you?
   – According to our records, we haven't received payment. And it was due on the 15th.
   – Let me get the details on screen. According to this, the invoice was passed for payment ten days ago. You should have received the money by now.
   – Well, we haven't received anything.
   – I'm sorry about this. Let me look into it – I'll call you back.

b – You've come through to Customer Service because your account is overdue and there's a bar on your phone.
   – But this is a company phone. My company pays the bill.
   – I'm afraid the account is overdue.
   – Really? So, how can we sort this out?
   – You need to talk to your accounts department and …
   – But there won't be anyone there at this time and I need to use the phone.
   – The only thing I can suggest is that you make a payment now and sort it out with them later.
   – I hope this isn't going to affect my credit record.

c – My card's just been declined; I'd like to know what's going on?
   – Yes, there've been some unusual transactions on your account and the automatic fraud protection is blocking your card. Can I ask what payments you have made today?
   – I haven't made any. I had to use another card.
   – Well, there have been some sizeable withdrawals.
   – Can you give me the details?
   – 500 and 200 this morning, 700 last night.
   – Oh no! Do you know when or where?
   – No, that's not on here yet.
   – So what do I do?
   – I'll cancel the card and order a new one, and you should call our fraud line as soon as possible. I'll give you the number.

d – So, how do I protect myself from ID theft?
   – There are a number of things you can do to reduce the risk. Do you have a shredder?
   – Yes, but I only use it for confidential documents.
   – Well you need to use it more than that. If they have your name and address they can find out your previous address, your date of birth, details of your parents.
   – Does that mean I shouldn't give people my business card?
   – Well, you need to make sure you know who they are. And very important – you must put your name on the anti-fraud register.

3 Listening

– Kolmex Conference Centre. Diana Fry speaking. How can I help you?
– Oh hello, it's Solo Associates here, part of the AFC group. John Mars speaking. As you know, we had a sales conference at your place in May and I've got what looks like an invoice here for accommodation. I passed it to our parent company in Belgium and they've written back to say that in fact this was paid by our sales manager at the time. Can I give you the details that are written on it?
– Yes, please. There should be a reference number in the top right-hand corner.
– Oh, oh yes, there is, but it isn't very clear. It's 123 stroke 321, reference 'Sonya'.
– Fine. It seems we've sent you a duplicate invoice by mistake. I'm very sorry. Could you send it back to us so I can check it?
– Yes, of course, but the problem is that the person in charge of purchasing here tells me that she has also paid this to you, so it seems that you have been paid twice for one invoice.
– Look, it seems there's been an administrative mix-up. Please send us the invoice which you have there and we'll sort it out. I'm sorry about any inconvenience this has caused you.

UNIT 16 Time management

1 Core practice

a – This company is very keen on training – so, I've recently been on a time management course.
– Was it useful?
– Well, you know, on these courses you usually don't learn anything you don't already know. What they do is remind you of the techniques you should be using anyway.
– So what did the course focus on?
– How to establish priorities, how to handle interruptions, the importance of delegating. All useful points.

b – I'd say I have a fairly high-pressure job. It's rewarding but we're under a lot of pressure. The secret is to stay calm and to have clear aims – you have to prioritise. However many interruptions there are, I try to do the important things first. I'm fortunate because I have a good assistant who screens my calls and handles routine matters. The phone would take up the whole day, if I let it. But the biggest time-waster, in my experience, is meetings. I now insist on an agenda, and if I'm in the chair I set time limits for each item. I like the job, but it's very demanding; I have to keep on top of it, otherwise it's a nightmare.

c – Look, I'm afraid we're having problems meeting the deadline on that consignment of water-filter parts for you. I know time is critical at your end.
– It is. What's the problem?
– I'm afraid because the changes in specification have caused more problems than we expected. We're not going to be able to complete on time.
– Well, that leaves us with a big problem – we have an export order to meet.
– I know, I'm sorry. I'm calling to see if we can work something out.

d – I think the course would benefit my work – not just my work but the department as a whole. RTL Training has a good reputation. Its courses are supposed to be good.
– What's our schedule like at the moment?
– Not too bad; we've just finished stock-taking. I thought it might be a good time.

– Well, it's OK by me providing you can get someone to cover for you. Ask HR to check it out, especially the cost; it'll come out of my training budget.

3 Listening

– What do you do to prepare for a successful meeting?
– Well it is a very interesting question because, of course, we need to make meetings as efficient and effective as possible because statistics show that 1% more of business people's time is spent in meetings each year. So how do we prepare for an effective meeting? And the essence of it is planning. And I quote you the old motto of 'Failing to plan is planning to fail'. So how do we plan for a meeting? We make sure, first of all, that everybody knows where it is, the sort of housekeeping details, where and when and ideally what time it is going to finish as well. The third thing is the agenda, a most important tool, but have we got too many things on the agenda? The fourth thing is, don't be tempted to include too many people in your meeting. Sometimes people want to just be in the meeting to be seen. Don't fall into that trap. Have the decision-makers and the people with the right information in that meeting. The other very important aspect is the chair person. Now it is no good just suggesting that somebody is the chair person; we have to make sure that that chair person has the experience and the authority with which to control that meeting. Otherwise we'll get somebody with a big mouth and lots of ideas and lots of enthusiasm taking over and the shrinking violets, shrinking into the corners and feeling that their time has basically been wasted. So that person with authority needs to stick to that agenda. There's a saying that goes with this: 'Be gracious with people, but be ruthless with time.'

UNIT 17 Delivering quality

1 Core practice

a – We find that many customers insist that suppliers have a quality certificate. You have to have one; if not, they won't deal with you. So from a marketing point of view, they're important.
– But they don't guarantee quality, do they?
– Not exactly. What they mean is that you've reviewed your systems and prepared a manual, and that you're keeping to the standards laid down. If you like, it shows that your systems are working properly.

b – We believe we have high production standards. Everyone in the company from top to bottom accepts the importance of quality in our work. We're always improving and updating our quality-check procedures. It's difficult for an American company to compete on price. Our main competitors tend to have a lower cost base, so generally our products sell at a slight premium. What we depend on is our reputation for excellence, not just of our products themselves, but also the aftersales service and so on.

c – Our best-selling product is a low-cost mouthwash called Aquarinse. We supply it direct to dentists – it's not available on the retail market. It's part of our range for the dental profession. We specialise in offering a complete 24-hour service. A dentist can call us at any time before 5.00pm and we guarantee next-day delivery. Our competitors may be able to beat us on price; some have particular lines that they claim are superior to ours, but none of them can offer the range and the service we offer. Our customers are prepared to pay a little extra in order to have the back up we provide.

d – A couple of months ago, we let a job go out that was below standard. Never again. What we should have done was re-run it, but we didn't. It was a rushed job that came in at the last minute – the customer had been let down by someone else. So they were screaming for it, and they told us to send it as it was, which we did in the end – because the customer is always right. But then the complaints started to come in and, of course, they blamed us. We lost an important account – and we didn't get paid. It was a lot of hassle for nothing.

3 Listening

INT = Interviewer
TSA = Technical Services Assistant
INT: Can you tell me something about what you do?
TSA: My official title is Technical Services Assistant and I deal basically with complaints, technical complaints and to a limited extent non-technical complaints.
INT: How does the system work exactly?
TSA: Well, basically we use our sales managers in the field to process complaints which are then handed on to me for technical evaluation. And then, after dealing with the technical evaluation … evaluation side of the complaint, I gain authority from my superior Charles Eden. And with this authority I then produce a credit note for the customer, in the case of justified complaints. If it's a one-off contract, I might have to organise a refund. That's about it.
INT: Um, what kind of record do you keep of complaints?
TSA: We produce a monthly report which tries to break down all the complaints into our process areas so that we can try to analyse them. Our major problems come from development work, some problems are inherent in the products and not produced by the machines or whatever.
INT: Can you give an example?
TSA: Well, when things go wrong it's often a design problem, not a quality control problem – there are design faults which need sorting out.
INT: So is quality assurance part of the technical department?
TSA: Yes, in a way – I actually work in the technical service department, which is just myself and Charles. Technical Service sits halfway between Quality Assurance and Research and Development.

UNIT 18 Working practices

1 Core practice

a – If your organisation is customer focused, the contacts and clients are well treated not out of politeness, but as part of your standard working practices. That's the situation in this company; in fact, were one of our customers to complain the person responsible would probably lose his or her job.
  – Do you maintain these standards in all areas?
  – We try to; we don't always succeed. At the moment our switchboard is letting us down a bit. We can't get the right kind of staff. It's a crucial job, but it's a bit repetitive.
b – Health and Safety comes under compliance. It's part of the Building Manager's job. He has to ensure that the regulations are properly applied – for example, that the fire alarms are tested regularly, that the evacuation procedures are clearly displayed – and he has to organise fire drills on a regular basis. He ensures we comply with all the legal requirements.

  – Who checks if they are being applied?
  – The inspectors do spot checks from time to time.
c – The atmosphere in my company is pretty easy going. The managers are all fairly young – the MD is only 36. The management style is generally informal; we all use first names and we have a dress-down policy. But they do expect you to pull your weight. The emphasis is on what works.
  – It wouldn't work in my business.
  – Why's that?
  – I'm a sales demonstrator with an estate agent. My bosses wouldn't want me to wear jeans, and neither would the customers; they expect us to be a bit traditional.
d – The main changes have been in the area of technology. I used to have an administrative assistant who worked with a number of us in a back-up capacity. Now we work on-line with terminals on our desks. We handle our own typing and filing. I have a few work-in-progress files, but most of our data is stored electronically. Another big change is that we no longer have agents or intermediaries – customers from around the world contact us direct, by email or phone. The connection is direct.
  – Do you have much flexitime or job sharing?
  – Yes, because we have a lot of women. But the main changes have been in the area of technology. We have to work harder and the pace is faster.

3 Listening

ERM = Employee Relations Manager
INT = Interviewer
INT: Could you tell me something about the style of management here at Alyces?
ERM: I think what we have tried to do here is to develop a distinctive Alyces style of management which is very open, informal, very flexible. French industry is sometimes troubled by industrial relations' problems. Some companies experienced difficulties and some of them went out of business because of these problems. But we've overcome that by having a very progressive style of management which, as I've said before, is very open and informal.
INT: And what about your relations with the unions?
ERM: Well, we have a very close cooperation with the staff Comité d'Enterprise – the equivalent to the staff committee. We try to involve them in the decision-making process.
INT: Does that mean you have a single-union agreement?
ERM: No, generally they don't exist in France; by law, companies with more than 50 employees must have a Comité d'Enterprise. These committees are elected by the workforce – and candidates are put forward by the national unions and there are also candidates who are not affiliated to any union.
INT: What about no-strike agreements?
ERM: Again, this type of agreement does not generally exist in France. All workers have the right to go on strike. This means that an agreement in advance not to strike would be illegal or non-legal.

UNIT 19 Advertising and promotion

1 Core practice

a – The draft report from the focus groups indicates that the main problem you face is that your potential customers

don't realise that what you provide is different from what they can get at the local supermarket.
– That's the conclusion we've come to.
– I think we should try a campaign based on radio ads. It's a low-cost medium, and the great thing is that we can target fairly closely, because we have a variety of radio stations with various listener profiles. Organised properly, the campaign should work.
– When will your report be circulated?
b – We sell a range of pre-packed frozen meals to the domestic market through retail outlets, and also to places like hospitals and canteens. For the domestic market we do promotions in shops and supermarkets, where we give away free samples and hand out information leaflets which have a tear-off, money-off-your-next-purchase section.
– Do you have anything promoting the brand?
– Yes, we have a glossy brochure that promotes the company as a whole, which has just been redesigned. And we have point-of-sale display posters.
c – In our business, reputation is crucial. We try to promote an image of quality and excellence. Whatever people spend, they don't want a piano that sounds cheap. So we do quite a lot of brand advertising, usually in upmarket lifestyle magazines. But it's expensive, and it's difficult to measure the results. More recently we've tended to concentrate more on special offers and one-off promotions in the musical press.
– Are you being advised by anyone?
– Yes, we are …
– Well, you should have been told this won't work if you want to reach a mass market.
– I know; we depend a lot on personal recommendation.
d – This is our company brochure; as you can see we're part of the Tango Group of companies.
– Can I take a copy?
– Yes, of course. What are you particularly interested in?
– I see you make micro pumps.
– Yes, it's an area we specialise in.
– Do you have a leaflet or something?
– Yes, here. These are the specifications for the standard C17 model – they give an idea of the products' capabilities. The price list is printed on the back.
– Umm … Considering what your competitors charge, these seem quite high.

3 Listening

Speaker 1: a computer software developer
The flexibility of our products is what makes a key selling point for us. And really that's because it allows us to deliver, as a whole package, solutions that meet business needs. And that's where the money's coming from and after all it's from the business user, not the IT department. And they want something competitive.

Speaker 2: a production director of a fork-lift truck manufacturer
We build a quality product with … high reliability, and this leads to improved profitability for the customer due to extremely low running costs.

Speaker 3: the manager of a fast-food chain
Key selling points of our product must be the nice environment in which you can sit and eat, the high standards of cleanliness, the friendliness of the staff – also, especially, the value for money. The staff are carefully chosen so they're nice, friendly, outgoing personalities that get on with people. As I say, the restaurant itself is maintained well. I mean, where else can you get a meal at this kind of price?

UNIT 20 Offers and orders

1 Core practice

a – We'd like to take you up on your offer; I'd just like to check the details. You quoted us £57.20 each.
– I'm afraid that was old stock – we now have the new stock in and the prices are higher.
– But we left it that we'd get back to you before the end of the month. You knew that when you gave us the quote.
– OK, fair enough; I can let you have them for £61 – I can't let you have them for less than that.
– £61; it's still a big increase.
– How many are you taking?
– Seven.
– OK, look, I'll tell you what I'll do – we're offering a quantity discount on this one. If you take ten, I can reduce the price to £58.
b – There seems to be an error in your invoice. You quoted us $9 per hundred, but you've charged us $13 per hundred.
– Our quote was subject to the costs of raw materials. As you know, paper is up by 19% since the beginning of the month. That's why our margins are very tight – we've had to put our prices up.
– But this was all agreed at the time. We've quoted our clients on the basis of the price you gave us.
– Well, all our quotes are subject to market variations. In our terms of trade, it says that we can increase prices without notice.
c – We're hiring 30 plasma screens from you and they're due to be delivered on Friday. I'm just ringing to see if I can increase to 35 screens and include glare filters.
– Let me just check if the courier has gone. No, apparently your order still being loaded. It should be OK. I'd better check with the warehouse if they have them in stock. If they haven't, I'll call you back immediately.
– OK thanks. Will they be at the same price?
– No that was a special offer – you got 15% off.
– Isn't it all part of the same order?
d – I'm afraid the job isn't going to be ready till Friday.
– But you said you'd be able to meet the deadline.
– Yes, I'm sorry …
– We made it clear that time is critical on this; our instructions seem to have been ignored.
– We are giving the job absolute priority. The reason for the delay is that the materials were late reaching us – there was a hold up at your end …
– OK. Er … can you send any of it on Wednesday?
– Yes, we can batch through about 25%. You can track the order on-line.
– OK.
– Just go to our website and click on 'My Order Status'.

3 Listening

a – Hello.
– Hello Sara. I'm just ringing to confirm that I've spoken to Kelly Mateja at TYH.
– Yeah.
– He said that we've got the 23 unit order for the HGF21s. I've checked the stock situation, and we only have 11 units ready. Fortunately, Karl has 12 in the warehouse. So we can do it, just.
– That's lucky.
– Yes it is, but I'm expecting another order for ten pieces next month, so we'll have to look at our production schedules.
– When do they want delivery?
– The week commencing the 26th.

- That's OK.
- Yes, that's fine, but there isn't much cushion.
b – Hello.
- Hello Donna. Just to let you know what's happening with the Rebal order. Apparently their buyer isn't happy with the initial delivery and is threatening to cancel the whole deal. I've offered to send one of our technical people over tomorrow morning at our expense, and this seemed to calm him down a bit.
- Do you know what the problem is?
- Something to do with the weight specifications being wrong. I'm sure that we did what was ordered, but anyway we'll find out tomorrow.
- Assuming that everything works out OK, is final delivery still set for the end of August?
- Yes. Let's keep our fingers crossed.

UNIT 21 Customer care

1 Core practice

a – We claim to put the customer first, but all it really amounts to is being polite on the telephone and when dealing with clients face to face. The organisation isn't customer focused in the real sense because we don't give customers what they want.
- And what's that?
- They want two things: an efficient service at a competitive price. So the way we can become more customer focused is to listen to what they want and provide it. Dissatisfied customers don't complain; they just go somewhere else. I read that attracting new customers can cost four times as much as retaining them.
b – I've had a lot of trouble getting through to you. Your call centre wouldn't put me through.
- I'm sorry, we've been very busy this morning. If you'll explain the problem, I'll see what I can do.
- OK – well, we are having problems with our C224 sorting machine. It keeps stopping. It makes a funny noise, then cuts out.
- It sounds as if it's overheating. Do you have a service contract?
- It's still under warranty. According to the contract, the call-out time is supposed to be two hours. We're very unhappy about the way we're being treated.
- I completely understand and I apologise. Leave it with me; I'll get a technician out to you immediately.
c – I was thinking of giving Marnix Busko tickets for the Cup Final.
- That's a good idea.
- He's an excellent customer. And he recommends us to other people; he brings in a lot of business. I think we need to show our appreciation.
- I agree, but we don't have a budget for entertaining.
- But the company spends a fortune on corporate entertaining. Couldn't we make a case and get the funding?
- We can try, I suppose.
- They want us to build the business – it's a legitimate expense!
d – I bought this bag a couple of days ago, and look, it's split.
- Have you got the receipt?
- Yes, here it is.
- We can get it fixed for you but …
- Would that be under the guarantee?
- Not really – the guarantee doesn't cover heavy use.
- But it's falling apart. I'd like my money back.

- Well, I can't give you a refund. This isn't the result of normal wear and tear – it's torn.
- Look, when I bought it, I was assured it was a tough, all-purpose bag. I didn't get what I paid for.
- OK, I'll tell you what I'll do … I'll send it to our laboratory for analysis, and if they say it's a design fault or there's something wrong with the material, I'll give you your money back. It's the best I can do.

3 Listening

Speaker 1

In Japan every company makes efforts to provide a better service for customers, so that normally we get very good service in Japan. For example, the working hours – if we go to a Japanese shop just before closing time, they will of course extend their working hours. But in London they don't like to do that; they just close the shop. They say: 'Come back later on, or tomorrow.' This is not good in customer relations. In Japan we believe the customer is always right. And staff in shops and in hotels are very, very polite. There are silent languages between customers and shop staff, you know. And a good sales clerk understands what customers need very quickly because he understands this kind of non-verbal language.

Speaker 2

Occasionally we do have major problems getting our books to the right people at the … at the right time. So we have to have an ongoing programme of good customer relations. Er … this means going out with … major suppliers, talking to them about their problems, seeing what we can do to assist them. It also means a certain amount of market research with students and teachers who use our books. So we try to find out on an ongoing basis what basically keeps them happy. Now sometimes we do actually budget for this, we have … what's called an entertainment and travel allowance. And when we go round visiting various people, obviously we take them out to lunch, we take them out to dinner, we occasionally arrange receptions, we occasionally arrange seminars. So there is quite a lot of corporate PR that goes into keeping people happy.

UNIT 22 Home and family

1 Core practice

a – We live in a modern apartment block; we're on the second floor. It's in a quiet neighbourhood. We have a fine view over the city.
- Do you own the apartment?
- No, we're renting because we're not sure how long we're going to be here – we have a three-year lease. But we're very pleased with the area. The facilities are excellent. There's a good golf course, and a swimming pool. And, of course, we're only 20 minutes from the mountains.
- What about parking?
- There's parking in the basement.
b We both work. The alarm goes off just before six and I make an effort to get up by about quarter past. I very often get back late, so I try to see the children in the morning. They are all old enough to look after themselves. But I try and have breakfast with them all the same. My wife's mother lives with us, so my wife has to make sure she's OK. We leave the house around 7.30, and drop the children off at school on the way to the station. My commute is about 45 minutes.
c – In this you can see the house where we live. In the front there you can see my wife.

- Is it a recent picture?
- Yep, it was taken last year.
- So your step-daughters are quite young.
- Yeah, they're five and seven. This picture here is of my father – that was his 63rd birthday party.
- Is that your mother?
- Uhmm …
- You don't resemble them at all, do you?
- No, but my brothers and sisters are all very similar to each other. It's funny.

d – I'm living in a company apartment at the moment. It's only a temporary arrangement, till I find a place of my own.
- Do you have a flat mate? I'm actually sharing with a colleague who is in the same situation as me.
- Did you know each other before?
- He's a friend of my sister's but I didn't know him before. We get along fine. We don't do much housework, but then the apartment is fully serviced so there's not a lot to do. I'm away on business every other week. It suits us very well because we're both on our own.

3 Listening

Speaker 1
This is a photograph of when we were on holiday a couple of years ago, in South Africa, where I was brought up as a child. And we were staying at this time with my brother and his wife who have a very small cottage. That's my sister-in-law, my brother is just behind her, … she is called Elizabeth, or more correctly, she is called Elizabet because she in fact comes from Denmark.

Speaker 2 (in conversation)
- That is actually my entire family, including my father who died … umm … but otherwise they are all still around who are on this picture.
- How long ago did your father die?
- This was seven years ago, so that picture was taken eight years ago. As you can see … umm … Raffi still is quite young. And Hannah is here … and she must have been at the time about eight … eight years old … nine. And Raffi was … umm … five, four or five.

Speaker 3
I've got four children. I'm there with my husband and all the children, and my brother-in-law is married to a … to a Scottish girl and they have three children. We've just finished the walk and we are coming back down just towards the car.

UNIT 23 Work / life balance

1 Core practice

a – My job is quite demanding. I try to get home in time to say 'good night' to my children. And when I'm away on business, I always call to keep in contact. To be honest, I find it difficult to get the right balance between my domestic and my work commitments. A lot of the time I get it wrong. But the fact is that I have to provide an income and if I don't do the job properly, they'll get someone else. So my wife has to handle many of the domestic demands single-handed.
- Does she accept that?
- Up to a point. She doesn't really agree with it, but it's easier for me to earn on a regular basis.

b – What I like best is meeting up with some friends and going out to a restaurant, or having them round for dinner. Of the two, I'd much rather eat out than

entertain at home because it's far more relaxing and it's a lot less hassle. During the week my socialising is really confined to work obligations – entertaining clients, going to official receptions and so on. Sometimes, I get to take a client to the opera. I'd love to go more often but the tickets cost a fortune.

c – Hey, Maria! We must get together for a meal or something.
- Yes, that would be nice.
- Well, how about this weekend?
- That sounds good.
- Which would suit you better, Friday or Saturday?
- Er … let me check – Saturday would be better for me.
- What sort of time?
- How about 7.30?
- Right, I'll look forward to that. Shall I see if I can get tickets for the new production at the National Theatre?

d – Saturday is a day for family and shopping – it's mainly a practical day. In the evening we might go to a film.
- What about babysitting?
- Our neighbour's daughter usually babysits for us.
- And Sunday?
- For me it's a time to relax and spend time with my family. We usually do something together. If the weather's bad, we might watch a film on television. If it's good, we might all go for a walk in the park which is fun and it helps me unwind.
- Do you ever take work home?
- Not if I can avoid it. I'll work late during the week rather than work over the weekend.

5 Feature

- Do you often go through an entire weekend without spending any time on work brought home from the office?
- Not that often. I tend to work on Sunday evenings, after the kids go to bed.
- Do events at work sometimes force you to miss occasions at home that your family have particularly asked you to get back for?
- No, my work tends to be flexible enough. I mean if I have … a sick nanny or something, I can usually get home, so … no I tend not to, I mean.
- Do you ever dream about work problems?
- Oh, all the time. I never not dream about work problems.
- Do you have at least three significant leisure interests that have nothing to do with your work?
- I don't think so. I don't think that I've ever been very good on hobbies, to tell you the truth. I think I've been working … I started working part time when I was 16, and … not that I had to … I didn't come from a terribly poor family or anything. There was kind of just … a work ethic.
- When you are ill, do you take work to bed with you?
- Umm … I'm not ill very often.
- Do you find it easier to talk to work colleagues than to your partner and friends?
- Well it depends what (we're) talking about, you know. Umm … I'm afraid … I mean … my work is very emotional and very intense, so in fact I bring a lot of the conversation home, and go on talking at home, and I am very lucky that … um … John, my partner, is terrifically tolerant and so he allows me to continue the conversation.
- How unusual is it for you to ring home and say that you are going to be back later than you had planned?
- Quite often I do that, I'm afraid. I quite often ring home.
- Have you ever had to cancel a holiday due to pressure of work?
- Very nearly. I never, but very nearly.

- When you are trying to read a book or a magazine for pleasure, do you find that your mind keeps wandering back to work problems?
- I don't think so, no I think I can switch off.
- Do you like to meet new people who have nothing whatever to do with your line of business?
- Not particularly, I mean, yes and no. I mean, I don't, I think, I am incredibly lucky with my business is that … in a sense … everything can fit into the business and … publishing gives one such an entree into so many interesting people, so actually I think I would use my work to meet interesting people rather than … try and avoid them.

UNIT 24 Getting away

1 Core practice

a – I want to get away for a few days, preferably somewhere warm.
   – Where to?
   – I don't mind really. I'll take whatever you've got.
   – Well, what about Rhodes? I have a special off-season break which includes flight and accommodation.
   – Are there any hidden extras?
   – Well, airport tax is extra, of course. In spite of that, it's very good value.

b – I was there last summer.
   – How long for?
   – Two weeks. The climate is great, although it can be chilly at night. They've got some wonderful unspoilt beaches. It's best to go in April before the high season.
   – Where were you?
   – Near Wichuchu, on the south island.
   – What are the people like?
   – They're a bit reserved. Even so, it's a good place to unwind. The lifestyle is very easy going.
   – What about formalities? Do you need a visa?
   – Yes, you do. And you need various jabs. Whatever you do, don't drink the water. My partner was ill …

c – I want to get to the Imperial Palace. According to this guide it's just outside Fulong.
   – Yes, it's slightly beyond Fulong. It's on the road towards Gretik. The best way to get there is by car.
   – Is it possible to go by public transport?
   – Yes, but it involves a few changes.
   – Could you write down the directions for me?
   – Yes, of course. I'd advise you not to use an unlicensed taxi.

d – I have to get back to my office.
   – When by?
   – Well, as soon as possible really. Where can I change my travel arrangements?
   – Are you booked on a regular flight?
   – No, it's a special package.
   – I think you'll have to upgrade your ticket. You really need to go to a travel bureau.
   – Is there one within walking distance?
   – There's one in the parade of shops just under the hotel.

3 Listening

Speaker 1

I like some time to sort of unwind and relax and laze around, and think about things. I like some time to read and I like something good to be able to go and look at, something kind of cultural if possible. I also like to get some kind of physical exercise like swimming or riding or something like that. I think my favourite place to go on holiday, of course, is Australia, because that combines all these things … usually if you go round Christmas time it is the summer, so it is nice and warm.

Speaker 2

I like to go to the seaside, especially the Mediterranean seaside of France and Italy. And … one of the things that I like to do when I'm on holiday, believe it or not, is I work. I bring my work along with me, I sit on the beach and read the things that I have to do. I like my work so I don't like to be away from it. I like to keep thinking about it, so I typically work in the morning and then in the afternoon I will usually have fun.

Speaker 3

My favourite place is Goa where it is … where it is so relaxed. I mean, even though I originate from Goa, the people are so relaxed and so friendly. The main thing is … it has sand, sea and sun. And that … with the traditional food … makes Goa an idyllic place to unwind.

UNIT 25 Politics and business

1 Core practice

a – We have very good relations with our neighbours most of the time. The one problematic area at the moment concerns fishing rights. Our government has set a ten-mile zone round the coast but this zone is not being respected.
   – But you say relations are still good.
   – They are. I am sure the fishing issue will be resolved. Otherwise things run very smoothly. They announced on the news recently that we are even considering a new trade agreement.

b – Government policies are having a disastrous effect on our business. We're a logistics company and a large part of our business is transporting livestock. The government has recently imposed strict restrictions on the distances that we can take the animals by road and some of our customers are thinking of using rail transport instead.
   – What is the reason for the government policy?
   – No good reason. There are a lot of pressure groups who have been trying to stop the trade in animals. They say it's cruel and propose that it's banned. I think they should hold a referendum on the issue.

c – The current government is a coalition between parties of the left and centre. It's actually a minority government and it could fall at any time.
   – What's the alternative?
   – Good question. We have so many parties and so many interests that I don't think we will ever have a strong government. I reckon that if this government is defeated, we will simply get another weak coalition. At the same time, I'm not in favour of changing the voting system.
   – Why not?

d – It's very difficult to predict who will win the next election. Nevertheless, I would say the National Democrats have a good chance. There's been a strong swing to the right, especially since the scandal involving the socialist defence minister.
   – Yes, I suppose that might make a difference. Alternatively people may just forget about it. I really don't think the country will elect a right-wing government this time.

3 Listening

An interview with Kathleen Kelly Reardon (KKR)

Int: What skills are necessary to win at office politics?

KKR: Learning to observe. Make a science of observing people who do well in your organisation. Look for contradictions between what's supposedly going on and what actually is. Train yourself to generate options when confronted by a problem. By staying on your toes, you keep others off balance. When in doubt about anything, ask some questions.

Int: If you put your foot in your mouth in a meeting with your boss, what's the best first step toward repairing relations?

KKR: Send a brief memo describing what you actually meant to say. While you don't want to overdo the apology, it's better to acknowledge your mistake than to leave the impression that you didn't even notice it. Everyone makes mistakes. It takes class to own up to them.

Int: What three actions top your list for the worst moves to make politically?

KKR: Trusting your assumptions. Being predictable. Winning at all costs.

(From *American Airlines Magazine*; the part of Ms Reardon is spoken by an actor.)

UNIT 26 Taxation

1 Core practice

a – As far as I know, to reclaim sales tax you have to show your passport when you buy goods and fill in a form. You take the form to the airport where they have an office which refunds the sales tax. As an alternative, you can buy things in the duty free shops. Is that the same system in your country?
– More or less, I think. It's not really my area.

b – I think the income tax system in this country is pretty fair. Twenty years ago the top rates were high. Now they're down to between 35% and 45%, depending on what allowances you're entitled to.
– What about company taxes?
– Basic corporation tax is currently 25%, and on top of that local taxes are high in this area. Three years ago the government announced it was going to cut the rate to 15%, but it didn't happen.
– So how much does a middle manager on an average salary pay in tax?

c – There are a number of share schemes that are an efficient way of avoiding tax. If you keep money in these schemes for a number of years, you can take your profits tax free. Then, of course, pension schemes are also a good investment. You can set the total value of the money you pay into a pension scheme against tax. It's very tax efficient.
– What about investment in property?
– It depends on the way the property market is going. You have to pay capital gains tax on any substantial profits. Generally, we get tax relief on gains under £30,000; that's about $52,000.

d – Tax evasion is a problem, but companies have to be above board. Everything must be properly accounted for; invoices must be produced, documentation checked, etc.
– Look, I'm not an expert but I don't believe all companies are angels. An accountant was telling me about a client of hers who claimed that some huge oil tanks were full. The following day she checked and there was nothing in them. The client insisted it was just a misunderstanding, but a couple of days later he admitted he'd sold the oil and banked the money – tax free.

3 Listening

Speaker 1
We didn't see why we should pass so much over to the taxman after our father died. There's no justice in that.

Speaker 2
We couldn't believe it. We were expecting a routine tax inspection, but they went through the accounts with a fine toothcomb – then presented us with a colossal bill. Obviously there'd been some gross misunderstanding, because they soon capitulated – after our accountants had sorted it out.

Speaker 3
I bought some shares, paying far less than I had expected to pay, yet my partner didn't lose anything. I'm not quite sure how the accountants sorted it out, but I was very happy about it.

Speaker 4
Basically, what they did was to provide us with an excellent new pension and bonus scheme with drastically reduced tax liability.

Speaker 5
We appealed against the assessment, and to our amazement we didn't have to pay anything.

UNIT 27 Legal matters

1 Core practice

a – We had to go to court over a patent issue.
– What happened?
– One of our salesmen was at an exhibition and he saw an exact replica of our BJI moulding machine. We put the matter in the hands of our agent in the country concerned and he took legal action against the firm.
– How did it turn out?
– Very well. We won the case. Their stock was seized and we were awarded substantial compensation. The court ordered them to give various undertakings and to sign guarantees for the future.

b – Are you prepared to consider arbitration?
– Look, the last thing we want is a lengthy court case. Our lawyers have advised us it wouldn't be worth going to court in this case.
– So why are you threatening them with legal proceedings if they don't pay up within seven days?
– Because that's the way we always handle matters like this. Sending a final demand notice is standard procedure for us. They'll pay up, but not until the last minute – you have to take a firm line.

c – I got a call regarding T2 Chemicals.
– The company that owes us for the shipment to Nigeria?
– Yes – apparently they had to call the receivers in.
– Oh … I knew they were having problems but I didn't realise it was that serious.
– Why haven't we been notified – we're a creditor?
– I thought it was required by law.
– By law I'm entitled to four weeks' annual holiday. That doesn't mean I get it.

d – I don't think this document is very clear.
– You're right – the layout is a bit of a mess. First the heading needs to be in bold, and I suggest that we delete the third line of the second paragraph. That's the sentence beginning 'Receipts make it clear'.
– Why is the word 'faulty' in inverted commas, three lines further down?

- I don't know. Let's take them out. And the logo needs to go in the top left-hand corner.
- Yes, did you run it through the spellcheck?
- Not yet. I'll do that now.
- Could you let me have a hard copy?

3 Listening

Many people will have been amazed that Harvard Medical School is actually encouraging doctors to apologise for medical errors. Are they mad? Surely that will just play into the hands of greedy trial lawyers? Conventional wisdom would suggest as much, but a policy of saying sorry has in fact been shown to reduce lawsuits and liability costs in hospitals across America. The first hospital formally to implement it was the Lexington VA in Kentucky. The hospital had been stung by two multi-million-dollar lawsuits, but after introducing the apology policy, its average malpractice payouts fell to $16,000. Other hospitals have likewise reported positive results from adopting this approach with people. They have all found that when doctors apologised for errors and offer a fair compensation, cases are settled quickly and reasonably. What's more, they have found that dropping their defensive posture also leads less people to bring unjustified malpractice cases against doctors.

(From *The Week*; Doug Wojcieszak's words are spoken by an actor.)

UNIT 28 Planning

1 Core practice

a – It was a pilot, wasn't it?
   – Yes. The purpose of the project was to organise a pilot scheme to test a new cash card. This was organised in three phases. Stage one was preparing the cards and making them look right. Stage two was signing up local suppliers and retailers in the area. The next stage was the promotion of the scheme in the local community. The first phases went pretty well; everything went according to plan. But then we had a couple of setbacks – there were problems with the technology, so the card was late. And some of the suppliers withdrew from the programme. So the start date had to be put back.
   – That led to other problems, didn't it?
   – Yes, it did – and a lot of confusion.
   – You haven't started yet, have you?
   – No.
b – At the moment we are involved in background analysis of the market, and research into the state of the art – which will help to show us which direction we should go in. Then we will develop the individual components for the system. After that, the components will be assembled and we will build a laboratory prototype. This will then be site-tested in a field study. And our role at every stage in the process is to coordinate the work …
   – It's mainly a trouble-shooting role isn't it?
   – Yes.
c – In the end the project was abandoned. It's a pity, really, because the feasibility studies were very encouraging. Looking back, I think the biggest mistake was not having proper contingency plans. There are often hold-ups with this kind of project. You have to be ready for them. You need a plan 'b'.
d – There's some junk mail which I want to look through before I throw it out. Most of it isn't urgent. Er, these documents relate to a court case I'm involved in. At the moment the ball's in their court – so no action is required from me. And this is a tax return – I'm waiting for information from my accountant. That's quite

important. What's this? Oh, I'd forgotten about that. I'd better make a 'to do' list, and promise …

3 Listening

We started with the concept of an automatic waste-sorting system. At the moment we have semi-automated systems – where workers identify objects on a screen and mark them on a touch-screen for sorting, and a robot then collects them, or removes them. And the aim of this project is to create a fully automated system, where the recognition and identification functions, which are manual at the moment, are done automatically. So, the first step was to create a consortium of different companies who are interested in the idea and can work together on the project. At the same time, we put in an application to the EU for funds for research and development. We talked to a number of companies who we thought might be interested, and the companies that were interested were invited to a special workshop. The main purpose of this event was to break the project down into a number of single-work packages, and then to define those packages so that the end result of each package is the starting point for the next package. And we also broke the packages down into sub-tasks. We planned the whole project in such a way that when all the work packages have been completed, the end result will be an automatic sorting system. The next step in the planning process was to decide who was responsible for each package, and who the participants have to pass results to. And finally, we established a timetable, and planned milestone meetings. We defined what should be achieved by each point. And then the project was ready to start.

UNIT 29 Work in progress

1 Core practice

a – What's the position on OK Cosmetics?
   – My information is that they've achieved most of their targets for the current period. They've had one or two problems in connection with their plans to reduce the amount of packaging they use. There was a lot of resistance from retailers, who like beauty products to be expensively packaged. I gather the scheme has fallen badly behind schedule.
   – Do you know when it'll be completed?
   – No, I don't have a date for that.
b – The project involves installing a voice recognition security system on all the main entrances. It's going fairly smoothly. The current state of play is that the new doors are in place, all the wiring and the equipment have been fitted – at the moment the subcontractor is in the process of testing the computer program. The only hold up is that they're having trouble making appointments with staff members to record the voice samples. They're about a week behind schedule, so the change-over may be delayed a little.
   – Do you have a contingency plan for that?
c – When do you think you'll finish? There's a lot of pressure at this end.
   – Well, the fire officer wants automatic time switches fitted on the emergency lighting. That's something we hadn't planned for.
   – How long is that going to take?
   – It shouldn't take more than a couple of days.
   – And what's the position with regard to the fire escape?
   – That's now OK. We made the modifications and the inspector approved them.
d This table shows sales over the last five years, and you can see that although we're maintaining our market share there isn't much growth. That's on the dotted line there.

Now compare that with the red line here which indicates sales of electronic products. As you can see, the rate of increase is very substantial indeed. It's clearly an important growth area. If we put more resources into this market, there'll be a number of knock-on effects. I'll say more about those in a moment. Did you all get a copy of the overview I circulated? If you didn't, there's one in the folder in front of you.

3 Listening

Speaker 1: Martin Doyle, Managing Director of Software Systems Solutions, Dublin, talks about putting in-flight entertainment systems on board an Aer Lingus Airbus.

The project has … thankfully finished on time. There was a danger where we were going to have a slight overrun when the monitor for the computer system on board the aeroplane … didn't arrive on time. They sent in the wrong piece of software, and the monitor and the software just wouldn't talk to one another. But thankfully we sorted that one out. And we have spent extra hours working on the project, and … it will now be completed on time.

Speaker 2: Joanna Van Heynigen, a partner in Van Heynigen and Haward, an architectural practice, comments on progress with a new building in Oxford.

It's going well on site because the builder is good and really does want to get the building finished on time. But it … it is late – part of it's late and that'll probably mean that the whole job is late. The reason it's late is that there was a change in the specification of one of the roofing materials so he had to order it and the whole of the rest of the roof depends on this particular material arriving in time. So it's not really his fault … even though we'd quite like to think it was. It's the fact that we changed the specification. This will mean that the building will probably open two weeks late. And we've talked to the client about this and they're reasonably calm about it. If it was very much later than that, they would begin to panic, and then we'd have to … start letting the builder work at weekends and evenings.

UNIT 30 Feedback and review

1 Core practice

a – What's your overall feedback?
   – Well, speaking as someone who isn't used to studying, I thought the programme was very well planned and easy to use. I like the way the material was clearly laid out in the workbooks.
   – So on a scale of one to ten how would you rate the programme?
   – Oh I'd say it was definitely eight, maybe more.
   – Do you have any comments that would help with planning future courses? Any areas for improvement?
   – Yes, I think the briefing before the course was below the general standard.
   – So, you had some disappointments. What were your main achievements?
b – Are you satisfied with the progress you've made?
   – Well, yes and no; I'm disappointed I didn't meet my targets, but perhaps they were a bit unrealistic. I'd hoped to get through the Grade 3 test. The trouble is I had a lot of conflicting commitments at the time, so I missed quite a few of the classes, which in turn meant I wasn't ready to take the test. But they said I should pass next time – so I didn't do too badly bearing in mind all the distractions and so on. I did make some progress.

c – How was your course?
   – OK. Some people thought the content was a bit difficult. As far as I'm concerned it was more or less on the right lines. The content was relevant and I thought the teaching was really first class. My only criticism is that it was too classroom-based. I wanted to do extra work in my own time. To my mind we weren't given enough to do on our own.
   – What about the administration?
   – Basically everything was fine – except the accommodation, which frankly was absolutely awful.
d – Have you decided on your next steps?
   – Well, the first thing I need is a break. After that I think my next step will be to put what I've learned into practice, and use it, especially in work. I have a long list of action points.
   – Looking ahead, are you planning to do any other courses?
   – Yes, I'd like to attend a course on sales documentation, maybe sometime next year.

5 Listening

SM = Sales Manager
SR = Sales Rep

Excerpt 1
SM: I'd like to talk you through the points I've made in this appraisal form to make sure that everything is clear. We can discuss my comments as we go through. OK?
SR: Yes, that's fine.
SM: So, your first area of responsibility – I think you did well here, but of course there's room for improvement. The rating I've given you is B+. And the comment I've made is that you 'need to plan your appointments more carefully'. I think that's an important point, 'in order to maximise your effectiveness on the road'. And something we've talked about quite a bit – I've put that your 'reports should be more concise'. Does that seem fair to you?

Excerpt 2
SM: In the fourth area here, under 'additional comments' and 'areas of future interest', I made a note of the fact that you're keen to work in our export markets. That's true, isn't it?
SR: Yes, I'd very much like to be able to use my language skills in my work. It's one of my strong points. I'm fluent in Dutch and German, and I know we do a lot of business in those markets.
SM: Yes, that's certainly something for the future.

Excerpt 3
SM: So, now we come to the section for your comments …
SR: Well, I'm enjoying the job very much. It's true, it's taken me a little time to get used to the size of my area. I'm not used to handling so many accounts. So, I've had to change my approach to cope with the workload. The thing I've found most difficult is the report writing – there never seems to be enough time. As I said earlier, it would help a lot if I could have the use of a laptop, because then I could write on the road while the details are still fresh in my mind.

Grammar / language index

Glossary of business-related terms

absenteeism: being absent from work; this can include staying away from work for no good reason

actuary: person employed to calculate risk, usually for an insurance company

advertising agency: office that plans, prepares and manages advertising for companies

advertising campaign: campaign designed to promote a product, service or company

allowance: part of an income which is not taxed

APAC: abbreviation for the Asia and Pacific area

appraisal: a review of a staff member by his / her manager, usually done once a year

appropriation: act of putting money aside for a special purpose, e.g. appropriation of funds to the reserve

arbitration: settling of a dispute by an outside person, chosen by both sides

asset(s): thing(s) that belongs to a company or person, and that has a value

audit: n examination of the books and accounts of a company; **v** to examine the books and accounts of a company

back office: clerical personnel who provide support services for customer-facing front office staff

backlog: work that is waiting to be done

balance: sum remaining (on an account)

balance of payments: comparison between total receipts and payments arising from a country's international trade in goods, services and financial transactions

balance sheet: statement of the financial position of a company at a particular time

bankrupt: to be unable to pay your creditors and to have your assets managed by the Court; to go bankrupt (idiomatic: to go broke / bust)

benchmark: a measure of performance that can be used to assess other performances

black economy: goods and services which are paid for in cash and therefore not declared for tax

bonus: special payment to workers for good work or extra productivity

boom: time when business activity is increasing rapidly

bottom line: last line on a profit-and-loss account indicating the total profit or loss

boycott: n refusal to buy or to deal in certain products; **v** to refuse to buy or to deal in certain products

brand: the symbolic embodiment of all the information connected with a product or service, including the name and logo

brochure: a publicity booklet

bulk: large quantity of goods

bullet points: a list of points usually identified with dots or asterisks

business unit (BU): part of an organisation, often treated as a separate entity within the parent organisation

buy in: willing agreement or cooperation

capital costs: money spent on fixed assets (property, etc.)

cartel: group of companies that try to fix the price or to regulate the supply of a product for their own profit

cashflow: cash which comes into a company from sales, or the money which goes out in purchases or overhead expenditure

casting vote: deciding vote usually by the chairperson

classified ads / advertisements: advertisers listed in a newspaper under special headings, e.g. jobs wanted

closed shop: system where a company agrees to employ only union members in certain jobs

commission: 1 money paid to a salesperson or agent, usually a percentage of the sales made; **2** group of people officially appointed to examine a specific problem

compliance: fully meeting the requirements of the laws, rules and regulations that apply

consignment: (generally) a delivery of goods, (technically) goods sent to someone who will sell them for you

consortium: group of companies which work together on a particular project

consumer research: research into why customers buy goods and what goods they really want to buy

contingency plan: alternative plan that can be put into action if something goes wrong with the other plan

contract staff: staff employed to do a particular job for a company; these staff are not usually permanent

cost effective: producing the best results in relation to the costs incurred

cost of living: money spent on food, heating, rent, etc.

credit control: check that customers pay on time and do not owe more than their credit limit

credit limit: fixed amount which is the most a customer can owe on credit

credit rating: amount which a credit agency feels a customer should be allowed to borrow

current liabilities: debts that may be repayable within 12 months, e.g. bank overdraft

customer relationship management (CRM): covers all aspects of the relationship a company has with its customers, related to sales or service

customer services: a department that provides support to customers by answering enquiries, handling complaints, etc.

cutting-edge: technically very advanced, at the front edge of development

deadline: date by which something has to be done

deadlock: the two sides can't agree

delegation: 1 group of people who represent others at a meeting; **2** act of passing authority or responsibility to someone else

depreciation: reduction in the value of an asset; provision to write off the cost of a fixed asset, e.g. a machine

direct taxation: tax, such as income tax, which is paid direct to the government

discount: reduction, reduced charge

dividend: percentage of profits paid to shareholders

dotted line: indicates a second (usually lesser) reporting responsibility, e.g. *I have a dotted line to ...*

downsizing: reducing the number of people employed in a company to make it more profitable

dress codes: rules or guidelines that specify how an employee should dress, e.g. formal, smart, casual

earnings: money earned / total earnings

EMEA: abbreviation for Europe, Middle East, Africa

equal opportunities: strategies to ensure different sexes and races receive equal opportunities at work

exchange rate: price at which one currency is exchanged for another

expenditure: any money spent

feasibility study: e.g. to carry out a feasibility study = to carry out an examination of costs and profits to see if the project should be started

fixed assets: property or machinery which a company uses, but which it does not buy and sell as part of its regular trade

fixed costs: costs that do not vary with sales, e.g. rent

(a) flat: US English, an apartment

flat rate: charge which always stays the same

flexitime: system where workers can start or stop work at different hours, provided that they work a certain number of hours per day or week

flier: brief, one-sheet, low-cost advertisement, often put through doors, left on car windscreens, or handed out in the street to passers-by

focus group: small group of target customers employed to give their views on products / services

franchise: licence to trade using a brand name and paying a royalty for it

fraud: making money by making people believe something that is not true

freehold property: property which the owner holds permanently and does not pay rent for

front office: the customer-facing operations of a company such as customer service, customer support, call centres and sales

global: referring to the world economy and world markets

golden handshake: large, usually tax free, sum of money given to a senior employee who resigns from a company before the end of his / her service contract

gross: total or with no deductions, e.g. gross earnings = total earnings before tax and other deductions

gross profit: sales less direct cost of sales, e.g. manufacturing costs

guideline: suggestion as to how something should be done

handout: information in the form of a document that is handed out during a lecture

hard currency: currency of a country which has a strong economy and which can easily be changed into other currencies

head-hunter: person or company which finds senior staff and offers them jobs in other companies

human resources (HR): workers which a company has available (seen from the point of view of their skills and experience)

incentives: e.g. staff incentives = pay and better conditions offered to workers to make them work better

indirect taxation: tax, such as sales tax, which is paid to someone who then pays it to the government

industrial relations: relations between management and workers

inflation rate: percentage increase in prices over a 12-month period

infrastructure: e.g. a country's infrastructure = the road and rail systems of a country

in-house: working inside a company's building

insert: a sheet of advertising information that is put in something, usually a magazine

investment: placing of money so that it will increase in value and produce interest

invoice: n note asking for payment for goods or services supplied;
v to send an invoice to someone

job sharing: situation where two people share a job, each working part-time

junk mail: unsolicited advertising material sent through the post

lay-off: action of dismissing a worker for a time

leaflet: sheet of paper giving information that is used to advertise something

lease: written contract for letting or renting a building, land or equipment against the payment of rent

leasehold property: property held on a lease

liability: legal responsibility for damage or loss, etc.

liabilities: debts of a business or person; anything that is owed to someone else (see current liabilities)

liquidation: closing of a company and selling of its assets

live testing: testing a product or system in real conditions

logistics: the management of materials, parts, supplies and finished goods moving into and out of the business

mail order catalogue: catalogue from which a customer can order items, which are then sent by mail

mail shot: leaflets sent by mail to possible customers

mark-up: amount added to cost price to give the selling price

merger: joining together of two or more companies

message (advertising message): key idea that an advertisement aims to communicate

middle office: responsible for financial reporting, internal auditing, risk management; in smaller organisations the role is performed by the back office

milestone: a significant marker or point, e.g. *We have reached our milestone, so now we need a new target*

moonlighting: doing a second job for cash as well as a regular job

mortgage: agreement where someone borrows money to buy a property using the property as security, and repays by regular mortgage payments

natural wastage: loss of workers because they resign or retire, not through redundancy or dismissals

net: after all deductions have been made; e.g. net income

offset: to balance one thing against another so that they balance each other out

offshore: transfer parts of the business to a different country where costs are lower

outgoings: any money spent

outsource: obtain goods or services from an outside supplier; to contract work out; not sourcing internally

overheads: costs not directly related to producing goods / services, e.g. directors' salaries

overrun: to go beyond a limit, e.g. *We have overrun our time allocation, so will need to end this meeting now*

oversee: to supervise other workers

pay differentials: differences in pay between workers

payroll: 1 list of people employed and paid by a company;
2 money paid by a company in salaries

PDA: personal digital assistant, a hand-held digital organiser

PDP: personal development plan

perks: extra items given by a company to workers in addition to their salary

picket: n striking worker who stands at the gates of a factory to try to persuade other workers not to go to work;
v to put pickets at the gate of a factory

piloting stage: stage at which a project is tested on a small number of people to see if it will work in practice

plant: machinery or large factory

poster: large advertisement designed to be stuck on a wall

premium: 1 e.g. insurance premium = annual payment made by a person or a company to an insurance company;
2 e.g. to pay a premium = to pay extra

private enterprise: businesses which are owned by private shareholders, not by the state

privatisation: selling a nationalised company to private owners

procurement: action of buying equipment, materials or services for a company

productivity: rate of output per worker or per machine in a factory

profile: brief description giving the basic characteristics of, e.g., a particular market

profit margin: percentage difference between sales income and the cost of sales

profit and loss account: statement of a company's expenditure and income over a period of time, almost always one calendar year, showing whether the company has made a profit or loss

promote: to improve the image of a product by a sales campaign, advertising, etc.

purchase order: official order made out by a purchasing department

quality standard certificate: certificate awarded after inspection showing that a company and its products are of a sufficiently high standard

quantity discount: reduction given to customers who buy large quantities

receipts: any money received

receiver: government official who is appointed to run a company which is in financial difficulties, to pay off its debts as far as possible and to close it down

receivership: the state of being in the hands of a receiver

redundancy: the state of being no longer employed, because the job is no longer necessary

redundancy package: various benefits and payments given to a worker who is being made redundant

reimbursement: paying back money

relocate: to move to a different place

rep: representative, e.g. sales representative

retail: n sale of goods to the general public; **v** to sell goods direct to the public

return on investment (ROI): actual or perceived future value of an expense or investment

revenue(s): 1 money received as sales, commission, etc.; **2** money received by a government in tax

running costs: money spent on the day-to-day cost of keeping a business going

sale or return: the retailer pays only for the goods he / she sells, the rest are returned to the supplier

sales forecast: estimate of future sales

sales ledger: book in which sales to each customer are recorded

screen (to screen calls): to check or filter calls and then connect only the most important

service company: company which does not make products, but offers a service

shares in a company: documents that show the owner is a shareholder and entitled to a share of the profits (dividend)

shareholder: person who owns shares in a company

shift system / shift work: a system where one group of workers works for a period and is then replaced by another group

shop steward: elected trade union representative who reports workers' complaints to the management

slogan: words that can be remembered easily, often used in publicity for a product

slump: period of economic collapse and high unemployment

small print: the conditions of a contract, often printed in a very small typeface

sponsor: n person who pays money to help a business venture in return for advertising rights; **v** to pay money to help research or business development

stakeholder: anyone who has an interest in the project

statutory: fixed by law and therefore cannot be changed, e.g. a statutory holiday

subcontract: to employ another company to do work on a particular project

subordinate: member of staff who is directed by someone in a more senior position

subsidiary: company which is owned by a parent company

subsidy: 1 money given to help something which is not profitable; **2** money given by a government to make something cheaper

surcharge: extra charge

surplus: income less all deductions

tax avoidance: avoiding tax illegally

tax bracket: tax category

tax deductible: items that can be deducted from income before tax is calculated

tax efficient: an arrangement that results in a small liability for tax

tax evasion: trying illegally not to pay tax

tax exempt: free from tax

tax rebate: money paid in tax which is returned

tax relief: allowing someone not to pay tax on certain parts of his / her income

tax return: completed tax form, with details of income and allowances

time management: the organisation of time so that it is spent in the most efficient way

to-do list: a list of things that you have to do

TQM: total quality management; a management approach that focuses on customer satisfaction

trade agreement: agreement between countries on general items of trade

trade customers: customers who buy not for their personal use but for use in their business or for resale

trade fair: large exhibition organised for related companies to advertise and sell their products

transfer: 1 to move money from one place to another; **2** to move people or products to a new place

trouble-shooting: problem solving

turnover: total sales of a company, including goods and services

unsocial hours: working hours when most people are not at work, e.g. evenings and public holidays

user-friendly: which a user finds easy to use

variable costs: costs that rise and fall with sales, e.g. materials

warranty: a legal document which promises that a machine will work properly, e.g. *the 12-month warranty covers spare parts but not labour costs*

wholesale: buying goods from manufacturers and selling in large quantities to traders

workflow: the process by which tasks pass from one person or department to the next

workload: amount of work that a person has to do

work to rule: to work strictly according to rules agreed between the company and the trade union, and therefore to work slowly

write off: reduce the book value of an asset to zero because it is lost or damaged